Integrating Music Across the Secondary Curriculum

Integrating Music Across the Secondary Curriculum

KRISTIN HARNEY

OXFORD
UNIVERSITY PRESS

OXFORD
UNIVERSITY PRESS

Oxford University Press is a department of the University of Oxford.
It furthers the University's objective of excellence in research, scholarship,
and education by publishing worldwide. Oxford is a registered trade mark of
Oxford University Press in the UK and in certain other countries.

Published in the United States of America by Oxford University Press
198 Madison Avenue, New York, NY 10016, United States of America.

Library of Congress Cataloging-in-Publication Data
Names: Harney, Kristin author
Title: Integrating music across the secondary curriculum / Kristin Harney.
Description: [1]. | New York : Oxford University Press, 2026. |
Includes bibliographical references and index.
Identifiers: LCCN 2025038641 (print) | LCCN 2025038642 (ebook) |
ISBN 9780197822005 paperback | ISBN 9780197821992 hardback |
ISBN 9780197822012 epub | ISBN 9780197822029 | ISBN 9780197822036
Subjects: LCSH: School music—Instruction and study—Activity programs |
School music—Instruction and study—Activity programs |
Music—Instruction and study—Outlines, syllabi, etc. |
Music—Instruction and study—Activity programs |
Education, Secondary—Activity programs
Classification: LCC MT10 .H2942 2026 (print) | LCC MT10 (ebook) |
DDC 780.71—dc23/eng/20251202
LC record available at https://lccn.loc.gov/2025038641
LC ebook record available at https://lccn.loc.gov/2025038642

DOI: 10.1093/9780197822036.001.0001

Paperback printed by Marquis Book Printing, Canada
Hardback printed by Lightning Source, Inc., United States of America

The manufacturer's authorized representative in the EU for product safety is
Oxford University Press España S.A. of Parque Empresarial San Fernando de Henares,
Avenida de Castilla, 2 – 28830 Madrid (www.oup.es/en or product.safety@oup.com).
OUP España S.A. also acts as importer into Spain of products made by the manufacturer.

Once again, to Jon, Minnie, and Frank, with thanks for their love and support.

Contents

Figures

Tables

Acknowledgments

I wish to thank all the people who supported me and made the creation of this book possible. I am especially grateful to the thousands of K–12, undergraduate, and graduate students I have had the privilege to teach over the past thirty-two years. Special thanks go to the late Dr. Claire W. McCoy, who inspired my journey into the interdisciplinary approach. Thank you to the practicing secondary teachers who reviewed and/or field-tested the lessons and strategies included in this text: Barb Bolte, mathematics; Stacey Boujoukos, English language arts; Charlotte Colliver, music; Nathan Hallauer, music; Patrick Hoffman, visual art; Chandra Lind, music; Talia Martin, science; Cynthia McBride, mathematics; Kelley Meyer, English language arts; Michelle Maurer, music; Quentin Miller, social studies; Margie Phillips, music; Steve Riccio, science; Tim Rooney, visual art; Michel Sticka, music; and Amy Wallner-Drake, social studies. Thanks to experts in their disciplines for their insightful reviews of the manuscript: Liana Bauman, visual art; Dr. Mary Alice Carlson, mathematics; Dr. Nicholas Lux, science; Dr. Allison Wynhoff Olsen, English language arts; and Dr. Christine Rogers Stanton, social studies. Thanks to my mom, Linda Zolnosky, who read every word of every draft. I would also like to express my gratitude to my niece Annika Harney, for her quality artwork and gracious efforts, and for all those who granted permission to reprint copyrighted and other material.

Introduction

Setting the Stage for Music Integration

This book is designed to support middle school and high school educators as they integrate music throughout the secondary curriculum. It contains detailed, practical ideas and examples, including full lesson plans and over 100 teaching ideas and strategies for integrating music with visual arts, language arts, social studies, science, and mathematics. It is my hope that the range of possibilities, imaginative lesson ideas, and extensive descriptions, examples, and starting points presented in the text will facilitate teachers' creativity and inspire innovative curriculum making.

Integrating Music Across the Secondary Curriculum is an extension of my earlier book, *Integrating Music Across the Elementary Curriculum.* The two texts share many features, especially their endorsement of the value of music integration and their emphasis on the importance of making valid, meaningful connections between and among disciplines. Both books contain chapters focused on integrating music with art, language arts, social studies, science, and mathematics, and each utilizes the same structure. My previous book focused on kindergarten through fifth grade students, while this book targets sixth through twelfth grade learners; the content of the lessons and examples are unique to each text. The one exception is that both texts employ the Arts Analysis Template, a tool I created based on the Facets Model from *Sound Ways of Knowing* by Barrett, McCoy, and Veblen (1997).

Just as in my earlier book, all the lesson plans and activities have been reviewed by practicing teachers and subject matter experts. I am tremendously thankful to all of them and their students for their time and input in this project. The feedback I received was overwhelmingly positive. For example:

- "I read over these lessons twice looking for things that were not feasible or unclear, but I *love* them. I especially love some of the extension ideas."
- "This idea is amazing! It hit on many of the standards and did so in a creative manner that engaged my students."
- "I like the tables with examples and suggestions—makes it nice and clear for the teacher to follow."
- "My students had so much fun with this."
- "This is such a cool idea! Love these questions."

Integrating Music Across the Secondary Curriculum. Kristin Harney, Oxford University Press. © Oxford University Press 2026.
DOI: 10.1093/9780197822036.001.0001

- "I love this simple, yet powerful, tool; cool (and engaging) activity—it worked perfectly as a culminating project for my 11th grade U.S. history course."
- "Very well put together and I liked all the figures you used, as well."
- "I absolutely love the inclusiveness of various artists from different cultural backgrounds that all address a similar topic."
- "I really love this approach, and I think it makes the science much more accessible to a broader audience!"
- "Absolutely LOVE this bit! The details are so rich and fully aligned with how we talk about graphic novels."
- "These figures you have inserted are AMAZING! I had no idea they existed. SO cool!"
- "Great scaffolding and modeling!"

I also received specific criticisms and suggestions for modifications; I incorporated those recommendations throughout the text. The teachers' and subject matter experts' feedback ranged from simple adjustments like reordering lesson sequences and inserting tables, to more in-depth revisions like adapting assessments and more clearly defining expectations. Here are some of the specific suggestions they offered:

- Provide more detailed information for teachers and students.
  - "It might help students/teachers to see some examples."
  - "I'd like more specific directions for presenting background information."
  - "Incorporate musical examples as introductory hooks in some lessons and provide more examples."
  - "My class needed additional supports for the student created geographic maps."
  - "You could include a Think-Pair-Share here, it sounds like that's already what you have them doing, but simply label the activity."
  - "This was too quick a shift from students doing a deep analysis to directing them into their own topic."
  - "This sentence is hard for me to understand. Can you break it apart for clarity?"
  - "I'm curious why you are not using a table or some other sort of visual scaffold here. It was so effective earlier."
- Spread lesson content over multiple days.
  - "I needed to break this down into micro baby-steps for my students."
  - "For this lesson to be truly successful, I needed many days of 'a little of this and a little of that' to cover all the concepts/possibilities."
  - "I broke this lesson down over several days."
  - "My students need healthy chunks of time to dig in and collaborate. Every time I do an improvisation/composition/drawing project, I'm always astounded with the time it takes because the students really get into it and revise and expound on their ideas. They are seldom satisfied with the amount of time I allot."

- Emphasize student choice and ownership of lesson content; promote open pedagogies, in which teachers and students search together for paths of inquiry and exploration.
  - "I like the open-endedness of what you presented, it helped level the playing field for my students. Can you include more opportunities for student independence?"
  - "I had my students share their conclusions in small groups or pairs. They were so engaged!"
  - "Often, students think their hands are tied in terms of change; guiding them through thinking about this topic helps them recognize the options and opportunities for agency that are possible."
  - "Add that we should ask students questions that allow them to bring in their unique backgrounds; these conversations can be natural springboards into related content."
  - "I like the idea of students creating their own awareness song or chant. I'd invite *them* to identify a current environmental issue for the focus, though. I think this is important because it allows students the ownership to choose what is an important global issue to them and have the freedom to 'create,' which we don't do as often in science."
- Actively enlist student musicians and elicit students' musical contributions.
  - "My students loved singing and playing along."
  - "I'd suggest more frequent performances."
  - "Great song choices. My students loved weighing in with their opinions. I had them brainstorm additional musical options, and that was engaging, too."
  - "You might organize a performance showcase following this lesson. (I did this with my high school students, and they ATE IT UP.)"
- Conclude lessons on a positive note.
  - "This is such an important but heavy topic. I made sure to end the lesson by encouraging student optimism."
  - "Maybe end by circling back to what is already being done to facilitate climate change issues."
  - "My students needed some positive affirmations after this valuable reflection."
  - "This lesson fosters a LOT of emotional labor/vulnerability. That is excellent, but I don't know many who want to be critiqued at this time. I highly recommend more of a celebration or a simple 'thank you' from the audience."
- By far, the most frequent suggestions were appeals for collaboration. While all the material in this book may be delivered by individual subject area teachers, most content area specialists (music, art, language arts, social studies, science, and math teachers) expressed a desire to deliver integrated content with a collaborative partner outside their discipline. This might look like teachers consulting subject area specialists in preparation for solo teaching, teachers planning integrated lessons together, teachers delivering separate portions of the

content in their respective classes, or teachers fully co-teaching and delivering lessons together.

- "I know you didn't ask for me to collaborate, but I immediately sent this lesson to one of my ELA colleagues. So excited to try this lesson again with a partner."
- "I asked the choir director at my school to teach the more technical aspects of the lesson, which she did during 7th grade choirs. We don't have all our students in common, but there is enough overlap between my pre-algebra classes and her choirs that it worked. Those students in just one class or the other missed out on some of the rich connections, but still had a worthwhile experience."
- "I taught this lesson fully on my own, but would love to try it with a social studies teacher next time."
- "I love the cooperative aspect! The whole idea of teaching collaboratively with teachers from other content areas invigorates me. I'm sure this will translate to my students!"

Outline of the Book

Chapter 1 provides an overview of the interdisciplinary approach, a teacher-tested model that allows educators to successfully create their own interdisciplinary lessons, and suggestions for selecting musical examples. Chapters 2 through 6 explore connections between and among music and other areas of the secondary curriculum. Each chapter begins with a section describing common links between music and the designated discipline for the chapter. Each chapter also includes a section addressing national standards with tables showing the specific standards that are included in each lesson and activity. This text utilizes the most recent National Core Arts Standards (2015) as well as the most recent standards in language arts, social studies, science, and mathematics. Each chapter includes four detailed, full-length lesson plans followed by an inventory of ideas cataloguing additional lesson topics, specific teaching strategies, and recommended activities.

The lessons in this book have not been assigned specific grade levels. There are three reasons for this decision. First, all the lessons and activities are adaptable to a variety of ability levels. Second, it eliminates the chance that teachers might discount a lesson simply because it is labeled with a different grade level from the one they teach. Finally, it accounts for school districts' varying curricular schedules.

Each lesson in this text has standards-based objectives and assessments. In many cases, the assessments are informal. This decision was primarily based on the feedback I received from curricular specialists who expressed a desire to informally assess the quality of the connections students made. As such, most lessons do not include formal rubrics. Of course, each teacher is welcome to add formal assessments if they wish.

You know your students best. All the lessons and ideas in this book are intended as tools for you to meet your students' needs. Most of the lessons will need to be spread over two or more class periods. Please adjust, adapt, or expand the content to work best for you and for your students. Seek out teachers with whom you can collaborate and please utilize the range of ideas and examples as starting points to facilitate your creativity and inspire innovative curriculum making. My hope is that you, your colleagues, and your students will be creative, think critically, and have fun.

1

Overview of Music Integration in the Secondary Curriculum

Music gives a soul to the universe, wings to the mind, flight to the imagination, and life to everything.

—Plato

Introduction

Music is not merely an accessory to the academic experience; it is a vital, transformative force that can enhance and illuminate every subject area. When we integrate music across the secondary curriculum, we create opportunities for students to explore complex ideas in new ways, making learning more engaging, interactive, and relevant. The primary aim of secondary education is to provide students with a comprehensive and challenging curriculum that prepares them for success in college, their career, and their life beyond graduation. Common areas of focus include critical thinking, communication, collaboration, and creativity. Researchers and educators across disciplines attest to the capacity of music integration to address these goals (Cslovjecsek & Zulauf, 2018; Fautley & Savage, 2011). Whether a lesson involves exploring the use of mathematical sequences in minimalist music, analyzing historical events through protest songs, or examining literary themes in song lyrics, integrating music across the secondary curriculum is a powerful means for nurturing these essential skills, meeting the current and future needs of our society and our students. Additionally, teachers who integrate music across the secondary curriculum provide students with opportunities to explore concepts from multiple perspectives, foster active engagement with content, and encourage the understanding of music as connected with all of life.

Defining Music Integration

Depending on the context, the term "interdisciplinary education" may or may not refer to cross-curricular projects, multiple intelligences, cooperative learning, cooperative teaching, theme-based teaching units, combined curriculum, creative curriculum, or curriculum integration. For consistency of language and common understanding, a discussion of definitions follows (see Box 1.1).

Integrating Music Across the Secondary Curriculum. Kristin Harney, Oxford University Press. © Oxford University Press 2026.
DOI: 10.1093/9780197822036.003.0001

> **Box 1.1 Definitions**
>
> - Discipline: A curricular area with a specific body of teachable knowledge
> - Interdisciplinary: A curriculum approach that consciously applies methodology and language from more than one discipline to examine a central theme, issue, problem, topic, or experience
>
> *Jacobs*, H. H. (1989). The growing need for interdisciplinary curriculum content. In H. H. Jacobs (Ed.), *Interdisciplinary Curriculum: Design and Implementation.* Association for Supervision and Curriculum Development.

Common synonyms for the term "discipline" are "subject," "field," and "area of study." To be more exact, a discipline is a curricular area with "a specific body of teachable knowledge" (Jacobs, 1989, Definitions section, para. 1). This definition assumes a school setting; a particular set of skills, elements, and concepts; and a methodology for teaching that knowledge. If one discipline is a single area of the curriculum, a working definition for the term "interdisciplinary" might be something like "combining disciplines" or "between disciplines." A more precise definition of "interdisciplinary" is a "curriculum approach that consciously applies methodology and language from more than one discipline to examine a central theme, issue, problem, topic, or experience" (Jacobs, 1989, Definitions section, para. 4). This definition clarifies that interdisciplinary lessons don't occur by chance; instead, teachers make intentional choices to structure lessons that utilize particular skills, elements, or concepts from at least two disciplines. Additionally, this definition highlights the need for a common theme, purpose, or objective that is addressed from the perspective of multiple disciplines. These shared associations might be concept connections (enduring ideas), topics (themes or focuses), or processes (any of the active modes by which students learn, such as reading, writing, moving, etc.). The term "music integration" refers to a specific subcategory of arts integration and can be defined in several ways. It is loosely defined as teaching through and with music, creating relationships between music and other curricular subjects (Burnaford, 2007). This perspective refers to the expanded definition of arts integration developed by ArtsEdge, a teaching and learning resource created by the Kennedy Center in Washington, DC. From this standpoint, music integration is an approach to teaching that, rather than being an isolated activity, is embedded into daily practice (Kennedy Center ArtsEdge, n.d.). Because the terms "integration" and "interdisciplinary" both occur regularly in related research and literature, I have used them interchangeably throughout this book.

Rationales for Music Integration and Overcoming Potential Problems

There are numerous justifications for incorporating music in secondary classrooms. Music provides a creative outlet for communication, allowing students to share ideas and express emotions. Performing music together promotes teamwork, collaboration, and communication skills; it also fosters empathy and emotional intelligence as students learn to interpret and present music cooperatively. Studying music from different cultures broadens students' perspectives by immersing students in diverse musical traditions, styles, and genres. Additional rationales highlight music as a way to promote physical responses, divergent thinking, self-discipline, and self-confidence. Finally, music grabs students' emotions in ways that words and numbers do not, and music integration can increase students' interest and engagement in learning. Music supplies insight and meaning to other subjects, giving understandings a human dimension and helping students experience curricular content in a more personal way. When we integrate music into the curriculum, we invite students to make cross-disciplinary connections that are both creative and meaningful.

In 2022, the President's Committee on the Arts and the Humanities (PCAH) posted an executive order. The policy states that the arts "are essential to the well-being, health, vitality, and democracy of our nation" (PCAH, 2022). The policy continues, affirming that the arts:

> inspire us; provide livelihoods; sustain, anchor, and bring cohesion within diverse communities across our nation; stimulate creativity and innovation; help us understand and communicate our values as a people; compel us to wrestle with our history and enable us to imagine our future; invigorate and strengthen our democracy; and point the way toward progress. (PCAH, 2022)

Unfortunately, music is often trivialized or used as an add-on in music integration lessons. Even in situations where teachers support the interdisciplinary approach, the lessons they teach may use music superficially. Ideally, in integrated learning, students will experience music as an essential aspect of the human experience, not as an inconsequential accessory. It is disappointing when music is integrated with another subject and the outcomes focus almost exclusively on the other discipline.

To address this issue, it is important to realize that music integration is not a substitute for a strong, sequential music education, taught by a certified specialist, as there are aspects of music education that can only be effectively taught in the context of music classes. Students must develop skills in music before they can apply musical skills to other learning situations; a strong background in music is necessary for students to connect new understandings in authentic ways.

Lack of time is another potential problem related to music integration. The planning time for creating interdisciplinary lessons is almost always more than the time required to plan lessons in isolation; however, teachers generally agree that the benefits to students are well worth any extra time spent. The lesson plans, ideas, and strategies in this book will facilitate teachers' planning and implementation of lessons that integrate music across the secondary curriculum. A best practice in music integration is for classroom teachers and music teachers to collaborate. While this approach may require extra time for cooperation and planning, "collaborative projects often evolve with a degree of richness that individual efforts cannot achieve"

(McCoy, 2000, p. 39). When I taught general music and collaborated with classroom teachers, it not only benefited the students but also was enjoyable and empowering for us as teachers. We became aware of connections between and among our content areas, drew on our own unique strengths and skills, and created lessons that would not have been possible had we taught them alone.

Review of the National Core Arts Standards

The National Core Arts Standards (NCAS) were designed as a framework to provide a comprehensive and clear approach to teaching and learning in the arts (2015). The NCAS are intended to guide educators in delivering high-quality arts education and to ensure that students gain the skills and knowledge necessary to engage with the arts in meaningful ways. Music shares common process standards with dance, media arts, theater, and visual arts. The four common arts processes are creating, performing, responding, and connecting; however, the music standards somewhat sidestep the power of connecting as one of the central processes. In the music standards, connections are woven throughout the other three processes, cross-referencing users to the creating, performing, and responding standards. As of this writing, the National Coalition for Core Arts Standards (NCCAS) and the National Association for Music Education (NAfME) are working on a revision of the arts standards. I am hopeful that the revised standards will unreservedly uphold all four common process standards for a variety of reasons: (1) placing connecting as a central process endorses the significance of the connecting standards and more strongly advocates for curricular integration within music education; (2) claiming all four process standards allows for a more straightforward reading of the various standards documents; and (3) this structure aligns with the standards in dance, media arts, theater, and visual arts. Throughout this text, I treat connecting as a central process.

The national standards in many disciplines, including the NCAS, highlight the importance of interdisciplinarity, reminding us that "although educational institutions segment knowledge into separate packages called 'subjects,' deep understanding often depends upon the intersections and interactions of the disciplines" (Barrett, 2001, p. 27). Some classroom teachers might be surprised by the quantity of information included in the NCAS, unsure about how to cite them; doubtful of their abilities to meet, let alone address, the standards; and apprehensive about even undertaking the task. Feeling overwhelmed does not have to be the typical response to the standards, though. The standards are a tool, and teachers are invited to make the standards work for them, not the other way around. A simplified, intuitive way of expressing the anchor standards that serves as a springboard to the rest of the standards follows.

There are three anchor standards that relate to creating music. In student-friendly language, they can be summarized as (1) generate musical ideas; (2) organize and write them down; and (3) finish your musical work. There are three anchor standards

Table 1.1 National Core Arts Standards: Simplified and original anchor standards

Process standard	Creating	Performing	Responding	Connecting
Simplified anchor standard descriptions	1. Generate musical ideas 2. Organize and write them down 3. Finish your musical work	4. Learn about a piece 5. Practice it 6. Perform it	7. Analyze music 8. Interpret meaning 9. Evaluate music	10. Connect music to self 11. Connect music to everything else
NCAS anchor standard descriptions	1. MU:Cr1 Generate and conceptualize artistic ideas and work. 2. MU:Cr2 Organize and develop artistic ideas and work. 3. MU:Cr3 Refine and complete artistic work.	4. MU:Pr4 Select, analyze, and interpret artistic work for presentation. 5. MU:Pr5 Develop and refine artistic techniques and work for presentation. 6. MU:Pr6 Convey meaning through the presentation of artistic work.	7. MU:Re7 Perceive and analyze artistic work. 8. MU:Re8 Interpret intent and meaning in artistic work. 9. MU:Re9 Apply criteria to evaluate artistic work.	10. MU:Cn10 Synthesize and relate knowledge and personal experiences to make art. 11. MU:Cn11 Relate artistic ideas and works with societal, cultural, and historical context to deepen understanding.

that relate to the performance of music. They can be expressed as (4) learn about a piece; (5) practice it; and (6) perform it. The process of responding also has three anchor standards. Their simplified descriptions are (7) analyze music; (8) interpret meaning; and (9) evaluate music. Finally, two anchor standards relate to connecting. They can be portrayed as (10) connect music to self and (11) connect music to everything else. This streamlined language may enable teachers to more easily incorporate NCAS in their curriculum planning, ultimately benefiting students (Harney, 2015a).

The anchor standards are already indexed in a way that facilitates citing them. MU:Cr1 corresponds to Music, Creating, Anchor Standard 1; MU:Pr4 corresponds to Music, Performing, Anchor Standard 4, and so forth. Table 1.1 contains the simplified anchor standard language along with the full NCAS versions of the anchor standards.

Selecting Music

There are hundreds of musical examples referenced in this book, but they represent only a minuscule fraction of the music that teachers could employ in lessons they create. As technology advances, students are exposed to a wide variety of musical styles, genres, and cultures that allow for deeper exploration of topics both inside and outside the classroom. Similarly, with the rise of digital music tools and accessible online resources, educators have more opportunities than ever before to incorporate music into their daily teaching practice. When setting out to expand the scope of musical examples on which to draw for use in your classroom, the sheer number of options may be stifling, rather than freeing. A simple suggestion is to start small. You might choose a different radio station each day of your commute to school (e.g., jazz Wednesdays or hip-hop Fridays). Strive to move beyond the suggested-for-you-type playlists, albums, and songs in apps like Spotify and AppleMusic. Keep a running list of the music you discover and invite your students to join the search for school-appropriate musical examples. You might first ask students to share music from their own listening libraries (their current music choices), then direct them into detective mode, offering specific prompts like "locate a notable song from the 1940s" or "track down a Portuguese folk song." You might also go into detective mode yourself, searching for examples that fit within a specific topic, genre, period, or relate to a specific theme (e.g., see Lesson 4.2 for a list of songs with place as a unifying theme).

Once you have located a musical example, there are some guidelines you can employ to ensure that the music you select serves the purpose of your lesson and meets students' needs. First, listen to your example the whole way through, following along with the printed lyrics, if applicable. Ask yourself the following questions:

- Will this song appeal to my students? Most of your musical selections should have at least a basic appeal.
- Will this piece inspire and engage my students?
- If there are lyrics, are they school-appropriate? Are there any vocabulary words or phrases that will require explanation?
- How long is the example? If it is a long work, can I use smaller excerpts?
- Will my students be performing the piece, or just listening? If they will perform, is it too challenging (range, complexity, etc.) or too simple?
- Is the song culturally authentic and historically accurate?
- Is the recording of good quality (audible, clear, etc.)?

You might also consider informally completing an analysis of your musical example, perhaps using a tool like the Arts Analysis Template found in chapter 2. The results of your analysis will likely point to logical activities and elements to explore with your students.

Creating Interdisciplinary Lessons

Beyond selecting music to use in lessons, the task for teachers who employ the interdisciplinary approach is to make meaningful connections between and among disciplines without compromising the integrity of any discipline. In those scenarios, music and other disciplines act as equal partners in interdisciplinary lessons, with each subject enhancing the other(s). The tools from this chapter can be used to analyze existing interdisciplinary lessons and to create your own. Ideas to keep in mind when reviewing or planning interdisciplinary lessons are (1) integrity within each discipline and (2) integrity between and among disciplines. Beyond these two ideas, consider that the central aims of education transcend disciplinary boundaries as well. Music integration enriches journeys within the school curriculum but also has the potential to inspire lifelong pursuits. These ideas were first introduced in the book *Sound Ways of Knowing: Music in the Interdisciplinary Curriculum* by Janet Barrett, Claire McCoy, and Kari Veblen, and further developed in *Seeking Connections: An Interdisciplinary Perspective on Music Teaching and Learning* by Janet Barrett.

Integrity Within Each Discipline

In an interdisciplinary lesson, when skills and understandings specific to each discipline are employed, each discipline maintains curricular integrity. One method for ensuring that essential skills in each discipline are employed is to design lessons that address standards for each subject. Music experiences have integrity when students are engaged in the processes of creating, performing, responding, and connecting, addressing the NCAS. Other disciplines have integrity when the skills and understandings of those disciplines are used in valid ways and standards are met. When designing your own lessons that integrate music, ask yourself: "Does the lesson I'm designing allow students to apply basic skills in music and another discipline?" True integration respects the integrity and uniqueness of each of the disciplines being combined. Every lesson and idea in this book includes standards for music and the respective connecting discipline. As you design your own interdisciplinary lessons, strive to incorporate standards from each of the relevant subject areas.

Integrity Between and Among Disciplines

In an interdisciplinary lesson, when the unique skills and understandings of each discipline are employed to examine a central idea, there is integrity between and among the disciplines. Integrity between and among disciplines is characterized by a sense of balance, complementary relationships, and mutual illumination. A rationale for integrating two or more content areas should describe a valid connection. Valid connections include concepts, topics, and processes that the disciplines have in common.

- Common concept: Common concepts are usually broad, overarching ideas. Establishing a common concept is the most straightforward way to ensure integrity between and among the disciplines. A list of potential connecting concepts between music and other disciplines is included at the beginning of chapters 2, 3, 4, 5, and 6.

- Common topic: There are often school-wide or grade-level units focusing on a single topic that is relevant to the community or the time. The presence of a common topic does not always ensure a valid connection, though. For example, a unit focused on the Great Depression would likely include multiple valid intersections with music, while a school-wide assembly might not have such straightforward musical connections.
- Common process: Interdisciplinary lessons often highlight processes that music and other disciplines share. Process connections that are often reinforced in music integration include creating, reading, writing, listening, presenting, analyzing, and evaluating.

When designing your own lessons that integrate music, ask yourself: "Is there a logical reason to integrate music with another content area in the lesson I'm designing? Is there a valid connection between or among the disciplines and a common idea that students can explore from multiple perspectives?"

When teachers integrate music in meaningful ways, students are led to connect knowledge and to recognize relationships between and among disciplines. Rather than keeping each content area separate, students discover connections and develop holistic understandings. It is my hope that this text will serve as a springboard for teachers, encouraging them to utilize their personal pursuits and affinities, varied histories in music and other disciplines, and unique bases of knowledge to creatively engage in interdisciplinary curriculum making; this book is just the tip of the iceberg. It is also my hope that the lessons and strategies in this book will enhance students' learning in powerful and authentic ways, inspire them to see the interconnectedness of knowledge and to appreciate the profound ways in which music can help us make sense of the world around us, and launch them toward deeper questions and explorations about the role of the arts in their lives.

2

Music and Visual Arts

Introduction

The arts are an essential aspect of human expression, and members of every culture and community create music and art to convey those unique perspectives. For example, the song "Fake Happy," released in 2017 by the American rock band Paramore, expresses the pressure some people feel to appear happy even when they aren't feeling that way. The lyrics include the following lines, "no one sees me" and "I've been doing a good job of makin' 'em think I'm quite alright" (Paramore, 2017, track 5), illustrating that smiles can be false and not actually reflect a person's emotional state. The main character in the song describes masking her sadness; however, the line "don't make me play pretend" (Paramore, 2017, track 5) also points toward a desire for authenticity. Relatedly, in 2020, Marcia Angus, an artist who openly acknowledges her struggle with mental health, painted *Matryoshka Doll* (see Figure 2.1). Her work was featured on the website Perspective Project, a site dedicated to promoting an open, creative platform for exploring mental well-being. Angus had this to say about *Matryoshka Doll*, "For me, the Matryoshka wears a painted smile which conceals many, deeper layers. There are so many of us putting on a mask, a brave face" (Perspective Project, 2023). Angus also points toward the optimism in the painting, noting that the doll appears to be leaning, but it does not fall over, and the green shoots sprouting around the doll's head suggest new ideas and better days ahead. These are two examples of artists using their respective mediums to promote awareness of mental health issues. Through the arts, students can know, experience, and express ideas that go beyond words and numbers. The arts enable students to encounter and communicate what otherwise cannot be expressed.

The arts teach divergent, flexible, creative thinking. Most of the time, problems in music and visual art have multiple solutions. When questions have more than one possible answer, students cannot only rely on strict rules, but must also engage in qualitative reasoning, make judgment calls, and defend their convictions. When multiple perspectives are celebrated, it naturally follows that there are a variety of acceptable and appropriate ways to interpret the world around us. In this digital age, we have access to virtually unlimited numbers of recordings and images. Analyzing and considering connections between music and art can facilitate students' development as knowledgeable lifelong consumers of the arts.

Music and art invite deep wellsprings of cognition, emotional response, critique, curiosity, and engagement—all transformative processes at the heart of experience. Integrating music and art in middle school and high school classrooms can promote

Integrating Music Across the Secondary Curriculum. Kristin Harney, Oxford University Press. © Oxford University Press 2026.
DOI: 10.1093/9780197822036.003.0002

Figure 2.1 *Matryoshka Doll* by Marcia Angus.
Image courtesy of the artist.

active engagement with the skills and elements of both disciplines. Active and meaningful engagement in music and visual art includes such varied activities as playing instruments, singing, moving, improvising, composing, drawing, painting, sculpting, sketching, designing, listening, perceiving, analyzing, imagining, interpreting, evaluating, and expressing. Opportunities for students to create diverse works of art, share their perspectives, and participate consistently over time are essential. Classrooms that embrace arts integration can be vibrant, inspirational, and transformational centers of learning. Through lessons that integrate music and visual arts, students can connect more deeply with the world around them, actively participate in multiple art forms, collaborate and forge social bonds, creatively solve complex problems, and foster personal identity.

The lessons and the strategies and activities included in the chapter 2 inventory of ideas promote in-depth interaction with visual arts and music content. These engaging lessons and activities draw on musical and visual arts examples that represent a wide variety of styles, cultures, and historical periods.

Common Links Between Music and Art

Concurrently exploring paired concepts, elements, or skills in music and art enhances students' understanding in both disciplines. For example, students who examine and differentiate the attributes of Sarah Emily Porter's 2021 painting *Village Fete* (see Figure 2.2) that characterize it as minimalist art (attributes such as geometric shapes, simplicity, orderly organization, repetition, and open space) will be better equipped to discern those same qualities in Isobel Waller-Bridge's 2013 minimalistic composition for strings, "Arise."

Similarly, imagine students engaged in a philosophical debate as they consider examples from visual art and music and deliberate the topic "what is art and who gets to decide?" Students' perceptions of intent, aesthetics, utility, and value would likely influence their viewpoints and personal positions. How might students categorize a bird call, the musicians of *Stomp* rhythmically sweeping a stage floor, Martin Kazimir Malevich's *White on White* (see Figure 2.3), or Martin Creed's artwork, titled *Work No. 227*, an empty room in which the lights clicked on and off every five seconds? The *Oxford English Dictionary* defines art as "the expression or application of human creative skill and imagination . . . producing works to be appreciated primarily for their beauty or emotional power" (Oxford University Press, n.d.). Given that definition, how might students revise their categorizations?

Additionally, many broad concepts may be explored through music and art, with each discipline addressing the theme from its own perspective. Enduring ideas that can be explored in music and visual arts include:

Balance
Change
Character
Communication
Conflict
Cooperation
Creativity
Direction
Diversity
Energy
Function
Identity
Insight
Interaction
Interdependence

Figure 2.2 *Village Fete* by Sarah Emily Porter.
Image courtesy of the artist.

Lens
Pattern
Preference
Power
Repetition
Responsibility
Ritual
Setting
Truth
Unity
Value

Figure 2.3 *White on White* by Kazimir Malevich.
Public Domain/Museum of Modern Art, 1935. Acquisition confirmed in 1999 by agreement with the Estate of Kazimir Malevich and made possible with funds from the Mrs. John Hay Whitney Bequest (by exchange)

National Standards

The disciplines of music and art are grounded by the same overarching standards document, the National Core Arts Standards. The two disciplines share four underlying artistic processes (Creating, Presenting/Performing, Responding, and Connecting) and eleven identical anchor standards. Each discipline has distinct, but related, Enduring Understandings and Essential Questions.

The National Core Arts Standards for Music and the National Core Arts Standards for Visual Arts call for interdisciplinary connections among the arts, with Anchor Standards 10 and 11 focused implicitly on multiple connections. Additionally, the Essential Question in music that is linked with Anchor Standard 11 asks, "How do the other arts, other disciplines, contexts, and daily life inform creating, performing, and responding to music?" (National Coalition for Core Arts Standards, 2015). Box 2.1 specifies the shared anchor standards in the National Core Arts Standards that are addressed in the chapter 2 lessons and inventory of ideas. Box 2.2 offers a framework for structuring lessons and activities.

Box 2.1 National Core Arts Standards for Visual Arts (VA) and Music (MU) Included in Chapter 2 Lessons (L) and Inventory of Ideas (I)

VA:Cr1 and MU:Cr1 *(Creating)*	Generate and conceptualize artistic ideas and work	L 2.3 L 2.4 I 4 I 6 I 13 I 14
VA:Cr2 and MU:Cr2 *(Creating)*	Organize and develop artistic ideas and work	L 2.3 I 4 I 7 I 8 I 15
VA:Cr3 and MU:Cr3 *(Creating)*	Refine and complete artistic work	L 2.2 L 2.4 I 6 I 8 I 13
VA:Pr4 and MU:Pr4 *(Presenting and Performing)*	Select, analyze, and interpret artistic work for presentation	L 2.1 L 2.2 I 1 I 3 I 9 I 12 I 14
VA:Pr5 and MU:Pr5 *(Presenting and Performing)*	Develop and refine artistic techniques and work for presentation	L 2.1 L 2.3 I 6 I 7 I 8 I 14
VA:Pr6 and MU:Pr6 *(Presenting and Performing)*	Convey meaning through the presentation of artistic work	L 2.2 L 2.4 I 1 I 6 I 9 I 12
VA:Re7 and MU:Re7 *(Responding)*	Perceive and analyze artistic work	L 2.1 L 2.3 I 2 I 5 I 8 I 11
VA:Re8 and MU:Re8 *(Responding)*	Interpret intent and meaning in artistic work	L 2.2 L 2.4 I 1 I 6 I 10 I 15

VA:Re9 and MU:Re9 (Responding)	Apply criteria to evaluate artistic work	L 2.2 L 2.4 I 3 I 5 I 9
VA:Cn10 and MU:Cn10 (Connecting)	Synthesize and relate knowledge and personal experiences to make art	L 2.2 L 2.4 I 2 I 3 I 7 I 10 I 13
VA:Cn11 and MU:Cn11 (Connecting)	Relate artistic ideas and works with societal, cultural, and historical context to deepen understanding	L 2.1 L 2.3 I 1 I 4 I 11 I 14

Box 2.2 Framework for Chapter 2 Lessons and Ideas

This chapter is designed to support middle school and high school educators as they integrate music and visual arts. The four detailed, full-length lesson plans are independent and not organized as a progressive series.

- Lesson 2.1: Arts Analysis Template
  - I chose this as the first full lesson in the book since the student-focused step-by-step Arts Analysis Template can be applied to the exploration of any piece of music or work of art in preparation for creating integrated lesson content. I selected *Viva la Vida, Watermelons* by Frida Kahlo to use as the exemplar for this lesson because of the unique story surrounding its creation.
- Lesson 2.2: Paul Klee: Inspired by Music and Inspiring Music
  - I am a huge Paul Klee fan, and to me, he's the perfect example of an artist whose artwork was clearly inspired by music as well as an artist whose work clearly inspired musical creations from others. It was really difficult for me to narrow my choice of examples for this lesson!
- Lesson 2.3: Replicating Artistic and Musical Techniques
  - In this lesson, I wanted to feature the notion of "play" as a way to reinforce creative risk-taking. In "playful" learning environments, studying specific artistic and musical elements or engaging in intentional practice can spark creative ideas. I chose contour, layering, and balance as concepts to highlight, then picked some of my favorite artistic and musical examples to represent those techniques. I am reminded that my

"favorites" are an ever-expanding list, often based on serendipity. For example, I first encountered Hilma af Klint's artwork at IKEA, then soon after saw a fantastic exhibit of her work at the Guggenheim Museum.

- Lesson 2.4: Musical and Artistic Expressions of Three Montana Rivers
  - I was first drawn to the work of artist Ben Miller because he is from my local community; second, because of his innovative techniques; and third, because his paintings are stunning. The idea to connect his artwork to the music of a local, innovative composer occurred following a concert in which my friend and colleague Linda Antas shared a work for flute and electronic sounds. I like the fact that both their works highlight locations close to Yellowstone National Park, a place that is recognizable to many students. Finally, this lesson is special to me because my niece, Annika Harney, created the Montana river artwork to accompany it.

The chapter ends with an inventory of ideas detailing fifteen additional lesson topics, specific teaching strategies, and recommended activities. The lessons and activities may be fully taught by individual subject area (art or music) teachers; however, ideally, the plans will facilitate partnerships and collaboration between art teachers and music specialists. All lessons and activities have been reviewed by practicing teachers, and most have been field-tested in middle school and high school classrooms. Most of the lessons will need to be spread over two or more class periods. Chapter 2 lessons are adaptable to a variety of grade levels and are intended as tools for you to meet your students' needs. You and your students bring your own knowledge and experiences to these encounters, and you are invited and encouraged to apply those skills and understandings. I hope you are inspired to locate additional works to explore, including musical examples students are likely to encounter in their lives beyond school (e.g., readily recognizable musical works, paintings, etc.) and those that are less likely to be encountered (e.g., contemporary works that have not yet received widespread recognition, works for specialized groups or audiences, or works that are rooted in specific geographic regions). See additional guidelines for selecting repertoire in chapter 1. All the images included in this chapter are printed in black and white. Consider accessing full-color images online when displaying photographs, artwork, and other graphics for students, especially when lesson content directly references aspects related to a work's color. Please adjust, adapt, or expand these lessons and ideas to work best for you and for your students. Seek out teachers with whom you can collaborate and utilize the range of ideas and examples as starting points to facilitate your creativity and inspire innovative curriculum making.

Lesson 2.1: Arts Analysis Template

Grade Level

Middle school and high school, depending on adaptations

Essential Question

How do artists and musicians analyze creative products and discern meaningful connections between specific artistic and musical works?

Objectives

- Following group practice, each student will accurately analyze a musical example and a work of art using an Arts Analysis Template.
- Students will discern and describe similarities and differences between a musical composition and a work of art.
- Students will present their research to the class, explaining and defending their interpretations of two selected works and the meaningful connections between them.

National Core Arts Standards Addressed

- VA:Pr4 and MU:Pr4: Select, analyze, and interpret artistic work for presentation
- VA:Pr5 and MU:Pr5: Develop and refine artistic techniques and work for presentation
- VA:Re7 and MU:Re7: Perceive and analyze artistic work
- VA:Cn11 and MU:Cn11: Relate artistic ideas and works with societal, cultural, and historical context to deepen understanding

Materials

- Arts Analysis Template (see Table 2.1)
- Optional music: "Viva la Vida" by Coldplay
- Optional artwork: *Viva la Vida, Watermelons* by Frida Kahlo
- Additional music (popular music, classical music, examples from other cultures, etc.) for students to access
- Additional art (contemporary art, folk art, pop art, examples from other cultures, etc.) for students to access

Procedure

As preparation for individual work, collaboratively analyze a piece of music as a whole class, then complete the Arts Analysis Template together (see Table 2.1). The Arts Analysis Template was adapted from a model I often employed with my

Table 2.1 Arts Analysis Template

Arts Analysis Template (5Ws + 1H)	
Who is the creator (artist, composer, and/or performer)?	
What is the title and what is the piece about?	
Where was it created and does the style of the piece reflect that culture or place?	
When was it created and does the style of the piece reflect that time?	
Why did you choose this example?	
How does it make you feel and what techniques did the composer or artist use to evoke those feelings? (text, tempo, harmony, instrumentation, dynamics, articulation, melody, structure, line, color, texture, light, content, etc.)	
References:	

Adaptation of the Facets Model, found in *Sound Ways of Knowing* (1997) by Janet Barrett, Claire McCoy, and Kari Veblen; further developed in *Seeking Connections: An Interdisciplinary Perspective on Music Teaching and Learning* (2023) by Janet Barrett.

students, the Facets Model. The Facets Model was first introduced in the book *Sound Ways of Knowing: Music in the Interdisciplinary Curriculum* by Janet Barrett, Claire McCoy, and Kari Veblen (1997), and further developed in *Seeking Connections: An Interdisciplinary Perspective on Music Teaching and Learning* by Janet Barrett (2023).

Depending on your chosen musical example, provide opportunities for students to sing, move, create, play a rhythmic accompaniment, or otherwise musically perform the piece. Model a variety of techniques for drawing conclusions about the piece. These techniques might include a close reading of lyrics, reviewing primary source material such as interviews with the composer, examining the composer's written comments about the piece, exploring firsthand accounts of performances, studying the printed music, inspecting copyright information, and, most important, focused, repeated listening.

Respond to each of the questions on the template:

Who is the creator? This question sometimes poses problems for students. In cases where the composer of a piece is not the performer, direct students to list both. Similarly, in cases where several people collaborated to create a piece, direct students to list them all. If the creator is unknown, students can simply list "anonymous."

What is the title and what is the piece about? When determining the subject or main idea of a piece, students can start with the title. Next, if the piece has lyrics or other text associated with it, students can examine them for clues. Beyond that, direct students to use additional print and online resources to search for answers and to use deductive reasoning based on what they hear or see.

Where was it created and does the style of the piece reflect that culture or place? When attempting to answer the first part of this question, students may need to make an educated guess. It may not be possible to identify the exact location where a work of art was created. Ideally, even if students can't pinpoint a specific place, they can narrow it down to a country or region. Determining whether the style of the piece reflects the culture or place will require three things. First, students need to research and thoughtfully analyze the artwork to identify its style or genre. Next, they will need to research the styles and genres that typify the piece's country or region of origin. Finally, they will evaluate and describe any similarities and differences they identify.

When was it created and does the style of the piece reflect that time? When answering the first part of this question, the most straightforward response is to cite the copyright date. If that is not possible, again, direct students to make an educated guess. Perhaps they can narrow it down to a decade, a century, or even an era.

Why did you choose this example? This is the most subjective response on the Arts Analysis Template. Push students to elaborate on their rationale for choosing the piece they did. If they say, "I chose this piece because I like it," encourage them to explain why they like it. What specifically about the piece draws them in?

How does it make you feel and what techniques did the composer or artist use to evoke those feelings? To answer this question, students first need to identify the mood of the piece. Direct them to consider a variety of adjectives that might describe the overall feeling, encouraging them to move beyond "happy" and "sad." Next, through repeated listenings, identify the specific techniques that the composer used that generated that particular response. For example, if students describe the mood of a particular piece as somber, they might also identify musical techniques such as a minor key and a slow tempo. Additionally, students can analyze a piece's text, tempo (fast/slow), harmony (major/minor or brighter/darker), instrumentation (what instruments they identify), dynamics (loud/soft), articulation (choppy/smooth), melody (the tune), and structural elements (phrases, overall form, repetition, etc.) and examine their impact.

References. The last section of the Arts Analysis Template encourages students to follow accepted research practice by citing the sources referenced during analysis.

Once the template is complete, use at least one category from the template as the inspiration for identifying a piece of visual art to examine. For example, if the song your class analyzed and performed was "Viva la Vida" by the British band Coldplay, you could focus on answers from the "what" and "how" categories in the Arts Analysis Template and you might choose to look at Mexican artist Frida Kahlo's painting *Viva la Vida, Watermelons* (see Figure 2.4), the artwork that inspired the creation of Coldplay's song. Depending on the works and the circumstances, exploring examples of music and visual art with shared titles can lead to substantive connections or to more superficial relationships. While Kahlo's artwork and the Coldplay song share a title, it is likely that students can find more differences than similarities between the works.

Frida Kahlo finished *Viva la Vida, Watermelons* in 1954, just eight days before she died. Her life had been full of physical pain due to disease, a bus accident, and the twenty-eight resulting surgeries she endured. Kahlo's artwork sometimes depicted these dark themes, but even in the face of death, *Viva la Vida* shares a message of beauty and joy. Famous during her life, but especially after it, Kahlo's works were declared Mexican artistic monuments in 1984 (Cultural Property News, 2018). Almost a quarter of a century later, Chris Martin, the lead singer-songwriter of Coldplay, was on tour in Mexico City. Martin happened to see Kahlo's painting and instantly loved its title. In an MTV interview, he discussed the theme of the album that includes *Viva la Vida*, stating, "We're aware of all the bad stuff in life . . . but that doesn't mean you should ever give in to it" (Montgomery, 2008).

Other ideas for works to collaboratively study as a whole class in preparation for later individual projects include pieces of music and visual art examples that share a common culture, style, or time period. After completing the analysis of your chosen musical work, use another Arts Analysis Template to record the results of your

Figure 2.4 *Viva la Vida, Watermelons* by Frida Kahlo.
© Paulo Quiros/Dreamstime.com, ID 123698766.

group research about the visual art example you choose. The template can be used for visual art examples in the same way you modeled using it for a musical example.

When both Arts Analysis Templates are completed, consider similarities and differences that emerged during the analysis of the music and the art, highlighting them in two different colors on the templates. These interactions may initiate further research. For example, in the "Viva la Vida" works discussed above, you would likely identify and discuss their different cultural origins, the recognition both works received, and the positive message they share.

Individually or in small groups, students will now use the same process to analyze a musical example and a visual arts example. You may wish to provide parameters regarding the musical examples students may choose and regulate students' search for visual arts examples. This could be a good opportunity for students to constructively use cellphones in the classroom. You could also offer students a set of three to four musical examples and works of art from which to choose. To manage noise levels when multiple musical examples are played simultaneously around the room, you could also have students visit a computer lab or use classroom computers with headphones. After students compare and contrast their musical examples and their works of art, they will prepare short verbal summaries that represent the significant relationships and/or relevant differences they identified.

Assessment

Set up a demonstration exhibit to highlight students' work. Project the visual arts images and listen to excerpts of the corresponding musical examples students have chosen. Ask students to present their findings to the class by expressing and defending their appraisals of their two selected works and the meaningful connections between them.

Collect two Arts Analysis Templates from each student, one for music, and one for art. Check each template for accurate information, correct labeling of similarities and differences, evidence of thorough research, and careful examination of creative works.

Lesson 2.2: Paul Klee: Inspired by Music and Inspiring Music

Grade Level

Middle school, but may be adapted

Essential Question

How do interactions with works of art and music impact our creative responses to those specific works and the ways we interpret the world?

Objectives

- Students will analyze representative artworks by Paul Klee and the musical compositions associated with them, appropriately identifying, describing, and evaluating the characteristic musical and artistic elements that define each work, through class discussions and in individual written responses.
- Students will apply their understanding of musical techniques to create a melodic and rhythmic improvisation, then correctly explain the specific elements of art they chose to represent and the musical techniques they employed.
- Students will apply their understanding of Paul Klee's artistic techniques to create a painting in Klee's style, then correctly explain the elements of music they chose to represent and the visual arts techniques they employed.

National Core Arts Standards Addressed

- VA:Cr3 and MU:Cr3: Refine and complete artistic work
- VA:Pr4 and MU:Pr4: Select, analyze, and interpret artistic work for presentation
- VA:Pr6 and MU:Pr6: Convey meaning through the presentation of artistic work
- VA:Re8 and MU:Re8: Interpret intent and meaning in artistic work
- VA:Re9 and MU:Re9: Apply criteria to evaluate artistic work
- VA:Cn10 and MU:Cn10: Synthesize and relate knowledge and personal experiences to make art

Materials

- Art supplies
  - White paper
  - Pens and pencils
  - Tempera or acrylic paint in white, black, red, blue, and yellow
  - Paintbrushes
  - Paper plates
  - Paper cups
- Musical supplies
  - Various pitched instruments for improvisations, such as students' band or orchestra instruments, bells, keyboards, recorders, ukuleles, and so forth.
- Musical examples
  - *Fugue in G Minor*, K. 401 by W. A. Mozart
  - *Klee: Suite for Piano*, "Messenger of Autumn," by Takashi Kako
  - *Seven Studies on Themes of Paul Klee*, 4. "Twittering Machine," by Gunther Schuller
  - *Five Klee Pictures*, Op. 12, 3. "Twittering Machine," by Peter Maxwell Davies
  - Symphony No. 2: *Kleetüden, Variations for Orchestra After Paul Klee*, 4. "Die Zwitschermaschine (Twittering Machine)," by Jason Wright Wingate

There are many excellent audio and video recordings available of all these pieces.

- Historical photo
  - Paul Klee (Figure 2.5)
- Visual art examples (Paul Klee)
  - *Fugue in Red* (Figure 2.6)
  - *Messenger of Autumn* (Figure 2.7)
  - *Twittering Machine* (Figure 2.8)
  - *Resting Ships* (Figure 2.9)
- Video examples

- *[Badura-Skoda-Demus] Mozart: Fuga for Piano Duet in G, K401(K375e)* (youtube.com/watch?v=3sNE374O7ws)
- *Mozart—Fugue in G Minor KV 401/375e, Part 2* (youtube.com/watch?v=gB5XqeEC1RU)

Procedure

Paul Klee (pronounced "clay"; see Figure 2.5) was born in Switzerland in 1879. His father was a German music teacher, his mother a Swiss singer, and unsurprisingly, Klee began his musical training at a very young age. He studied violin, voice, piano, and organ, and was on track to follow in his parents' footsteps and become a professional musician himself. Even as a young student, though, Klee expressed a dislike for classical music composed during his lifetime and felt it didn't have meaning for him. In part because of his opinions about contemporary music, he decided to focus on visual art, rather than music, for his profession. As a teenager, he stated, "I didn't find the idea of going in for music creatively particularly attractive in view of the decline in the history of musical achievement" (PaulKlee.net, n.d.). While Klee did not pursue a career in music, he maintained a deep respect for and love of music, especially that of Bach and Mozart. Throughout his life, music remained a major influence on his art. He was fascinated with the connections between art and music, and across his artistic career, he sought to translate sounds into images. In particular, he believed that rhythm was the primary link between music and art. As might be inferred from the title, Klee's *Fugue in Red* (see Figure 2.6) likely represents one of his early attempts at representing musical structures in a visual form.

In general, a fugue is a contrapuntal, polyphonic musical composition in which a musical theme (the subject) is introduced by one voice or part and then repeated by other voices. The theme is then systematically developed with variations and is interwoven among the various voices. As a comparison, Mozart's *Fugue in G Minor*, K. 401 follows this same structure. Listen to a recording of the piece and aurally identify the points where different iterations of the theme enter. Alternately, listen to an arrangement for piano duet while viewing the musical score in the video *[Badura-Skoda-Demus] Mozart: Fuga for Piano Duet in g, K401(K375e)* (tnsnamesoralong, 2013) or while viewing a visual animation of the sounds in the video *Mozart—Fugue in G Minor KV 401/375e, Part 2* (aniMIDIfy, 2012) to perceive the structure of the fugue more clearly. In *Fugue in Red*, Klee employs various shapes, overlapping them and gradually shifting their color, perhaps representing the sequential recurrences of the musical subject.

Like *Fugue in Red*, many of Klee's over 9,000 artworks were influenced by music. Given music's central role in his artwork, it is not surprising that numerous composers were moved to create music directly inspired by Klee's works. The heart of this lesson focuses on closely examining two of Klee's paintings and some of the musical compositions those works inspired. Lead students to systematically analyze

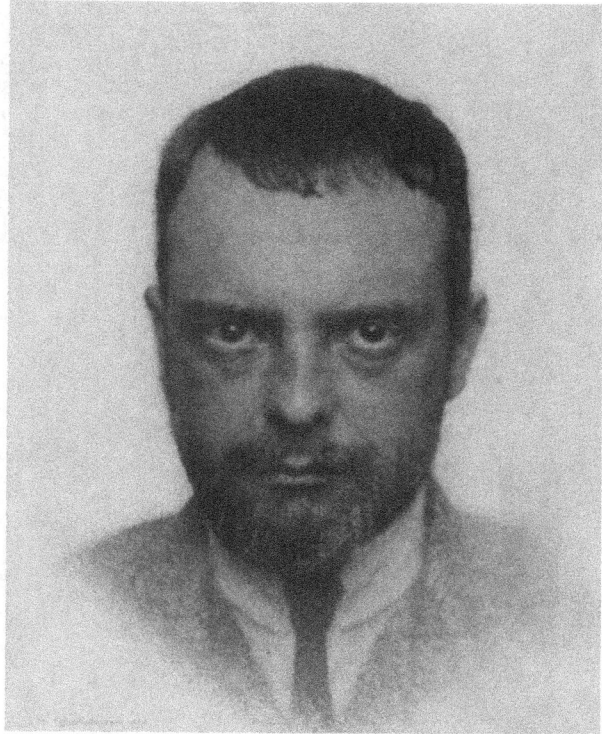

Figure 2.5 *Paul Klee Portrait* by Hugo Erfurth, 1922.
Public Domain/Wikimedia.

each work of art and each composition. Direct students to use the Arts Analysis Template from Lesson 2.1 for each work. Alternately, ask guiding questions such as:

What explanation do you have for ____?
How did the artist portray ____?
What can you infer about ____?
Why might the artist have constructed ____?
How would you distinguish ____?
How could you compare the ____ with the ____ in this work?
How would you evaluate ____?
What categories of ____ can you generate?

Students' subsequent explanations and conclusions may or may not align with the analytical descriptions of works included with this lesson. Treat the content provided here as one viewpoint among the many possible analyses.

1. *Messenger of Autumn*

Paul Klee's *Messenger of Autumn* (see Figure 2.7) consists primarily of columns of horizontal stripes in various shades of blue, green, and white. Departing from the

Figure 2.6 *Fugue in Red* by Paul Klee, 1921.
Zentrum Paul Klee, Bern, Switzerland/Wikimedia.

repetitive pattern of cool colored stripes are a few triangles and diagonally falling stripes in the outer columns. The foremost exception to the blue and green stripe configuration, however, is a single two-dimensional golden-orange oval on a vertical trunk, suggesting a tree contained within two stripes of a single column. Perhaps this single warm-toned "tree" represents the first tree to change the color of its leaves at the beginning of the fall season, signifying it as the "messenger of autumn." An enlarged white half oval is the final departure from the abstract geometric grid of the composition, echoing the shape of the tree, and acting as a sort of reverse shadow of the work's focal point.

Japanese jazz pianist Takashi Kako released *Klee: Suite for Piano*, "Messenger of Autumn" in 1986. The short work for solo piano has a repetitive ostinato accompaniment figure in the bass that anchors the entire composition, and a simple melody that floats above. The piece has a meditative, contemplative character.

In the second section of the piece, Kako creates a sense that "wrong notes" are being played. This is achieved by writing the left-hand accompaniment figure and the right-hand melody in different keys. This juxtaposition of melody and accompaniment reflects the visual juxtaposition of the cool background colors and the warm tree figure in Klee's work.

2. *Twittering Machine*

Twittering Machine (see Figure 2.8) is one of Paul Klee's best-known works. It is a watercolor, pen, and ink oil transfer depicting four birds perched on a wire that is attached to a hand crank. The background is a blue wash of color surrounded by what almost appears to be a pink stain, setting off the twittering machine as a focal point. Klee used oil paint to transfer the line-drawn twittering machine to the paper.

Figure 2.7 *The Messenger of Autumn* by Paul Klee, 1922.
Public Domain/Yale University Art Gallery, Gift of Collection Société Anonyme.

According to the Museum of Modern Art's website, the black smudges are most likely an accidental result of this process (MoMA.org, 2024).

There are many different interpretations of Paul Klee's *Twittering Machine*, ranging from whimsical and lighthearted to darker and more sinister. Have the birds simply chosen a pleasant place to land and sing, or are they tethered to the device against their wills? Is the lighter rectangle under the birds simply the base of the machine, or is it a pit or trap designed to capture prey? Is the machine purely mechanical, or is it some dangerous mix of industry and nature?

Klee's *Twittering Machine* has inspired over 100 musical compositions. Three of the most well known were composed by Gunther Schuller, Peter Maxwell Davies, and Jason Wright Wingate.

- Gunther Schuller wrote *Seven Studies on Themes of Paul Klee* in 1959 and 1960. "Twittering Machine" is the fourth movement of this work that represents a fusion of jazz and classical styles. The two-minute movement opens with spiraling sounds that seem to mimic or indicate the turning of the machine's hand crank. Soon after, a seemingly random assortment of woodwind, brass, and percussion instruments squeak, chirp, chatter, honk, and twitter various bird-like sounds. Approximately two-thirds of the way through the movement, we hear what appears to be the twittering mechanism winding down, expressed in the lower strings. Instead of fading away, though, the machine springs back to fervent action, and we again hear the varied and layered bird songs with their discordant sound. Finally, with a conclusive sputter, the movement ends.

- Peter Maxwell Davies first wrote *Five Klee Pictures* in 1959 for his school orchestra, then set the piece aside. When he came across a copy of the parts in 1976, he created *Five Klee Pictures*, Op. 12 for full orchestra. The third movement of the piece, "Twittering Machine," opens with overlapping ideas presented by the low brass and the piano. The somewhat plodding brass melody gently steps up and down, perhaps representing the turning of the twittering machine's handle. The piano's escalating ascending fragments intersect with the brass melodies, suggesting the connection between the movement of the mechanism's perch with its handle. A range of instruments play over this backdrop, representing a strident, noisy group of birds. As the piece continues, Davies seems to envision that the twittering machine cranks faster and faster. The escalating tension is evident in the ensuing dissonance, increased dynamics, and concentrated texture. Immediately following the frenetic climax, we hear echoes of the turning handle, the revolving perch, and the distinct utterances of various birds. One could imagine that we are hearing the fading remnants of a wind-up toy after the handle is no longer being turned.

- The most recent of our examples, Jason Wright Wingate's Symphony No. 2: *Kleetüden, Variations for Orchestra After Paul Klee*, was written for orchestra in 2009 and contains twenty-seven short movements. Each movement of the symphony is a variation on a melodic theme created to represent

Figure 2.8 *Twittering Machine* by Paul Klee, 1922.
Public Domain/Museum of Modern Art/Wikimedia.

the artist's name. Using the numerical position of the letters P.A.U.L.K.L.E.E in the alphabet as pitch class integers, Wright Wingate converted them to the pitches E.C#.A.C.B.C.F.F. In the fourth variation of the work, "Die Zwitschermaschine," or "Twittering Machine," this series of notes is repeatedly played by the harp, serenely spelling Klee's name throughout the movement. The overall quality of Wright Wingate's "Twittering Machine" is not tranquil, however. Instead, we hear the rotation of the device's handle in the plucked pitches of the string section and the disorderly chorus of bird calls in a sort of fugue for piccolo and flutes. Unlike Schuller's or Maxwell Davies's twittering machines, Wright Wingate's piece ends with a single emphatic accent.

Next, invite students to create their own musical improvisatory compositions inspired by the art of Paul Klee. Examine Klee's *Resting Ships* (see Figure 2.9) as students begin to conceptualize their pieces and prepare to improvise. During 1927, Klee visited the French islands of Porquerolles and Corsica (PaulKlee.net, n.d.). It is possible that his travels there inspired him to create *Resting Ships*, a work he painted in that same year. In the painting, Klee placed brightly colored triangles, diamonds, squares, and semi-circles on a vivid, blue background. The arrangements of abstract shapes appear as sailboats drifting on the Mediterranean Sea. Elements and design aspects of the work students might consider representing musically include line, shape, color, contrast, pattern, repetition, and tone.

Direct pairs of students to improvise short musical passages using available pitched instruments. Just as the composers in this lesson represented various characteristics of Paul Klee's artwork in the compositions they created, students' musical improvisations should align with what they see in Klee's *Resting Ships*. Review some of the characteristic qualities of the work and ask students to demonstrate how they might incorporate those qualities in their improvisations. For example, students could demonstrate a sense of fluidity and flexibility by playing without a strong pulse and without maintaining a consistent tempo. They could emphasize contrasts by playing high and low sounds, perhaps including broad glissandos that sweep between pitch extremes. They could portray the map of shapes by playing clusters of notes, eliminating a sense of tonal center, or experiment with soft and loud sounds to show the difference between denser and more open areas of the painting. If students have access to laptops, tablets, or phones, invite them to audio record their compositions for later sharing.

Assessment

Ask students to explain a direct connection between music and art to a partner, using specific examples of musical and artistic techniques to support their generalizations. As the partner discussions conclude, pass out index cards. On their index cards, have students write one to two sentences about the relationship between the two art forms.

After students' compositions are complete, have students sit in a circle with their partners. Allow pairs of students to take turns sharing their recorded compositions or live performances. After each example, the students will clarify the connections

Figure 2.9 *Resting Ships* by Paul Klee, 1927.
Public Domain/National Museum of Fine Arts/Wikimedia.

between their compositions and Klee's work, justifying their musical choices based on the analysis of *Resting Ships*. Foster a positive atmosphere by encouraging students to offer commendations and compliments to their peers.

Extensions

1. Listen to music by Bach or Mozart, Paul Klee's favorite composers. Invite students to create a work of art that is inspired by Paul Klee by manipulating two-dimensional shapes to reflect at least one specific musical characteristic of the piece. Depending on the musical example, students might choose to create their artwork with mostly one tone of color (warm or cool). To reflect the musical stimulus, they might vary the sizes, arrangement, or layering of the specific geometric shapes they select.

2. Klee's drawing *Bad News from the Stars* was owned by musician Serge Gainsbourg; he created a musical composition inspired by the work. Without knowing what Klee's *Bad News from the Stars* looks like, listen to Gainsbourg's "Bad News from the Stars." As a digital image of the artwork is not readily available online, invite students to extrapolate the musical information contained in the song to imagine the drawing.

3. Some composers have created multi-movement musical works with each variation or section inspired by a different Paul Klee work. Print or digitally

display all the artwork associated with a single composer's composition. Play the musical representations and have students infer which musical movement is connected to each image by analyzing and evaluating each work. Some possibilities:

- Peter Maxwell Davies's *Five Klee Pictures*, Op. 12 is a single piece for orchestra with five separate movements.
- Jim McNeely's *Paul Klee* (2007) is a complete jazz album written for the Swiss Jazz Orchestra that includes eight compositions.
- Gunther Schuller's *Seven Studies on Themes of Paul Klee* (1959–1960) is a large work for orchestra in seven movements.
- Sándor Veress's *Hommage à Paul Klee* (1951) is a set of seven fantasies for two pianos and string orchestra.
- Jason Wright Wingate's Symphony No. 2: *Kleetüden, Variationen für Orchester nach Paul Klee* (2009) includes twenty-seven short movements.

4. Return to Klee's *Fugue in Red* example from the beginning of this lesson, an artwork that was likely inspired by a musical composition, perhaps one like Mozart's Fugue in G Minor, K. 401. Listen to Jason Wright Wingate's Symphony No. 2: *Kleetüden; Variationen für Orchester nach Paul Klee*, "14. Fugue in Red," a musical composition inspired by Klee's artwork. Compare and contrast the two musical works. Consider taking the next step in the sequence and have students create an artwork titled *Fugue in Red* based on Wright Wingate's piece. The sequence would be music (Mozart) possibly inspiring art (Klee) inspiring music (Wright Wingate) inspiring art (students).

5. Compare various other Klee paintings with the musical compositions they inspired. See Table 2.2 for suggestions:

Lesson 2.3: Replicating Artistic and Musical Techniques

Grade Level

Middle school or high school, depending on adaptations

Essential Question

How does learning about specific creative elements and following established traditions encourage people to take creative risks and generate creative ideas?

Table 2.2 Paul Klee artwork and associated musical compositions

Paul Klee's Artwork	Associated Musical Compositions
Senecio (1922)	Peter Maxwell Davies: *Five Klee Pictures*, Op. 12, IV. "Stained Glass Saint" (1976)
Diana in the Autumn Wind (1934)	Gap Mangione: "Diana in the Autumn Wind" (1972)
Bust of a Child (1933)	Jim McNeely: *Paul Klee*, 3. "Bust of a Child" (2007)
Glass Facade (1940)	John Pennington: "Glass Facade" (2008)
Little Blue Devil (1933)	Gunther Schuller: *Seven Studies on Themes of Paul Klee*, 3. "Little Blue Devil" (1959–1960)
Pastorale (Rhythms) (1927)	Gunther Schuller: *Seven Studies on Themes of Paul Klee*, 7. "Pastorale" (1959–1960)
All in Twilight (1932)	Tōru Takemitsu: "All in Twilight" (1987)
Ancient Harmony (1925)	Sándor Veress: *Hommage à Paul Klee*, 3. "Alter Klang" (1951)
Up and Down (1932)	Sándor Veress: *Hommage à Paul Klee*, 4. "Unten und Oben" (1951)
Rock Collection (1932)	Sándor Veress: *Hommage à Paul Klee*, 5. "Steinsammlung" (1951)
Fatal Bassoon Solo (1918)	Jason Wright Wingate: Symphony No. 2: *Kleetüden, Variationen für Orchester nach Paul Klee*, 12. "Fatal Bassoon Solo" (2009)

Objectives

- Students will demonstrate their understanding of a variety of creative elements (contour, layering, balance) by accurately distinguishing those elements in existing visual art and musical works.
- Students will apply their knowledge to correctly reproduce a variety of creative elements (contour, layering, balance) in their paintings and musical performances.

National Core Arts Standards Addressed

- VA:Cr1 and MU:Cr1: Generate and conceptualize artistic ideas and work
- VA:Cr2 and MU:Cr2: Organize and develop artistic ideas and work
- VA:Pr5 and MU:Pr5: Develop and refine artistic techniques and work for presentation
- VA:Re7 and MU:Re7: Perceive and analyze artistic work
- VA:Cn11 and MU:Cn11: Relate artistic ideas and works with societal, cultural, and historical context to deepen understanding

Materials

- Art supplies
  - Large, thick sheets of paper (for painting) divided into four equal segments
  - Acrylic or tempera paint in red, blue, yellow, black, and white
  - Pens and/or pencils
  - Paintbrushes
  - Paper plates
  - Paper cups
- Musical examples
  - "Children's March" by Percy Grainger
  - "The Loop Song" by Peter Bence
  - *Concerto a cinque in C Major*: I. "Allegro" by Silvius Leopold Weiss
- Visual art examples
  - Detail from center of Van Gogh's *Wheat Field with Cypresses* (Figure 2.10)
  - *A Bear Walking* by Leonardo da Vinci (Figure 2.11)
  - *A Woman with a Folk Plate* by Mikuláš Galanda (Figure 2.12)
  - *A Toast II, 1893* by Anders Zorn (Figure 2.13)
  - *The Ten Largest No. 1—Childhood* by Hilma af Klint (Figure 2.17)
  - Collection of vintage radios (Figure 2.18)
  - *Tulip Pattern* by William Morris (Figure 2.19)
  - *Hens and Chickens*, Library of Congress (Figure 2.20)
  - *Rosette from Stylized Flowers and Leaves* by Julie de Graag (Figure 2.21)
- Musical scores
  - Melody excerpt, "Children's March," by Percy Grainger (Figure 2.14)
  - Melody and accompaniment excerpt, "Children's March," by Percy Grainger (Figure 2.15)
  - Graphic score excerpt, "Children's March," by Percy Grainger (Figure 2.16)
- Video recordings
  - *Grainger, Children's March* (youtube.com/watch?v=mJZR91YggAw)
  - *The Loop Song—Peter Bence* (youtube.com/watch?v=Tb9wgI9bASI)

Procedure

For this lesson, students will analyze elements and principles of art in existing works, then reproduce those elements to better understand the artists' processes. This respectful imitation is standard professional practice and allows students to intentionally practice specific techniques. (See number 11 in the inventory of ideas at the end of this chapter for an exploration of the distinction between educationally inspired replicating and forgery.)

Given the close relationship between visual art and music, it is logical to connect students' study of artistic techniques with an exploration of ways those same elements are expressed musically. Recognizing and considering an element such as texture in multiple disciplines can reinforce students' understanding in each. In this lesson, before students replicate various visual art techniques, they first interpret the expression of those techniques in existing works of art and in existing pieces of music. For example, students might explore ways that texture is expressed in Vincent van Gogh's 1889 oil painting *Wheat Field with Cypresses* (see Figure 2.10) and then use gradation, layering, and a thick medium that stands out from the surface to display texture in their own paintings.

Prepare paper plate "palettes" with red, yellow, blue, black, and white acrylic or tempera paint. Pass out palettes, paintbrushes, pencils, and papers divided into four segments. Three of the segments on students' papers will be separate replicas, allowing students to demonstrate three isolated artistic techniques. In the final segment, students will create paintings giving their interpretation of a recorded piece of music. Alternately, you might choose to have your students explore each individual technique in separate, sequential lessons. The works of art and musical compositions included with this lesson highlight each of the three separate artistic techniques, but there are endless art and music examples from which to choose. All the visual art examples are shown here in black and white but are available through public domain in color.

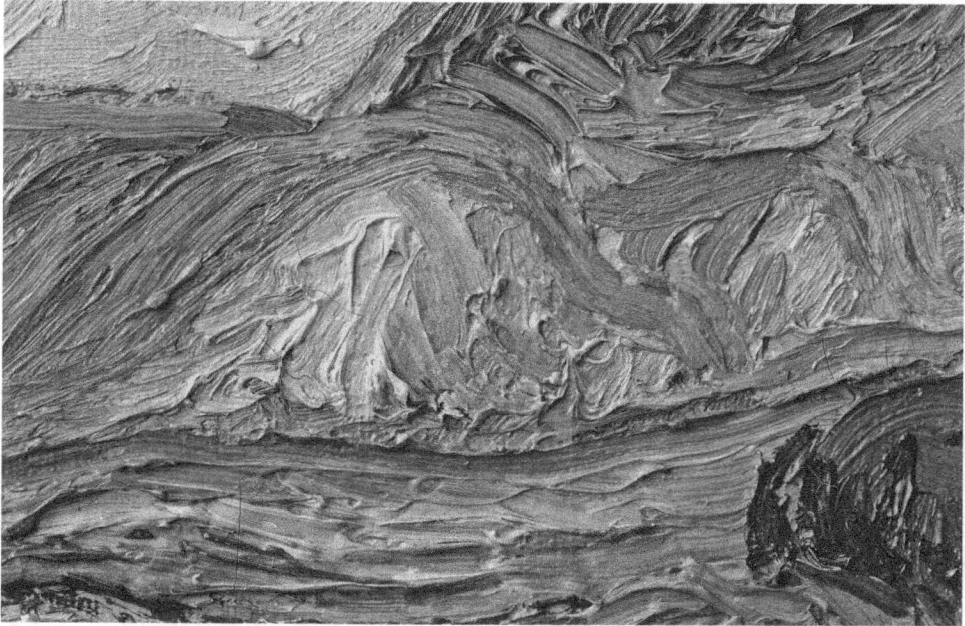

Figure 2.10 Detail from center of Van Gogh's *Wheat Field with Cypresses.*
Public Domain/Metropolitan Museum of Art, Purchase, The Annenberg Foundation Gift, 1993.

1. Contour

Contour is an essential feature in both visual art and music. In art, contour refers to the outline of a figure or subject. The contour is the border edge or line that defines the outer limits of an object. In *A Bear Walking* (see Figure 2.11), Leonardo da Vinci used contour lines to depict a bear mid-stride. The lines create the illusion of depth and impart a sense of movement to the sketch. The faint contour outline of a human figure appears beneath the bear, suggesting that Leonardo recycled this paper.

Contour outlines feature prominently in *A Woman with a Folk Plate* (see Figure 2.12) by Mikuláš Galanda. The contour lines bound the figure and their relative thinness or thickness create depth, further defining the figure. Additional details such as the embellishment on the figure's sleeve and the decorated plate above the figure's shoulder complement the contour lines.

In *A Toast II, 1893* (see Figure 2.13), Swedish artist Anders Zorn uses contour hatching to define the edges of figures and objects. Hatching typically involves placing closely spaced parallel lines in an artwork to produce shading or tonal effects. Cross-hatching utilizes perpendicular lines for the same effects. With contour hatching, rather than straight lines, the hatch marks follow the curves of figures

Figure 2.11 *A Bear Walking* by Leonardo da Vinci, 1484.
Public Domain/Metropolitan Museum of Art, Gift of the Robert Lehman Collection, 1975.

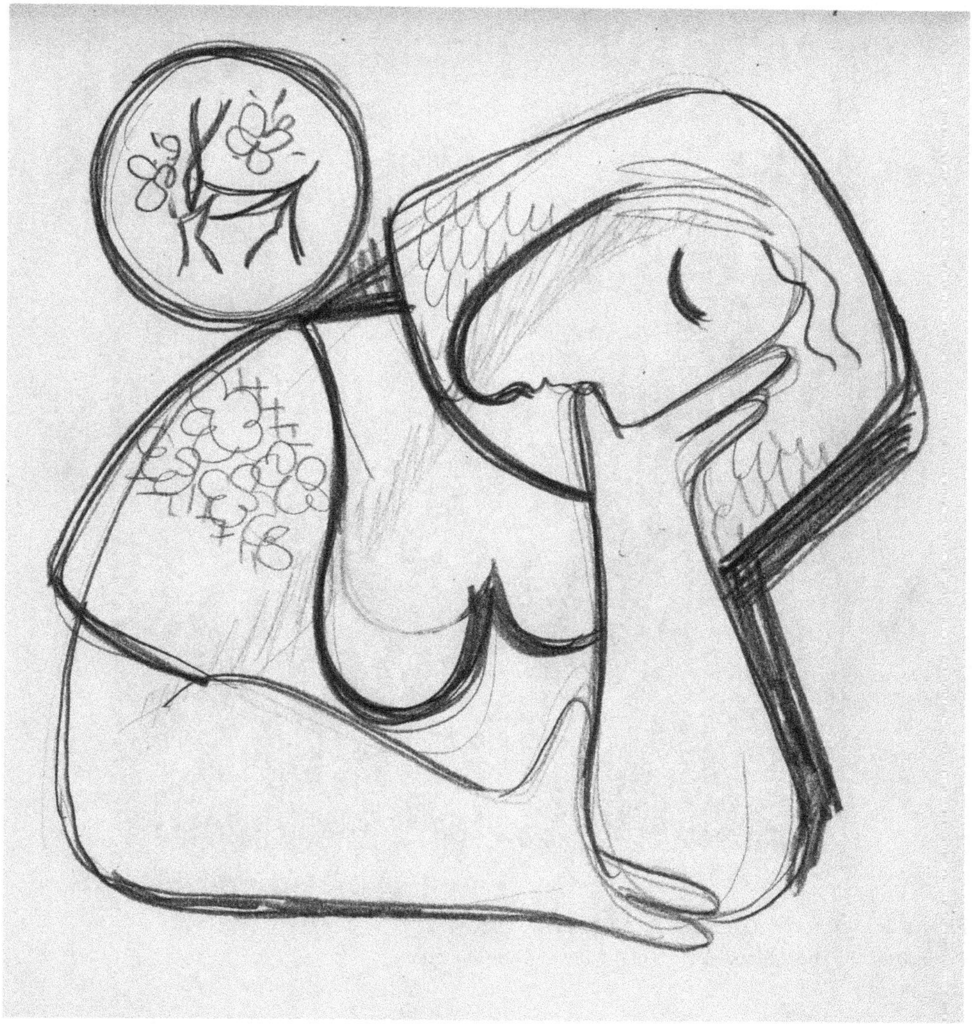

Figure 2.12 *A Woman with a Folk Plate* by Mikuláš Galanda, 1938.
Public Domain/Artvee.

and objects, enhancing the sense of three-dimensional space, in addition to providing shadowing.

In music, contour almost always refers to the shape of a melodic line. Melody lines can ascend by steps or leaps, descend by steps or leaps, repeat pitches, or any combination of those actions. The beginning few measures of Percy Grainger's *Children's March* contain a melody line for piano that rises and falls three times. The first two arcs remain in the bass clef, and the third reaches up into the treble (see Figure 2.14). Sing or hum along and trace the contour of the melody using broad arm gestures.

Just as in visual art, the contour of the melody line is often supplemented with other elements. Grainger's *Children's March* was originally written for two pianos. In this original form, the melody is played by Piano II, while the Piano I part adds

Figure 2.13 *A Toast II, 1893* by Anders Zorn, 1893.
Public Domain/The National Gallery of Art, Rosenwald Collection.

Figure 2.14 Melody excerpt, *Children's March* by Percy Grainger.
Original publication G. Schirmer, 1920. Image courtesy of author.

Figure 2.15 Melody and accompaniment excerpt, *Children's March* by Percy Grainger.
Original publication G. Schirmer, 1920. Image courtesy of author.

accompaniment and depth (see Figure 2.15). Listen to a recording to aurally discern the melodic contour and the complementary accompaniment.

To further explore visual representations of Grainger's *Children's March*, view the animated graphical score video created by Stephen Malinowski (see Figure 2.16). This version of *Children's March* features an arrangement for wind ensemble, performed by the United States Marine Band.

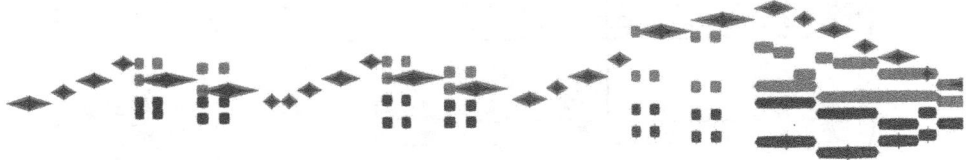

Figure 2.16 Grainger, *Children's March* graphical score excerpt.
Image courtesy of Stephen Malinowski (@smalin on YouTube).

Instruct students to create a contour drawing or painting in the first quadrant of their papers. They might choose to focus on a contour outline or explore various hatching techniques. The subject of their artwork might be a tangible object or a visual representation of the musical contours of a work of their choice.

2. Layering

Visual artists use layering for a variety of purposes. These include adding details, correcting errors, and building visual interest, depth, or complexity. Among the diverse approaches to layering in artwork, the most common involve painting and collage. In painting, layers are created by adding one or more coats of paint on top of another. In collage, materials such as cloth, paper, photographs, or other objects are glued or attached onto a surface. In both these approaches, the artist gradually adds dimension by progressively adding layers of color or additional components to their work.

Layering in visual art involves the stacking of specific elements on top of one another. Sometimes, each individual layer of a work remains visible. Scrutinize *0 Through 9* by Jasper Johns (numerous versions are available online, e.g., the Minneapolis Institute of Art). Are you able to discern each individual numeral in the work? Sometimes, a later layer in a work conceals a layer that was previously applied, creating the impression that a certain shape or object is in front of another. Additionally, layers can be translucent, developing complex colors and textures in combination. In Hilma af Klint's *The Ten Largest No. 3, Youth* (see Figure 2.17), note instances where specific images appear to be layered on top of another and points where layering has created subtle blending of colors.

In music, layering occurs when multiple sounds occur simultaneously. Often, this involves different musicians performing together, with each person contributing to a specific aspect of the whole. For example, a drummer maintains a rhythmic foundation, a pianist provides harmonic accompaniment, a guitar player adds the bass line, and a singer layers on the melody. Alternately, a single voice or instrument can be recorded multiple times, with multiple tracks layered on top of each other after the fact. Sound technicians also can create layers of sound using frequency effects and sonic processing.

Figure 2.17 *The Ten Largest, No 3, Youth,* by Hilma af Klint, 1907.
Public Domain/Wikimedia.

Watch the video of "The Loop Song," a piece written for piano in 2020 by Peter Bence, which is a clear example of layering in a musical composition. The work is based on different combinations of musical fragments that are recorded sequentially, then layered or looped in various combinations throughout the performance. During the piano performance, Bence uses a loop pedal to stop and start the various tracks. The first fragment is played continuously throughout the entire composition, while additional fragments are layered intermittently. Just as you attempted to discern individual numerals layered in Jasper Johns's *0 Through 9*, try to aurally discern concurrent fragments in "The Loop Song."

Direct students to create a layered composition with multiple tracks using a free app like GarageBand, Cakewalk, or Reaper. Have small groups or individuals create discrete tracks that can then be compiled and played back simultaneously. Alternately, small groups of students can create spoken or rhythmic ostinatos and perform them together.

The sculpture *Babel* by Cildo Meireles exhibited layering in both visual art and music. The piece consisted of hundreds of analog radios (see Figure 2.18) stacked in concentric circles with older radios on the bottom, and newer radios on the top. Meireles tuned the radios to different stations and set their volume to the lowest setting at which they could still be heard. The effect was a cacophony of incomprehensible, layered, continuous sound. Ask students about the work: How could someone construe meaning if they could not understand the speech or musical lyrics? What effect would the constantly changing sound produce? What is the impact of the placement of older and newer radios within the work? What ideas do they have for items that could be layered in a work of art?

Ask students to create an example incorporating layers of paint in the second quadrant of their papers. Students who wish to employ collage to demonstrate their understanding of layering will require additional materials or supplies.

Figure 2.18 Collection of vintage radios, circa 1940s and 1950s.
Joe Haupt/Wikimedia, Creative Commons Attribution 2.0 Generic.

3. Balance

Balance is a principle of design that applies to both visual art and music. In music, balance indicates the degree to which two or more different tones or sounds are integrated to attain a complementary sound. Balance is often associated with the dynamic level at which each musician is performing; however, factors such as the size of the ensemble, instrumentation, amplification, and the performance space also affect balance. Additionally, musical balance is relative. For example, listen to the first movement of *Concerto a cinque in C Major*, by baroque composer Silvius Leopold Weiss. The lute melody is prominent in some sections, with all other instruments playing supporting roles; in other sections, no one instrument is conspicuous.

Just as balance in music relates to the integration or distribution of sounds, balance in visual art refers to the integration or distribution of visual elements such as line, color, shape, and form. The arrangement of these elements impacts viewers' perception of the visual weight or sense of equilibrium in an artwork. In visual art, balance is often described as symmetrical, asymmetrical, or radial. In works with absolute symmetrical balance, each portion on either side of the center line is a mirror image of itself, as is seen in William Morris's *Tulip Pattern* (see Figure 2.19).

With asymmetrical balance, the two halves of a work are not identical; however, a sense of balance is achieved by equalizing the theoretical visual weight of the elements incorporated in each half. In *Hens and Chickens*, the five small chicks balance the visual significance of the single hen on the other side (see Figure 2.20). Julie de Graag's *Rosette from Stylized Flowers and Leaves* displays radial symmetry, in which the center of a work is the focal point, and visual elements are consistently arranged around that point (see Figure 2.21).

Ask students to create a painting that displays symmetrical, asymmetrical, or radial balance in the third segment of their papers.

4. Put it all together

In the last remaining segment of students' papers, they will use the techniques they've practiced in the previous three segments (contour, layering, and balance) to create their own work of art. As the inspiration for their work, direct students to listen to and analyze a final piece of music such as "Fiddle-Faddle" by Leroy Anderson or "Ready Wednesday" by Snarky Puppy, both of which are instrumental only. Remind students that they will not be "painting what they feel" or "painting a picture that the music suggests." Instead, they will scrutinize the musical composition and determine its primary features and component elements, based on their previous analyses of the replica examples.

Ask students to create a visual reconstruction of the musical elements they identified and paint their design in the final segment of their paper. Play the music

Figure 2.19 *Tulip Pattern* by William Morris.
Public Domain/Metropolitan Museum of Art/Rawpixel.com.

while students work. Allow students to share their artwork and explain how it is connected to the music.

Figure 2.20 *Hens and Chickens*, Library of Congress, 1901.
Public Domain/Image courtesy of the Library of Congress.

Figure 2.21 *Rosette from Stylized Flowers and Leaves* by Julie de Graag, 1918.
Public Domain/Wikimedia/Rijksmuseum, Gift of J. de Graag, Arnhem, Creative Commons CC0 1.0 Universal
Public Domain Dedication.

Assessment

Informally assess students' responses during collaborative analysis of representative music and art examples, checking for in-tune singing, accurate performance of rhythms, musical independence when performing in parts, and correct identification and descriptions of creative elements.

Collect students' replicas and evaluate the precision with which students were able to express and accurately compile painted examples of contour, layering, and balance.

Extension

Explore additional concepts that music and art have in common such as shape, form, structure, color, positive/negative space, shading, depth, perspective, proportion, unity, and contrast.

Lesson 2.4: Musical and Artistic Expressions of Three Montana Rivers

Grade Level

High school, but may be adapted

Essential Question

How does nature inspire visual artworks and musical compositions? How is natural beauty portrayed in the arts?

Objectives

Students will explore the transformation of location data into music through the process of sonification and the transformation of site-specific visual data into art through the process of action painting, accurately identifying and characterizing the natural characteristics of water and its representation in various media.

Students will collect and quantify visual and aural data, compose a musical work by manipulating musical tools within a sonification app, and share their creative products with the class, describing and defining data points, explaining the compositional adaptations they employed, and clarifying the relationships between the Yellowstone River and their compositions.

National Core Arts Standards Addressed

- VA:Cr1 and MU:Cr1: Generate and conceptualize artistic ideas and work
- VA:Cr3 and MU:Cr3: Refine and complete artistic work
- VA:Pr6 and MU:Pr6: Convey meaning through the presentation of artistic work
- VA:Re8 and MU:Re8: Interpret intent and meaning in artistic work
- VA:Re9 and MU:Re9: Apply criteria to evaluate artistic work
- VA:Cn10 and MU:Cn10: Synthesize and relate knowledge and personal experiences to make art

Materials

- Musical example
  - *Meru: Tracing Earth*, II. "Ruby River" by Linda Antas (https://soundcloud.com/linda-antas)
- Video recordings
  - *The Rhythms of the River* (https://www.benmillerartist.com/videos)
  - Yellowstone National Park Water Sounds (youtube.com/watch?v=1Jj22Tipe2Q)
- Images
  - Map of all Montana rivers (Figure 2.22)
  - Map of select Montana rivers (Figure 2.23)
  - Ben Miller painting on the Jefferson River (Figure 2.24)
  - *Jefferson River* by Ben Miller (Figure 2.25)
- Technology needs
  - TwoTone sonification app
  - Spreadsheet program

Note to teachers: This lesson focuses primarily on the ways artists and musicians utilize unique methods and materials to represent nature in their work. For a further exploration of music as a direct response to experiences in nature and the relationship between listening, performing, and creating in music and environmental awareness, involvement, and action, see Lesson 5.1.

Procedure

Student prompts: "Think of a natural environment that includes water. When you imagine how the water looks and sounds, what characteristics come to mind? Do you picture ocean swells, crashing breakers, or lapping waves? Trickling or crashing waterfalls? A pounding downpour or a light sprinkle? Babbling brooks, roaring rivers, or torrential floods? Rippling lakes or silent ponds?" Ask students to share the particular sights and sounds connected to the water they envisioned. Note if the water anyone describes is a natural feature in Montana, perhaps a bubbling hot spring or an erupting geyser.

Montana's landscape is filled with rivers (see Figure 2.22). In this lesson, students explore artistic and musical representations of three Montana rivers: the Ruby River, the Jefferson River, and the Yellowstone River (see Figure 2.23). The Ruby River originates in southwest Montana in the Ruby Mountain Range and is a tributary of the Jefferson River, joining that river near the town of Twin Bridges. The Jefferson then joins with two other Montana rivers, the Madison and the Gallatin, to form the headwaters of the Missouri River at Missouri Headwaters State Park near Three Forks. The Jefferson River is also a portion of the Lewis and Clark National Historic Trail. The Yellowstone River, at nearly 700 miles long, is the longest unrestricted, free-flowing river in the lower forty-eight states. The headwaters of the Yellowstone River are just south of Yellowstone Lake in Yellowstone National Park. Waters of the Ruby River, the Jefferson River, and the Yellowstone River eventually converge when the Yellowstone, the principal tributary of the Missouri, joins about a mile east of the Montana–North Dakota border.

Linda Antas is a music technology professor at Montana State University in Bozeman, Montana. She reports spending most of her waking hours using technology and teaching others how to use it, but also articulates a deep connection with mountains and the wilderness. Antas weaves together these two essential parts of her life, technology and nature, through the creation of music. Her composition

Figure 2.22 Map of Montana rivers.
Image courtesy of Annika Harney.

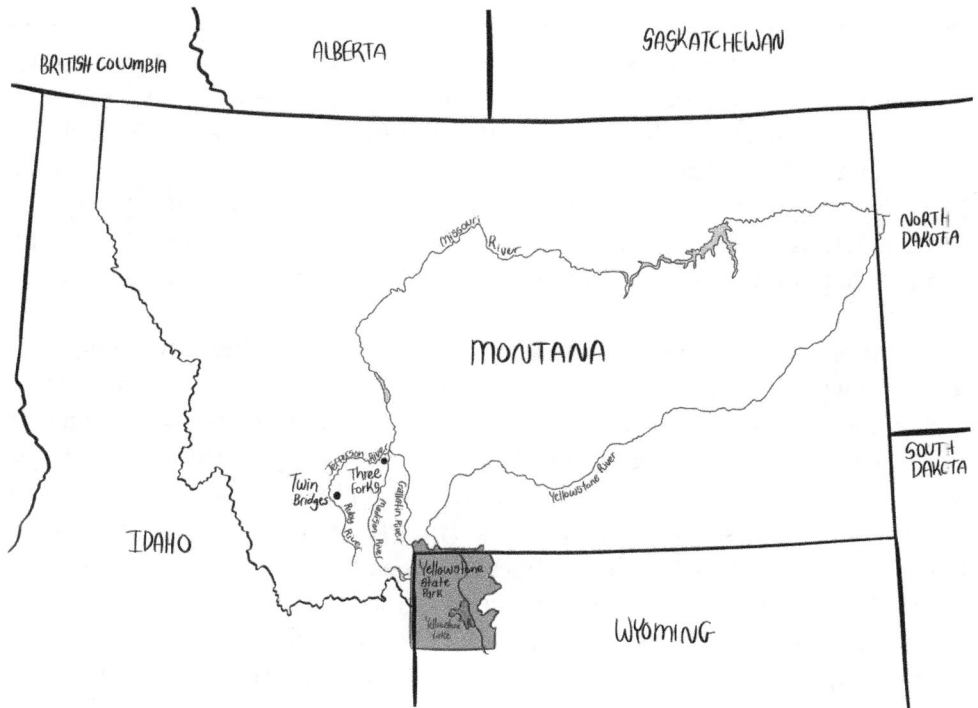

Figure 2.23 Map of select Montana rivers.
Image courtesy of Annika Harney.

Meru: Tracing Earth, for flute and electronic sounds, exemplifies that notion, combining her interest in sonification and her need to be connected to the mountain wilderness.

Sonification is to sound as visualization is to image. Sonification usually involves the use of algorithms to translate numerical data into audible sound by directing information from a data set through a computer program that generates digital audio, then into a converter that translates the digital signals to analog musical sounds. It is one way of experiencing and understanding data. Just as someone might create a line graph to show rainfall in inches over a specified period of time, that data could be expressed musically, as well, with the numerical data transformed into pitches and rhythms.

Meru: Tracing Earth is a sonification of location data Antas collected in southwestern Montana. The title *Meru* refers to the mythical Mount Meru, a fabled five-peaked mountain at the center of the universe that serves as a metaphor for size and stability in Buddhist tradition. The second section of *Meru: Tracing Earth* characterizes the Ruby River. On a float trip, Antas collected continuous information about her GPS location, elevation, speed, and the specific cardinal headings of her drift boat on the Ruby River. She collected 631 data points over the 8.9-mile float including elevations that ranged from 4890.5 feet to 4473.4 feet, speeds of 0 to

5.8 mph, and headings of 0 to 364.5 degrees. Antas mapped the data onto musical parameters to create several aspects of the electronic accompaniment; the drift boat headings were transformed into the flute melody.

Listen to "Ruby River," the second section of *Meru: Tracing Earth*, available on SoundCloud at https://soundcloud.com/linda-antas. Visually trace the path of the Ruby River (Figure 2.23) as the forty-six-second excerpt plays, focusing on the specific characteristics or general impressions of the river that are alluded to in the music. What additional meanings are conveyed through a musical presentation of data?

Like Antas, Ben Miller lives in Bozeman, Montana. He has been flyfishing since he was eight years old. A visual artist, Miller developed a unique painting technique, dubbed fly-cast painting or action painting. He works outdoors, standing about twenty feet away from Plexiglas "canvases" on the banks of the rivers he portrays. Miller creates his own flies, specially designed to apply paint rather than to catch fish. He loads the flies with paint, then strikes the Plexiglas as he repeatedly casts the flies from one of his flyfishing rods. Miller creates each painting over the course of a day, reading the river and the light as he chooses the specific colors and flies. When a painting is complete, Miller turns the Plexiglas over. The first hits of the day appear as the top layer of the finished product, displaying the surface reflection and ripples, while the layers of paint applied later in the day become shadows, rocks, and finally, the bed of the river. View the fifteen-minute video *The Rhythms of the River* for an intimate look at Miller's process (Miller, 2022). Figure 2.24 shows Miller working on

Figure 2.24 Ben Miller painting on the Jefferson River.
Image courtesy of Ben Miller and www.oxbowgallery.art.

one of his paintings. If you look closely at the photograph, you can see the canvas in front of Miller, who stands on the bank of the Jefferson River.

The resulting artwork, *The Jefferson River*, is shown in Figure 2.25. In addition to examining the layers of paint that represent the strata of the river from the surface to the riverbed and the colors that represent a range of elements from bubbles to rocks, invite students to analyze the unique shapes of the assorted splotches, blots, daubs, and flecks and to postulate the relationship between distinctive patterns and features and the various flies shaped as loops, lines, balls, or knots. What other characteristics of the natural environment are portrayed in the artwork?

Next, students will use a simple sonification app to design and generate musical compositions based on a third Montana river, the Yellowstone River. TwoTone is a free open-source web-based app that turns data sets into music, allowing students to sonify and manipulate data without having to write their own code.

To get started, scrutinize a video recording of the river, captured in 2021 within the borders of Yellowstone National Park, *Yellowstone National Park Water Sounds* (Relaxing White Noise, 2021). Direct pairs of students to record their perceptions about the sights and sounds they observe, utilizing the following prompts, if needed: What does the water sound like? What other sounds do you hear? What variations in the sound are apparent? How would you describe the sounds in terms of

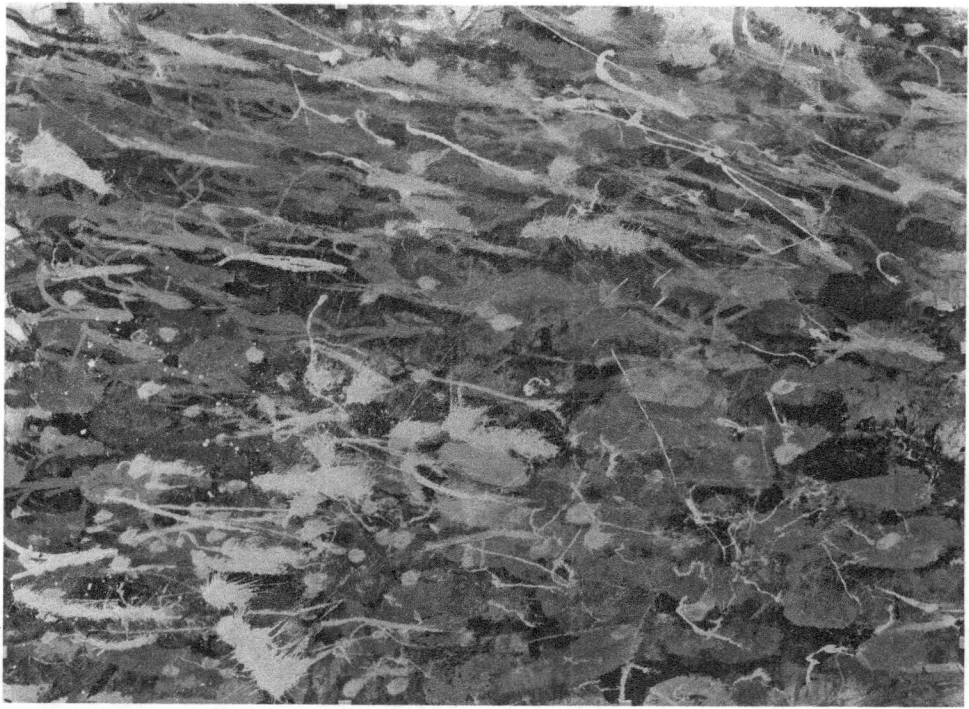

Figure 2.25 *The Jefferson River* by Ben Miller.
Image courtesy of Ben Miller and www.oxbowgallery.art.

dynamics, pitches, rhythms, accents, or tempo? What does the river look like? What distinguishes the river from the landscape surrounding it? What are the prominent shapes, forms, colors, lines, textures, or shading you observe?

The TwoTone app includes free data sets in the form of sample spreadsheets for students to utilize. These include everything from Mars weather reports to data about honey production in the United States. Choose one of the sample data sets to model the sonification process for the class. TwoTone will automatically generate a basic audio track from the selected data set, but employing the optional creative alternatives substantially varies the musical output. Take student suggestions as you develop the class demo composition: Change a track's data source or instrument; adjust the total duration of the piece; change the duration of different portions of the data; or modify the tempo of the compositions. The app also includes advanced features that allow students to adjust dynamics, filter data according to specific attributes, change keys, and adjust registers. After each adjustment, click the play button within the app to listen to the sound generated from the data. The app also allows students to export their compositions as audio files in MP3, PCM, or MIDI format.

For this lesson, rather than using the prefabricated data sets in TwoTone, students will generate and upload a set of numerical data in spreadsheet form based on the Yellowstone River video recording they viewed. Each pair of students will choose at least one visual and one auditory aspect of the first minute of the Yellowstone River video to quantify and enter in a spreadsheet. Students will record a visual and an auditory datapoint every five seconds, resulting in twenty-four total datapoints. For example, students might focus on bird calls and waves, noting whether any bird sounds are apparent and describing the specific type of waves present on the screen at the :05 point, the :10 point, and so forth of the video (see Table 2.3).

Next, students must quantify their data, so that it can be entered numerically in a spreadsheet (see Table 2.4). Using the previous example, since the presence of bird songs is a variable with only two possible responses, students might assign the

Table 2.3 Preparing data for spreadsheet

Time stamp, Yellowstone River video	Audio Attribute: Presence of bird songs	Visual Attribute: Type of waves present in lower right-hand corner of screen
:05	Yes	Ripples
:10	Yes	Smooth—none
:15	No	Ripples
:20	Yes	Splashes
etc.	etc.	etc.

Table 2.4 Quantified spreadsheet data

Time stamp, Yellowstone River video	Audio Attribute: Presence of bird songs	Visual Attribute: Type of waves present in lower right-hand corner of screen
:05	1	1
:10	1	2
:15	2	1
:20	1	3
etc.	etc.	etc.

integer 1 to all "yes" responses and the integer 2 to all "no" responses. Similarly, if students identified three separate codes to label the type of waves they perceived (ripples, smooth, and splashes), each description would be assigned a corresponding number. After students' spreadsheets are complete, they will upload their data sets to the TwoTone app and create a composition using the previous process.

Assessment

Invite pairs of students to present to the class. Students will justify their selection of specific audio and visual to collect, describe and define the resulting data points, explain the compositional adaptations they employed, and share their creative products, clarifying the relationships between the Yellowstone River and their compositions.

Inventory of Ideas

The following collection of ideas contains additional lesson topics, specific teaching strategies, and recommended activities.

1. If your students are studying a specific topic or issue, consider exploring musical and visual artworks associated with that theme. The diverse viewpoints and purposes different artists and musicians bring will likely lead to a richer understanding of the subject. For example, during a unit about Antarctica, look at visual art and listen to musical works that express distinct perspectives on the topic. You might first view *The Floyd Bennett Wings Its Flight over Antarctica* (Figure 2.26) and *Sastrugi Snow Formations Between the Ceremonial and Geographic South Poles* (Figure 2.27).

Next, listen to "The Harshest Place on Earth" from Alex Wurman's score for the movie *March of the Penguins* and "Penguin Ballet," the third movement of

THE "FLOYD BENNETT" WINGS ITS FLIGHT OVER ANTARCTICA

Figure 2.26 *The Floyd Bennett Wings Its Flight over Antarctica* by Francis Trevelyan Miller, 1930.
Public Domain/Newberry Library.

Nigel Westlake's *Antarctica Suite for Guitar and Orchestra*, a stand-alone piece he adapted from his film score for the IMAX documentary *Antarctica*. For additional insights, listen to Georgia Shackleton, a descendent of Antarctic explorer Sir Ernest Shackleton, playing a piece she composed. You can see her performance on the YouTube video *Relative of Ernest Shackleton Composes on a Violin Made from the Explorer's Floorboards* found at youtube.com/watch?v=R35f2epz5q0 (SWNS, 2022). In the video, Shackleton performs on a violin made from Ernest

Figure 2.27 *Sastrugi Snow Formations Between the Ceremonial and Geographic South Poles* (2023).
Photograph by Travis Groh, USAP. Image courtesy of the National Science Foundation, Creative Commons CC BY-NC-ND 4.0.

Shackleton's floorboards (see Figure 2.28). Finally, perform an Antarctic sledging song, pieces written and sung by Antarctic explorers to pass the time and to synchronize the physically demanding task of pulling a sledge across the ice. "Southern Sledging Song" was written by Frank Hurley in 1913 and is sung to the tune "Sailing, Sailing."

> Hauling, toiling, tireless on we tramp
> O'er vast plateau, sastrugi high, o'er deep crevasse and ramp
> Hauling, toiling through drift and blizzard gale
> It has to be done, so we make of it fun,
> We men of the Southern Trail (Watson, 2015, p. 191)

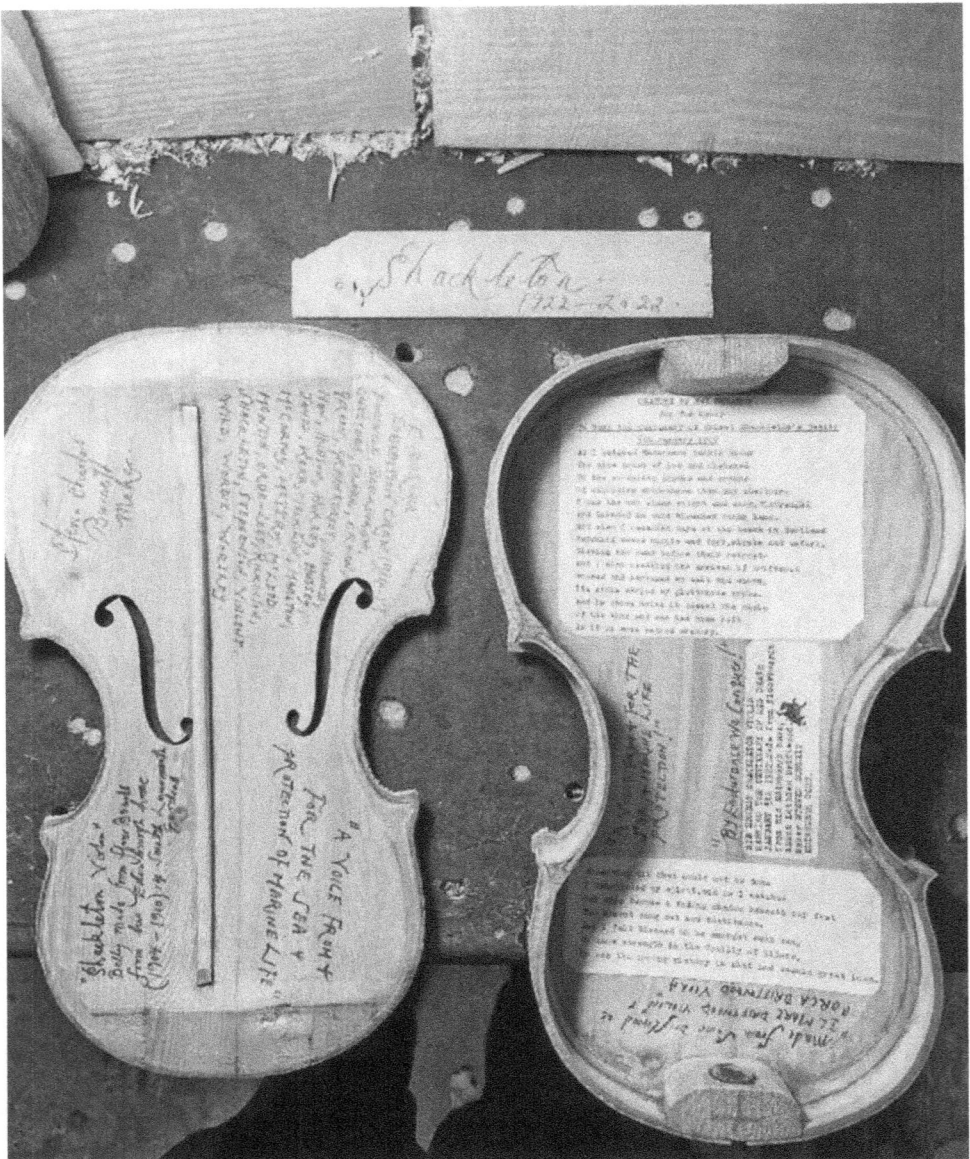

Figure 2.28 Shackleton violin inscribed with all twenty-eight names of the Endurance Antarctic Expedition crew members.
Image courtesy of luthier Steven Burnett.

Why might artists choose to emphasize the desolation and isolation of the landscape? The natural beauty? The heroism or nationalism of exploration? What specific elements of each work convey those ideas?

2. As a whole class, brainstorm eight adjectives that describe different moods. Write each word on a separate large sheet of paper and post the sheets around the classroom space. One by one, display a variety of visual art examples representing

various mediums, genres, and subjects. Without talking, students must move to stand near the mood word they believe best exemplifies each artwork. Repeat the process with a variety of short musical excerpts. Urge students to defend their choices by citing the specific artistic and musical elements present in the works that drove their decisions.

3. For a different exploration of the expression of emotion in visual art and music, rather than asking students to interpret given musical and artistic works, direct them to reflect about aspects of music and art that typically are used to portray emotions. Group students in pairs and pass out notecards, each labeled with a single word representing a particular emotion. Direct students to brainstorm artistic characteristics that are associated with their assigned emotion and record at least three ideas or elements on their notecard (e.g., they might focus on specific colors, style of line, and quality of texture). Next, have them consider musical elements that are related to their assigned emotion and again ask them to document at least three ideas (e.g., they might emphasize certain dynamics, rhythms, and instruments). Still working in pairs, ask one partner to summarize how the visual art elements they chose convey a sense of emotion. Repeat the process for music, asking the other partner to articulate their thoughts. Finally, invite the pairs of students to verbally share their interpretations with the whole class. As a large group, complete a T-chart to compare the two data sets to demonstrate interrelated ways of conveying emotions in music and art.

4. Major world events often inspire the creation of art and music, and the COVID-19 pandemic was no exception. Studying artistic products created during the COVID-19 lockdown provides unique snapshots of people's firsthand experiences at a specific point in time and gives insights about their thoughts and feelings. Examine various works to infer the artists' perspective. What musical and artistic techniques do the artists employ to transmit specific messages? One musical suggestion is "Gotta Be Patient" by the Spanish musicians Rai Benet, Guillem Boltó, and Klaus Stroink, who recorded the song on their rooftop during the quarantine. It was later re-recorded by Michael Bublé, Barenaked Ladies, and Sofia Reyes on Warner Records. Another song with a positive message that originated during the lockdown is "I Believe That We Will Win (World Anthem)" by Pitbull. An example of visual art created during the lockdown is *Hope*, a linocut created by Helen Maxfield in gratitude for the UK's National Health Service and all essential workers (see Figure 2.29). Invite students to create their own artwork or compositions based on their remembrances of the COVID-19 lockdown or select another contemporary world event to explore creatively.

5. Consider the appeal of hidden gems, objects that have an unrecognized beauty, significance, or value. The idea that one could go to a thrift store and pick up a lost masterpiece for a few dollars is compelling, but improbable; however, that is just what Jessica Vincent of Richmond, Virginia, did. In 2023, she purchased a rare Italian glass vase at her local Goodwill store for $3.99. It later sold for over $107,000. Sometimes forgotten valuables are right under one's own roof. In 2009, Vicki and

Figure 2.29 *Hope* by Helen Maxfield, 2020.
Image courtesy of Helen Maxfield.

Darrell Gatwood, of St. Anne, Illinois, were renovating a home and found stacks of musical scores. The manuscripts turned out to be the lost works of African American composer Florence Price (see Figure 2.30); the home had once been Price's summer residence. The Gatwoods donated the complete set of documents to the University of Arkansas, and Price's rediscovered works can now be performed and recorded. A representative example of Price's work is the playful third movement of her Symphony No. 3. Gather students' ideas about the value of lost or forgotten artifacts. What determines an object's actual value? What constitutes an authentic work of art?

6. A still life is a work of art in which the subject matter is limited to manufactured or natural inanimate objects. Essentially, a still life depicts non-living things that are "still." These works of art can suggest a mood or exhibit an artist's technical skill. Often, the artist evokes a sense of fleeting beauty or alludes to the impermanence of life by portraying perishable flowers, fruit, or other food at the peak of freshness. French painter Louise Moillon follows that practice in *Still Life with a Basket of Fruit and a Bunch of Asparagus* (see Figure 2.31) but breaks slightly with convention by including three flies in her painting, suggesting a sense of humor or whimsy.

Figure 2.30 Photograph of Florence Price by George Nelidoff.
Public Domain/Wikimedia.

Like many still life artworks, the song "Still Life" by the South Korean K-pop band BigBang expresses life's constant change. The lyrics discuss the ongoing cycle of the seasons, including nostalgia for change that has already occurred as well as hope for the changes to come. Listen to "Still Life" and identify passages that suggest change, both those that seem to indicate reminiscing about the past and those that project optimism for the future. For example, students might extract lyrics such as "Goodbye now to my beloved young days" and "I'm going to change more than before; a good person more and more" (BigBang, 2022). Beyond the lyrics, what aspects of the music can students isolate that point toward nostalgia or hope? Consider rehearsing the song "Still Life" with students and organize a presentation for another class or group. Students might sing, add percussive accompaniments, create dramatic movements, or generate their own representative artwork to display.

7. Explore the different end results or consequences when visual artists and composers utilize either mixed media or a single medium in a work. Artistic

Figure 2.31 *Still Life with a Basket of Fruit and a Bunch of Asparagus* by Louise Moillon, 1630. Public Domain/Chicago Institute of Art.

mediums or materials for drawing include pencil, pen, chalk, and crayon; typical mediums for painting are watercolor, tempera, acrylic, and oil; and mediums for sculpting include metal, wood, stone, and ice. In visual art, mixed media describes artworks that incorporate more than one material. While it is not the norm to describe a piece of music's instrumentation as its "media," the characterization fits. According to the Library of Congress, "Musical mediums of performance are defined as the voices, instruments, and other entities needed to perform a piece of music, such as a children's chorus, electronic organ ensemble, flute, orchestra, or a soprano voice" (Library of Congress, 2017). An example of a piece written for a single medium is a piano solo; a typical "mixed media" musical composition is a work for symphony orchestra. Direct students to use their phones (if allowed) or classroom computers to locate a single-medium artwork, a mixed-media artwork, a single-medium musical example, and a mixed-media piece of music. Ask students to present their findings in small groups and to share their conclusions about the suitability of the mediums for the purpose and function of each work.

8. Lesson 2.2 explores music inspired by the artwork of Paul Klee, but there are abundant art/music connections to consider. As in the Klee lesson, invite students to analyze individual works, investigate connections, perform musical examples, and create personal musical and artistic products. Additional suggested connections include:

Figure 2.32 *Dog Days Are Over* by Ugo Ronginone, 1998.
© Ugo Rondinone, Photo: Studio Rondinone.

- Dan Fogelberg's "Bones in the Sky," written as a tribute to Georgia O'Keeffe
- Swedish band Peter Bjorn and John's "Blue Period," an homage to Picasso's period of the same name
- Florence and the Machine's song "Dog Days Are Over," composed by lead singer Florence Welch after daily bike rides past a huge art installation in London, *Dog Days Are Over*, by Ugo Ronginone (see Figure 2.32)

9. While some visual artworks have a single piece of music with which they are associated, others, such as Leonardo da Vinci's *Mona Lisa* (see Figure 2.33), have inspired dozens of musical compositions. As a class, choose three songs inspired by the *Mona Lisa* to analyze. Besides Nat King Cole's iconic "Mona Lisa," consider "Mona Lisas and Mad Hatters" by Elton John, "Mona Lisa (When the World Comes Down)" by The All-American Rejects, "Portrait of My Love" by Matt Monro, and "Masterpiece" by Madonna. Compare and contrast the pieces selected by the class using a three-way Venn diagram. Sing along with all three songs to analyze and compare musical elements such as melody, range, tempo, rhythm, and text more straightforwardly. Additional elements to examine in each song include instrumentation, harmony, texture, dynamics, and structure. Hold a class vote to determine which piece "wins" as top connection with Leonardo's work.

10. In 2021, figurative artist Lynette Yiadom-Boakye curated a playlist of songs to accompany her exhibition of oil paintings at the Tate Gallery in London. The playlist includes songs by Miles Davis, Bill Evans, Nina Simone,

Figure 2.33 *Mona Lisa* by Leonardo da Vinci, 1550.
Public Domain/Musée du Louvre.

James Brown, and Solange, and is available on Spotify. Music plays an important role in Yiadom-Boakye's artistic process. Gather a set of artwork and invite students to curate a playlist that aligns with the collection. Alternately, gather a set of musical examples and direct students to curate a set of artworks that fit each piece.

11. In Lesson 2.3, students explored the respectful replication of works of art, often undertaken for educational purposes or to pay homage to an artist. Conversely, a forgery, counterfeit, or hoax is a dishonest replication or wrongful attribution of a work. Following a European tour during the early part of the twentieth century, Austrian violinist Fritz Kreisler (see Figure 2.34) reported finding numerous lost masterpieces of Bach, Vivaldi, and others.

He began performing the pieces in concerts, and they made their way into the standard classical repertoire. In reality, the pieces were not "found" by Kreisler; he had written them himself. On his sixtieth birthday in 1935, a *New York Times* reporter jokingly asked Kreisler if he had written the now-famous pieces. Surprisingly, Kreisler unapologetically admitted the hoax, revealing his conviction that whether a piece was credited to "Bach" or "Kreisler," the significance of the piece was the same. Kreisler's admission instigated fierce debates, but ultimately, his reputation was not harmed, and he remained a highly regarded musician. Listen to "Tempo

Figure 2.34 Photograph of violinist Fritz Kreisler with his violin, 1913.
Public Domain/Library of Congress.

di Minuetto," a piece written for violin and piano by Kreisler that was originally attributed to the composer Paganini.

One of the greatest mysteries, and perhaps one of the greatest deceptions in the art world, surrounds the artwork *La Bella Principessa*, attributed to Leonardo da Vinci (see Figure 2.35). In 2008, art dealer Peter Silverman reported finding the drawing at a friend's home. If the artwork is truly by Leonardo da Vinci, it could be valued at more than $160 million. If shown to be a forgery, it would be worthless. Experts on both sides disagree about the work, with some using scientific techniques such as carbon-14 testing, infrared photography, and fingerprint analysis to make their cases, and others citing a lack of provenance, analysis of artistic techniques, and materials not typical of Leonardo to make theirs. Following an investigation of "Tempo di Minuetto" and *La Bella Principessa*,

Figure 2.35 *La Bella Principessa*, attributed to Leonardo da Vinci.
Public Domain/Wikimedia.

invite students to locate other potential musical or artistic forgeries and research their circumstances.

12. Unlike forgeries, composition studies are early drafts or preparatory models done by an artist in preparation for a later work. We sometimes have records of these training pieces, as is the case with *Composition Study for "The Street Pavers"* (see Figure 2.36) by the Italian artist Umberto Boccioni. He created the work in pen and brown ink in 1914 as a precursor to *The Street Pavers* (see Figure 2.37). Compare the relationship between *Composition Study for "The Street Pavers"* and *The Street Pavers*, noting similarities and differences between the two. How might the creation of a composition study have helped Boccioni paint *The Street Pavers*?

Figure 2.36 *Composition Study for "The Street Pavers"* by Umberto Boccioni, 1914.
Public Domain/The Metropolitan Museum of Art, The Michael D. Dingman Foundation Gift, 1990.

In music, an arrangement is an adaptation of another musical work. *Ancient Airs and Dances Suite*, No. 1 by Italian composer Ottorino Respighi is a well-known arrangement, based on a collection of lute pieces from the Renaissance. Sing the opening melody of "Passo Mezzo Bonissimo" (see Figure 2.38) and the first and second themes of "Mascherada" (see Figure 2.39 and 2.40). These anonymous works are two of the lute pieces on which Respighi based his composition. Next, listen to the two Renaissance pieces performed on the lute. Both recordings can be found on *Ancient Airs and Dances*, a CD produced by Hyperion, with Paul O'Dette, lute. Finally, listen to the fourth movement of Respighi's *Ancient Airs and Dances, Suite No. 1*, "IV. Passo Mezzo e Mascherada," written for symphony orchestra in 1917. Many excellent recordings are available. Direct students to consider the relationship

Figure 2.37 *The Street Pavers* by Umberto Boccioni, 1914.
Public Domain/The Metropolitan Museum of Art, Bequest of Lydia Winston Malbin, 1989.

Figure 2.38 Opening melody of "Passo Mezzo Bonissimo."
Image courtesy of author.

Figure 2.39 Opening melody of "Mascherada."
Image courtesy of author.

Figure 2.40 Second theme of "Mascherada."
Image courtesy of author.

YOUR PERSONAL "FLYING CARPET" Step into it, press a button, and off you go to market, to a friend's home, or to your job.
Take off and land anywhere; no parking problems. Plug in to any electric outlet for recharging. They're working on it!

MORE POWER TO YOU!

America's independent light and power companies build for your new electric living

Figure 2.41 *Your Personal "Flying Carpet"* electric flying car advertisement, 1958.
Public Domain/Jim Griffin/Flickr.

between the earlier lute pieces and Respighi's arrangement. Can they identify the melodies they sang in the orchestral arrangement? What other aspects of "Passo Mezzo Bonissimo" and "Mascherada" can they hear in Respighi's work? Why might artists or musicians create drafts? Why might artists or musicians seek inspiration from previous artworks and compositions?

13. Contemplating the future is a universal human characteristic. Throughout history, people have described future events and situations in songs and art. These works reflect our collective hopes and fears, at times expressing our aspirations, and at other times, our apprehension. Some depictions of the future appear fantastical or unrealistic, while some seem like calculated forecasts. For example, the 1958 power company advertisement, *Your Personal "Flying Carpet,"* included the language, "Take off and land anywhere; no parking problems. Plug into any electric outlet for recharging. They're working on it!" (AIELPC, 1959), suggesting that flying cars were imminent (see Figure 2.41). The lyrics of Joni Mitchell's 1970 song "Big Yellow Taxi" were less optimistic and included the phrase "they paved paradise and put up a parking lot" (Mitchell, 1970, track 10), serving as a cautionary message about the future. Direct students to envision a specific aspect of their lives in the future. Ask everyone to represent their vision of the future musically and artistically by composing a set of lyrics and drawing an image. In both works, they should strive to depict the predicted situation and express their associated frame of mind. Invite students to perform their compositions and share their artworks with the class.

14. Musical blend occurs when two or more different tones or sounds are merged into a single, unified sound. The term "blend" is frequently used when describing a single section of an ensemble; for example, if someone says, "the altos have a good blend," they are referring to the singers' homogeneous sound. Listen to *Seoithín Seó*, a traditional Irish song collected in County Waterford, Ireland, in the late 1930s and

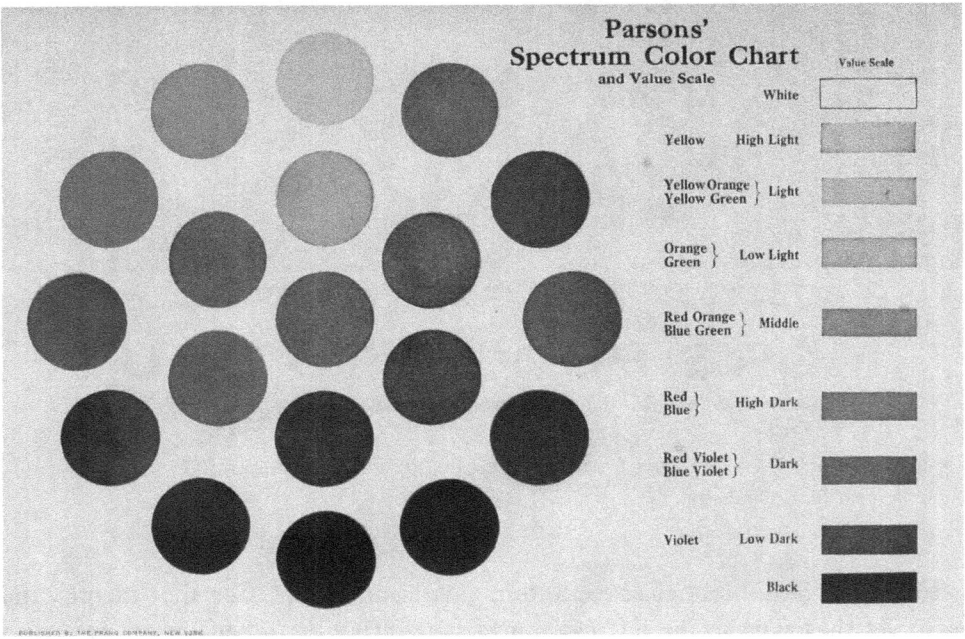

Figure 2.42 Illustration from *The Principles of Advertising Arrangement* by Frank Alvah Parsons, 1912.

Public Domain/University of California Libraries.

arranged by Rosaleen Molloy for unison choir. In the faster A section, notice the uniform timbre, or tone quality, of the treble choir as multiple singers produce a consistent, cohesive sound. In the slower B section, a soloist sings above the unison harmony line. Invite students to select a song whose melody is familiar to the class. Sing the melody in unison, listening to each other carefully to produce a balanced, unified sound.

In visual art, blend most often refers to the mixing or blurring of colors to create a new amalgamation. Show a color wheel or spectrum chart such as Figure 2.42. Pass out red, yellow, blue, black, and white paints, along with papers and brushes. Direct students to blend primary colors with various amounts of white or black to explore assorted hues, and to blend primary colors with each other to create secondary and tertiary colors. Identify the analogous colors students create. Analogous colors are those that lie next to each other on the color wheel such as red, red-orange, and orange, or yellow-green, green, and blue-green. Vincent van Gogh utilized analogous colors to create *Sunflowers* (see Figure 2.43). Invite students to create a painting

Figure 2.43 *Sunflowers* by Vincent van Gogh, 1889.
Public Domain/Van Gogh Museum, Amsterdam.

incorporating one set of analogous colors they blended. With students, explore why a composer might choose to write music for a single type of voice or instrument and why an artist might choose to create with analogous colors.

15. Select twelve artworks and print them in notecard-sized sets, with one complete set for each group of students in your class. Guide groups of students to establish discrete categories in which they can arrange their artworks into four distinct sets, with three artworks per set. Examples might include works with animals, works that are drawings, works that incorporate a vanishing point, and works in black and white. Invite groups to share their categorizations with the whole class. Share a twelve-song playlist with the class and repeat the activity, asking students to classify the songs into discrete categories.

3

Music and Language Arts

Introduction

Music and language arts are deeply connected through their emphasis on human expression. Narratives, whether novels, stories, poems, songs, or symphonies, impart information and communicate emotions. Interacting with narratives in music and language arts encourages students to appreciate a wide variety of texts, critically analyze compelling themes, and develop empathy for another's point of view. By reinforcing the relationships between music and language arts, teachers encourage students to develop understandings in both disciplines and draw connections between them. Integrating music and language arts enriches the learning environment, makes learning relevant, and builds a sense of classroom community.

The creative and self-expressive aspects of music and language arts are also strongly associated. In verbal communication, students might use vocal inflection, volume, and stress to effectively convey their intent. In a musical performance, students might sing with varied dynamics, rhythmic accents, and differing registers. These connections can encourage student writers and composers to compare the way sounds come together to make words and the way pitches come together to make tunes. Additional connections between music and language arts can also inspire creativity. Music can serve as a writing prompt; lyrics can be examined as poetry; texts can be analyzed for structure, rhyme, and literary devices; and students can create new lyrics to align with existing songs.

The lessons included in chapter 3, as well as the strategies and activities in this chapter's inventory of ideas, promote a balanced approach to integrating language arts and music content. These lessons and strategies incorporate examples that represent a wide variety of styles, cultures, and historical periods.

Common Links Between Music and Language Arts

Lessons that explore elements, skills, and broad concepts in music and language arts enhance students' understanding in both disciplines. Enduring ideas that can be explored in music and language arts include:

Action
Cause/effect

Integrating Music Across the Secondary Curriculum. Kristin Harney, Oxford University Press. © Oxford University Press 2026.
DOI: 10.1093/9780197822036.003.0003

Character
Color
Conflict/resolution
Contrast
Fluency
Form/structure (beginning–middle–end; climax–resolution)
Literal and nonliteral meaning
Mood
Pattern
Perspective
Phonemic awareness/pitch discrimination
Power
Repetition
Rhythm
Setting
Sequence
Storyline
Style
Subject/main idea/theme
Texture
Unity
Voice
Writing process

National Standards

Both the National Core Arts Standards for Music and the Common Core State Standards (CCSS) for English Language Arts encourage interdisciplinary connections. For example, to meet Music Anchor Standard 11, students are expected to "demonstrate understanding of relationships between music and other arts, other disciplines, varied contexts, and daily life" (National Coalition for Core Arts Standards [NCCAS], 2015). Similarly, in the CCSS for English Language Arts there is an explicit focus on integrating and evaluating information from a variety of sources, including musical examples (National Governors Association Center for Best Practices, Council of Chief State School Officers, 2010a). The following boxes specify the standards that are addressed in the chapter 3 lessons and inventory of ideas:

- Box 3.1, Common Core State Standards for English Language Arts: Reading
- Box 3.2, Common Core State Standards for English Language Arts: Writing
- Box 3.3, Common Core State Standards for English Language Arts: Speaking and Listening

- Box 3.4, Common Core State Standards for English Language Arts: Language
- Box 3.5, National Core Arts Standards for Music

Box 3.6 offers a framework for structuring chapter 3 lessons and activities.

Box 3.1 Common Core State Standards for English Language Arts (Reading) Included in Chapter 3 Lessons (L) and Inventory of Ideas (I)

READING

Key Ideas and Details	R.1	Read closely to determine what the text says explicitly and to make logical inferences from it; cite specific textual evidence when writing or speaking to support conclusions drawn from the text	L 3.2 I 7
	R.2	Determine central ideas or themes of a text and analyze their development; summarize the key supporting details and ideas	L 3.3 I 12 I 14
	R.3	Analyze how and why individuals, events, or ideas develop and interact over the course of a text	L 3.1 I 2
Craft and Structure	R.4	Interpret words and phrases as they are used in a text, including determining technical, connotative, and figurative meanings, and analyze how specific word choices shape meaning or tone	L 3.4 I 1 I 4 I 8
	R.5	Analyze the structure of texts, including how specific sentences, paragraphs, and larger portions of the text (e.g., a section, chapter, scene, or stanza) relate to each other and the whole	L 3.2 I 9 I 11
	R.6	Assess how point of view or purpose shapes the content and style of a text	L 3.4 I 11
Integration of Knowledge and Ideas	R.7	Integrate and evaluate content presented in diverse formats and media, including visually and quantitatively, as well as in words	L 3.1 I 2 I 5 I 7 I 13
	R.8	Delineate and evaluate the argument and specific claims in a text, including the validity of the reasoning as well as the relevance and sufficiency of the evidence	L 3.3 I 15
	R.9	Analyze how two or more texts address similar themes or topics in order to build knowledge or to compare the approaches the authors take	L 3.4 I 2 I 8 I 15
Range of Reading and Level of Text Complexity	R.10	Read and comprehend complex literary and informational texts independently and proficiently	L 3.2 I 6

Box 3.2 Common Core State Standards for English Language Arts (Writing) Included in Chapter 3 Lessons (L) and Inventory of Ideas (I)

WRITING

Text Type and Purposes	W.1	Write arguments to support claims in an analysis of substantive topics or texts using valid reasoning and relevant and sufficient evidence	L 3.3 L 3.4 I 10 I 13
	W.2	Write informative/explanatory texts to examine and convey complex ideas and information clearly and accurately through the effective selection, organization, and analysis of content	L 3.3 I 8 I 11
	W.3	Write narratives to develop real or imagined experiences or events using effective technique, well-chosen details, and well-structured event sequences	L 3.1 L 3.2 I 9
Production and Distribution of Writing	W.4	Produce clear and coherent writing in which the development, organization, and style are appropriate to task, purpose, and audience	L 3.4 I 1
	W.5	Develop and strengthen writing as needed by planning, revising, editing, rewriting, or trying a new approach	L 3.1 L 3.4 I 11
	W.6	Use technology, including the Internet, to produce and publish writing and to interact and collaborate with others	L 3.2 L 3.4 I 8
Research to Build and Present Knowledge	W.7	Conduct short as well as more sustained research projects based on focused questions, demonstrating understanding of the subject under investigation	L 3.3 I 5
	W.8	Gather relevant information from multiple print and digital sources, assess the credibility and accuracy of each source, and integrate the information while avoiding plagiarism	L 3.3 I 15
	W.9	Draw evidence from literary or informational texts to support analysis, reflection, and research	L 3.4 I 6
Range of Writing	W.10	Write routinely over extended time frames (time for research, reflection, and revision) and shorter time frames (a single sitting or a day or two) for a range of tasks, purposes, and audiences	L 3.2 I 10

Box 3.3 Common Core State Standards for English Language Arts (Speaking and Listening) Included in Chapter 3 Lessons (L) and Inventory of Ideas (I)

SPEAKING & LISTENING

Comprehension and Collaboration	SL.1	Prepare for and participate effectively in a range of conversations and collaborations with diverse partners, building on others' ideas and expressing their own clearly and persuasively	L 3.4 I 3
	SL.2	Integrate and evaluate information presented in diverse media and formats, including visually, quantitatively, and orally	L 3.1 I 4 I 5 I 6
	SL.3	Evaluate a speaker's point of view, reasoning, and use of evidence and rhetoric	L 3.3 L 3.4 I 13
Presentation of Knowledge and Ideas	SL.4	Present information, findings, and supporting evidence such that listeners can follow the line of reasoning and the organization, development, and style are appropriate to task, purpose, and audience	L 3.1 I 3 I 14
	SL.5	Make strategic use of digital media and visual displays of data to express information and enhance understanding of presentations	L 3.2 L 3.3 I 10 I 13
	SL.6	Adapt speech to a variety of contexts and communicative tasks, demonstrating command of formal English when indicated or appropriate	L 3.3 I 1 I 7

Box 3.4 Common Core State Standards for English Language Arts (Language) Included in Chapter 3 Lessons (L) and Inventory of Ideas (I)

LANGUAGE

Conventions of Standard English	L.1	Demonstrate command of the conventions of standard English grammar and usage when writing or speaking	L 3.1 I 3
	L.2	Demonstrate command of the conventions of standard English capitalization, punctuation, and spelling when writing	L 3.2 I 12

Knowledge of Language	L.3	Apply knowledge of language to understand how language functions in different contexts, to make effective choices for meaning or style, and to comprehend more fully when reading or listening	L 3.2 L 3.4 I 11 I 14
Vocabulary Acquisition and Use	L.4	Determine or clarify the meaning of unknown and multiple-meaning words and phrases by using context clues, analyzing meaningful word parts, and consulting general and specialized reference materials, as appropriate	L 3.2 I 7
	L.5	Demonstrate understanding of figurative language, word relationships, and nuances in word meanings.	L 3.1 I 9 I 12
	L.6	Acquire and use accurately a range of general academic and domain-specific words and phrases sufficient for reading, writing, speaking, and listening at the college and career readiness level; demonstrate independence in gathering vocabulary knowledge when encountering an unknown term important to comprehension or expression	L 3.1 I 4

Box 3.5 National Core Arts Standards for Music Included in Chapter 3 Sample Lessons (L) and Inventory of Ideas (I)

MU:Cr1 (Create)	Generate and conceptualize artistic ideas and work	L 3.1 L 3.3 L 3.4 I 4 I 8 I 13
MU:Cr2 (Create)	Organize and develop artistic ideas and work	L 3.2 L 3.3 I 5 I 6 I 14
MU:Cr3 (Create)	Refine and complete artistic work	L 3.2 L 3.4 I 6 I 11 I 13

MU:Pr4 (Perform)	Select, analyze, and interpret artistic work for presentation	L 3.4 I 8 I 10
MU:Pr5 (Perform)	Develop and refine artistic techniques and work for presentation	L 3.2 I 2 I 3 I 13
MU:Pr6 (Perform)	Convey meaning through the presentation of artistic work	L 3.2 I 3 I 10
MU:Re7 (Respond)	Perceive and analyze artistic work	L 3.1 L 3.3 I 1 I 6 I 11 I 15
MU:Re8 (Respond)	Interpret intent and meaning in artistic work	L 3.2 L 3.4 I 2 I 4 I 9 I 14
MU:Re9 (Respond)	Apply criteria to evaluate artistic work	L 3.1 L 3.4 I 1 I 5 I 7 I 12
MU:Cn10 (Connect)	Synthesize and relate knowledge and personal experiences to make art	L 3.1 L 3.3 I 2 I 7 I 9 I 10
MU:Cn11 (Connect)	Relate artistic ideas and works with societal, cultural, and historical context to deepen understanding	L 3.2 L 3.3 I 1 I 5 I 8 I 12 I 15

Box 3.6 Framework for Chapter 3 Lessons and Ideas

This chapter is designed to support middle school and high school educators as they integrate music and language arts. The four detailed, full-length lesson plans are independent and not organized as a progressive series.

- Lesson 3.1: Storytelling and Music: Key Ideas, Details, and Structure of *Slalom* by Carter Pann
  - I first heard Carter Pann's *Slalom* on the radio and instantly connected with the fun topic and the exiting, relatable sound. It is a great example of programmatic music that incorporates various musical devices to communicate a narrative.
- Lesson 3.2: Visual Devices in Graphic Novels and Graphic Musical Notation
  - Secondary students will certainly encounter examples of this contemporary genre, ideally both in and out of school. I was especially excited to connect this approachable literary style with examples of graphic musical notation, exposing students to alternative, accessible ways of expressing musical ideas.
- Lesson 3.3: Stage an Informal Debate: Musical Expression vs. Written Communication
  - Informal debates foster critical thinking, enhance communication skills, and encourage respectful dialogue, all essential life skills. I chose an accessible and relatable debate topic for this lesson, comparing music and writing as ways to convey messages to audiences.
- Lesson 3.4: Poetic and Musical Elegies
  - Students and communities who have suffered losses or tragedies were my inspiration for this lesson. The content prompts an opportunity to explore the functions of music, art, and poetry in contemporary life as we turn to the arts in moments of grief, despair, anxiety, and mourning, as well as moments of commemoration.

The chapter ends with an inventory of ideas detailing fifteen additional lesson topics, specific teaching strategies, and recommended activities. The lessons and activities may be fully taught by individual subject area (ELA or music) teachers; however, ideally, the plans will facilitate partnerships and collaboration between language arts teachers and music specialists. All lessons and activities have been reviewed by practicing teachers, and most have been field-tested in middle school and high school classrooms. Most of the lessons will need to be spread over two or more class periods. Chapter 3 lessons are adaptable to a variety of grade levels and are intended as tools for you to meet your students' needs. You and your students bring your own knowledge and experiences to these encounters, and you are invited and encouraged to apply those skills and understandings. I hope you are inspired to locate additional works to explore, including musical examples students are likely to encounter in their lives beyond school (e.g., readily recognizable musical works, poems, etc.) and those that are less likely to be encountered (e.g., contemporary works that have not yet received widespread recognition, works for specialized groups or audiences, or works that are rooted in specific geographic regions). See additional guidelines for selecting repertoire in chapter 1. All the images included in this chapter are printed in black and white. Consider accessing full-color images online when displaying photographs, artwork, and other graphics for students, especially when lesson content directly references aspects related to a work's color. Please adjust, adapt, or expand these lessons and ideas to work best for you and for your students. Seek out teachers with whom you can collaborate and utilize the range of ideas and examples as starting points to facilitate your creativity and inspire innovative curriculum making.

Lesson 3.1: Storytelling and Music: Key Ideas, Details, and Structure of *Slalom* by Carter Pann

Grade Level

Middle school, but may be adapted

Essential Questions

How does programmatic music utilize narrative tools to communicate a story without words? How does this differ from the use of language to communicate narratives, shape mood, and emphasize themes?

Objectives

- Students will analyze the musical features of *Slalom* related to structure, tempo, and style, and use domain-specific terms when discussing the piece with classmates.
- Students will create a narrative describing an activity or event that is typically portrayed as fast-paced, designing an event sequence in which each segment of their narrative aligns with a corresponding segment of *Slalom*.
- Students will demonstrate an understanding of the relationship between musical and narrative characteristics of the different episodes of *Slalom* by generating an event sequence that exhibits precise words and phrases, relevant descriptive details, expressive sensory language, and a command of standard English.

Common Core State Standards for English Language Arts Addressed

- CCSS:R3: Key ideas and details
- CCSS:R7: Integration of knowledge and ideas
- CCSS:W3: Text type and purposes
- CCSS:W5: Production and distribution of writing
- CCSS:SL2: Comprehension and collaboration
- CCSS:SL4: Presentation of knowledge and ideas
- CCSS:L1: Conventions of standard English
- CCSS:L5, CCSS:L6: Vocabulary acquisition and use

National Core Arts Standards for Music Addressed

- MU:Cr1: Generate and conceptualize artistic ideas and work
- MU:Re7: Perceive and analyze artistic work
- MU:Re9: Apply criteria to evaluate artistic work
- MU:Cn10: Synthesize and relate knowledge and personal experiences to make art

Materials

- *Slalom* by Carter Pann, performed by University of Kansas Wind Ensemble, John P. Lynch, conductor (2007). Naxos Wind Band Classics. Album: Redline Tango.
- Copies of Table 3.1

Procedure

Initiate a class discussion by asking students to list as many synonyms for the word "fast" as they can. Keep a running list on the board. Student responses might include terms like quick, speedy, rapid, high-speed, and swift. Next, ask them to brainstorm activities that are often completed at a very fast pace, again, keeping a record on the board.

Introduce the wind-band composition *Slalom* by the contemporary American composer Carter Pann. As the title suggests, this piece expresses the adventure of downhill skiing. On the first page of the printed musical score, Pann includes a special note for conductors of the piece, stating, "The most important element of *Slalom* is the speed at which it is performed . . . every fragment, gesture, and flourish was fashioned to be executed at break-neck speed" (Pann, 2008). Pann's *Slalom* is an example of programmatic music, a composition that tells a story without the use of text. The work is organized in a collection of scenes a skier might witness on the slopes. In the piece's program notes, Pann states that the ten-minute length of *Slalom* is "precisely the amount of time I need to get from Storm Peak (the peak of Mt. Werner, Steamboat Springs) to the mountain base, skiing full throttle" (Pann, 2008). Notify students that they will each write a narrative that aligns with characteristics of *Slalom* and conveys their interpretation of the "break-neck speed" activity of their choice.

Listen to *Slalom* with the goal of gathering initial impressions about the character of the piece. You might listen to just a few small segments, based on your students' attention spans. As students listen, invite them to choose a quick-paced activity that will be the basis of their narrative. Direct them to jot down aesthetic qualities that are suggested by the music and any words or phrases that describe the piece or their selected activity.

Next, pass out copies of Table 3.1 and engage students in a more in-depth examination, listening to the piece in chunks, and pausing after each section to allow students to record their impressions and any ideas suggested by the music. Table 3.1 outlines a plan for dividing the work into sections, based on the labels Pann devised and included in his musical score. Following this categorization will afford students a framework for how to delineate and characterize fifteen segments in their narratives. The longest sections are around a minute in length, but some segments are very short. For example, the section "Jumps!" is just nine seconds long but contains four quick ascending then descending melodic figures, representing the ups and downs of four different ski jumps. All timings align with the University of Kansas recording referenced in the materials list.

Both music and language are forms of communication; both mediums allow creators to evoke emotions and convey ideas. In the case of *Slalom*, Pann's labels clearly relate to downhill skiing and the musical features he incorporates express and expand the story of a ski run. As students analyze and interpret what they hear, direct their attention to general ways Pann uses musical elements to suggest specific aspects of the narrative. These include the consistently fast tempo, ascending and descending scale patterns, triumphant-sounding brass, syncopated rhythms, dreamy glissandos, slides and swells, and variations in dynamics. How might students utilize Pann's musical structure and translate these ideas to the fast-paced activities they have decided to portray?

You might also draw students' attention to specific moments in the music. For example, what do they imagine the slapstick sounds toward the middle of the "First run" section represent?

What musical elements can they identify that Pann uses to produce an "off-balance" feeling in the "One ski gyrating" section? What do they think of the neighing siren-type sound toward the beginning of the "One ski gyrating" section? What is the effect of the two segments where the piano stands out most prominently? Again, how could students incorporate those musical features in their own narratives and what role could they play?

The storyline of *Slalom* unfolds in a series of episodes and various elements of the story interact. The setting shapes the plot, and listeners can discern repeating themes, variations, conflict, climaxes, and resolutions. As students begin to draft their narratives and chronicle their unique account of a fast-paced event or activity, encourage them to utilize precise words and phrases, relevant descriptive details, sensory language, and well-structured event sequences that align with the episodes in *Slalom*.

Table 3.1 Labeled sections of *Slalom* by Carter Pann and associated timings

Timing	Carter Pann Label	Impressions	Ideas
0:01	–		
0:09	First run		
1:23	Out of bounds; no one in sight		
2:04	Snaking the terrain		
2:23	Scent of pine		
2:54	Jumps! (helicopter, spread-eagle, daffy)		
3:05	On one ski, gyrating		
3:49	Straight down, TUCK		
4:15	Open meadow, champaign powder		
5:04	Approaching vista		
5:41	Valley view, EPOCHAL		
6:36	Molto vivace! Come prima		
6:44	Second run, to the bottom		
7:45	Mountain base in sight		
8:22	Gliding all the way in		

Assessment

- Invite students to share their narrative drafts in small groups. When students act in a reviewer role, direct them to consider the structure of the event sequence portrayed and to review their peer's use of expressive language. Following constructive criticism from peers, direct students to edit and revise their work. Collect final narratives and assess the structure of their event sequences, the alignment of each episode of their story with the structure of *Slalom*, and their use of descriptive details and sensory language.

Extension

- Listen to the opening measures of the second movement of Beethoven's Symphony No. 9 a few times, inviting students to tap the recognizable opening rhythm on their desks. Next, play the opening few bars of *Slalom* and solicit students' perceptions about why Pann might have chosen to open his work in a way that so obviously referenced Beethoven's.

Lesson 3.2: Visual Devices in Graphic Novels and Graphic Musical Notation

Grade Level

Middle school

Essential Question:

How do authors and composers effectively communicate meaning with visual storytelling techniques and graphical notation?

Objectives

- Students will demonstrate an understanding of visual devices in language arts by creating a storyboard with a clear narrative and precise use of specific visual storytelling techniques.
- Students will scrutinize their storyboards, then identify and compose musical sound effects and background accompaniment to enhance their projects' storylines and moods.

- Students will demonstrate an understanding of visual devices in music by creating graphic scores incorporating precise use of specific visual techniques that accurately represent their compositions.
- Students will refine their creative works, present final projects to classmates, and reflect ways the projects effectively integrated visual and auditory cues to convey meaning and evoke responses.

Common Core State Standards for English Language Arts Addressed

- CCSS:R1: Key ideas and details
- CCSS:R5: Craft and structure
- CCSS:R10: Range of reading and level of text complexity
- CCSS:W3: Text type and purposes
- CCSS:W6: Production and distribution of writing
- CCSS:W10: Range of writing
- CCSS:SL5: Presentation of knowledge and ideas
- CCSS:L2: Conventions of standard English
- CCSS:L3: Knowledge of language
- CCSS:L4: Vocabulary acquisition and use

National Core Arts Standards for Music Addressed

- MU:Cr2: Organize and develop artistic ideas and work
- MU:Cr3: Refine and complete artistic work
- MU:Pr5: Develop and refine artistic techniques and work for presentation
- MU:Pr6: Convey meaning through the presentation of artistic work
- MU:Re8: Interpret intent and meaning in artistic work
- MU:Cn11: Relate artistic ideas and works with societal, cultural, and historical context to deepen understanding

Materials

- Graphic novel previously read by class, such as *El Deafo* by Cece Bell
- Examples of graphic musical notation
- Storyboard panel templates, if desired
- Art supplies such as markers or colored pencils
- Objects to produce sound
- Video examples
  - *Iannis Xenakis—Pithoprakta (w/ graphical score)* (youtube.com/watch?v=nvH2KYYJg-o&t=14s)

- *John Cage "Water Walk"* (youtube.com/watch?v=gXOIkT1-QWY)
- *Music Machine 41* (https://simonbelshaw.co.uk/mm41/mm41Intro.html)

Procedure

Following a class reading of a graphic novel such as *El Deafo* by Cece Bell, review visual storytelling techniques and the ways graphic novels convey narratives through images and text. Refer to specific panels as you discuss different techniques. Next, ask pairs or small groups of students to find examples within the graphic novel that show each device. You might ask students to locate:

- Panels
- Gutters
- Text boxes or captions
- Verbal dialogue in the form of speech balloons
- Inner dialogue in the form of thought bubbles
- Various placement of characters within panels
- Various angles such as close-up, pan-out, overhead shot, or bug's-eye view
- Differentiation between foreground and background
- Visually based sound effects

For example, students might identify speech balloons, a thought bubble, off-center character placement, and a visually based sound effect in the panels found on a single page of *El Deafo*.

Next, introduce the concept of graphic music notation, in which composers utilize symbols, shapes, or other images in unconventional ways to represent musical elements. The use of graphic notation, rather than traditional notation with pitches and rhythms on staff lines, allows performers to interpret a written musical score in a more exploratory manner. Some graphic musical scores are rooted in traditional notation (see Figure 3.1). Others seem to bridge the gap between conventional and alternative notation (see Figure 3.2), and still others are clearly nontraditional in their design (see Figure 3.3). When composers move away from traditional notation, they typically employ symbols to represent individual sounds, notes, or musical characteristics. Any shape or symbol can be used, as long as there is a detailed key or legend. Dots, circles, squares, diamonds, and triangles are common choices; when dashes and lines are used, often the length of the line represents the length of the note. The relative height of symbols or lines on a page often represents the approximate pitch; often the letter x is used when a sound does not have pitch. Changes to the thickness of a line or the size of an object can indicate changes in dynamics, and different colors might indicate specific instruments, combinations of instruments, or changes in timbre.

Figure 3.1 *Selfie* by John Dante Prevedini.
Image courtesy of composer.

Ask pairs or small groups of students to collaborate to find examples of the shapes, symbols, and other visual techniques that represent various musical elements within a sample graphic musical scores such as *Iannis Xenakis—Pithoprakta (w/ graphical score)* (Carré, 2017). You might ask students to locate visual elements corresponding to:

- Timing
- Pitch or melody
- Tempo, duration, or rhythm
- Instrumentation
- Dynamics
- Articulations

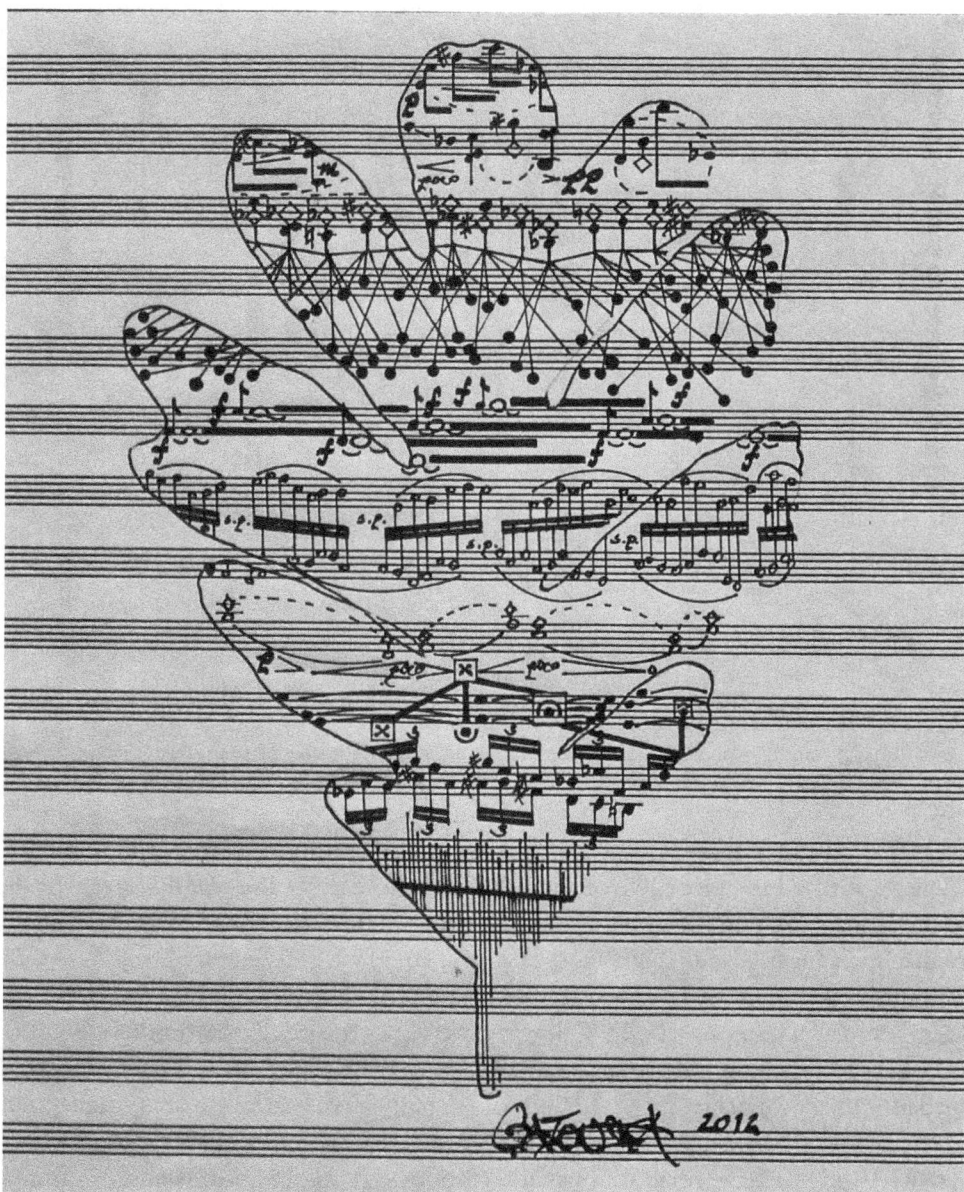

Figure 3.2 *Ex. 9—Eastern White Oak* by Michael Gatonska.
Image courtesy of artist.

A classic example of graphic music notation comes from the twentieth-century American composer John Cage, a pioneer of chance music, the non-standard use of musical instruments, electroacoustic music, and alternative forms of notation. Cage wrote his composition "Water Walk" in 1959. The complete score for the three-minute work includes a list of materials, a map showing the placement of each object and instrument, and three frames, each with text and pictures describing the order

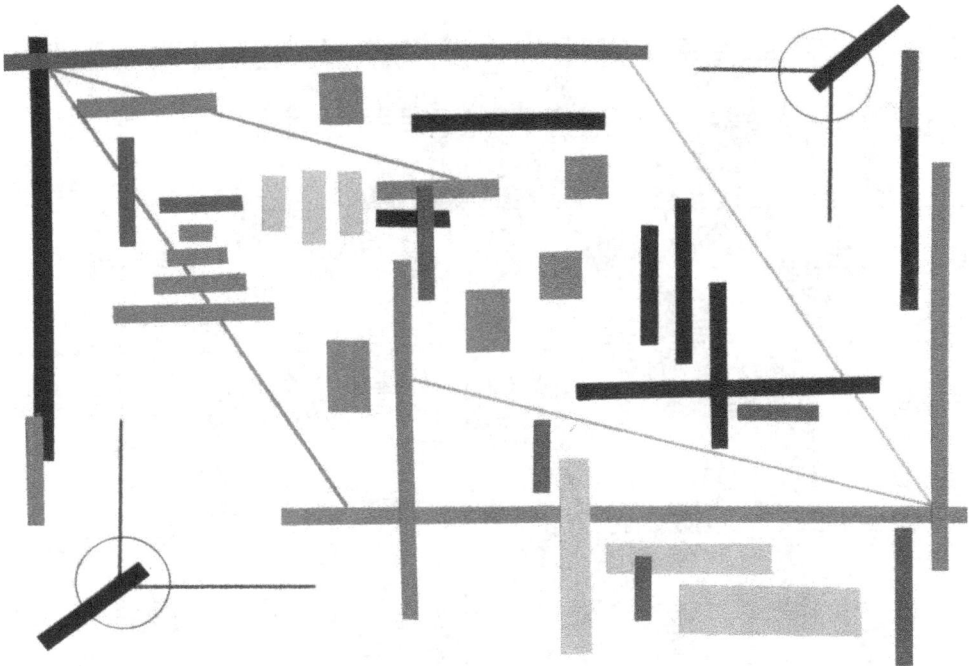

Figure 3.3 Graphic score for Sound Creation Workshop by Leonardo Luigi Perotto.
Leonardo Luigi Perotto/Wikimedia, Creative Commons Attribution-Share Alike 3.0 Unported.

of events within a single minute of the piece, divided in five-second increments. Cage performed the piece live on the 1960 TV game show *I've Got a Secret*. Locate and examine the graphic musical notation online, then view a video of the performance *John Cage "Water Walk"* (Nave for Eva, 2014) with students.

Reinforce students' understanding of graphic notation by inviting them to perform a musical composition by following the video recorded notation of a graphic musical score, Simon Belshaw's *Music Machine 41* (Belshaw, 2017). Divide students into four groups. Each student will play or sing for a given duration on a single pitch of their choice, based on the color that appears in their assigned quadrants.

After students have reviewed visual techniques in graphic novels and examined visual devices in graphic musical scores, they will create between four and six panel storyboards, compose music to accompany their stories, and create single-frame graphic musical scores to represent the music they compose. Table 3.2 details the steps students might take in creating their storyboard panels.

Just as visually based sound effects impact a reader, audible sound effects and musical accompaniments impact listeners. Explore the use of sound effects and dialogue in graphic novels, and have students create accompanying audio elements for their panels.

Direct students to utilize audio elements to compose short musical pieces to accompany their storyboards. Students will notate their compositions using graphic

Table 3.2 Guidelines for creating storyboards

Steps	Details
1. Choose a topic	Facilitate a brainstorming session in which students generate ideas for the themes of their stories. Alternately, provide a common topic for all student projects such as "the future" or "the best surprise." Ask questions such as: • What is the main idea of the story? • Where does the story occur and what is the specific setting? • When does the story take place? • How many characters are in the story? • Who is the main character? • Who are any supporting characters? • What is the main conflict? • How does the story end?
2. Finalize the sequence of events	Each story needs a beginning, middle, and end. The opening panel aligns with the beginning of the story, the next 2–4 panels tell the middle of the story, and the last panel corresponds with the end of the story, making a total of 4–6 panels for the complete story. Each panel represents a different moment in time and should include some action.
3. Add frames	Sketch freehand or use a ruler to create 4–6 panels on a single sheet of drawing paper. The simplest shapes are squares and rectangles, but many shapes and designs are possible. Be sure to include gutters, the empty space between panels. Alternately, there are many free graphic novel templates and storyboard templates available online.
4. Add core elements	In pencil, use basic shapes to sketch the core elements: • one or more empty text boxes • one or more thought bubbles • one or more speech balloons • at least one visually based sound effect • at least one character; vary the placement of the character within the panels • at least two perspectives (e.g., pan-out, close-up, overhead shot, and bug's-eye view)
5. Add text	Complete the written portions of each panel.
6. Add remaining details	Complete the background of each panel, add remaining details, shading, contours, etc.
7. Finishing touches	Trace images and text in pen and add colors.

musical notation. Table 3.3 outlines the steps students might take in creating their graphic musical scores.

Assessment

- Following time for students to finalize their storyboards and musical compositions, allow each individual to present their project to the class or in

Table 3.3 Guidelines for creating and notating compositions

Steps	Details
1. Review and brainstorm	Review storyboards, then brainstorm instruments and explore the use of sound effects in musical accompaniment; identify key moments where specific sound effects, accompaniment, or background sounds could be used to enhance the narrative.
2. Improvise and explore	Aim for 30–60 second composition that aligns with the time it would take someone to read the storyboard; improvise and experiment with various sounds, combinations of sounds, techniques for producing sounds, pitches, dynamics, timbres, and tempos. Students might use traditional instruments, digital music creation tools, classroom objects, or their own voices to perform their compositions.
3. Draft legend	Assign graphic elements to various musical elements; clearly define all aspects of the notation.
4. Notate core elements	Notate composition on a single page. Include the following core elements: • Two or more distinct colors • Two or more distinct shapes • At least one instance of a change to the thickness of a line or the size of an object • At least one visual device related to pitch • At least one visual device related to rhythm • At least one visual device related to dynamics
5. Add key to final score	Sketch the complete legend onto the musical score.
6. Rehearse composition	Rehearse the completed composition, following the notated score. Students may enlist classmates to perform their works as an ensemble.

small groups. Project or display storyboards and graphic scores as students perform their corresponding compositions. Informally assess student participation and collaboration, encouraging classmates to ask questions, provide constructive feedback, identify the visual techniques used by each author/composer, and celebrate successes. Conclude the lesson by reflecting on the connections between graphic novels and graphic music notation, and the ways in which visual and auditory elements can work together to tell a story and evoke emotions. If desired, complete a checklist of required storyboard and composition elements as a formal evaluation (see Table 3.4).

Lesson 3.3: Stage an Informal Debate: Musical Expression vs. Written Communication

Grade Level

High school, but may be adapted

Table 3.4 Required storyboard and composition elements

Project	Element	Checklist
Storyboard	Clear topic	
	4–6 panels, each representing a specific moment in time	
	Clear narrative sequence showing beginning, middle, and end	
	One or more text boxes	
	One or more thought bubbles	
	One or more speech balloons	
	At least one visually based sound effect	
	At least one character; varied placement of the character within the panels	
	At least two perspectives (e.g., pan-out, close-up, overhead shot, and bug's-eye view)	
Composition	One-page graphic notation	
	Alignment between storyboard and composition	
	Score includes complete legend	
	Two or more distinct colors	
	Two or more distinct shapes	
	At least one instance of a change to the thickness of a line or the size of an object	
	At least one visual device related to pitch	
	At least one visual device related to rhythm	
	At least one visual device related to dynamics	
	Performance of composition takes between 30-60 seconds	

Essential Questions

How does a strictly organized debate allow participants to constructively engage in critical thinking and deliberation while fostering diverse perspectives and respectful dialogue?

Objectives

- Students will evaluate how music and writing convey messages to audiences, consider the unique capabilities of each medium, and critically compare the merits of musical and written expression and communication.
- Students will collaborate with teammates to construct cohesive arguments, gather relevant information and evidence, and develop persuasive rebuttals.
- Students will apply critical thinking skills to analyze arguments presented by both sides of the debate and evaluate the strength of evidence.
- Students will engage in respectful and constructive dialogue, listening to and considering opposing viewpoints while articulating their own perspectives.
- Students will communicate their ideas clearly and persuasively in both oral and written formats, demonstrating proficiency in argumentation, expression, and the critical examination of musical and written examples.

Common Core State Standards for English Language Arts Addressed

- CCSS:R2: Key ideas and details
- CCSS:R8: Integration of knowledge and ideas
- CCSS:W1, CCSS:W2: Text type and purposes
- CCSS:W5, CCSS:W6: Production and distribution of writing
- CCSS:W7, CCSS:W8: Research to build and present knowledge
- CCSS:SL3: Comprehension and collaboration

National Core Arts Standards for Music Addressed

- MU:Cr1: Generate and conceptualize artistic ideas and work
- MU:Cr2: Organize and develop artistic ideas and work
- MU:Re7: Perceive and analyze artistic work
- MU:Cn10: Synthesize and relate knowledge and personal experiences to make art

- MU:Cn11: Relate artistic ideas and works with societal, cultural, and historical context to deepen understanding

Materials

- Timer or stopwatch
- Access to research materials (books, internet, etc.)

Procedure

Begin with an overview about the debate. Some key ideas to highlight:

- A debate is a formal discussion on a specific topic, with opposing sides presenting and refuting evidence for an audience or judge
- Debates foster critical thinking, offer opportunities for public speaking, and promote teamwork
- Evidence-based arguments and respectful dialogue are essential
- Describe the general purpose of a debate, review the particular format the class will use, and explain the ground rules (see Table 3.7)

Introduce the debate topic, "The relative effectiveness of music versus writing in expressing emotions and communicating ideas." Divide the class into two teams of debaters and assign each a position to argue: Team Music or Team Writing.

Provide teams with resources and set a time limit for research and preparation. Teams prepare for the debate by conducting background research, collecting exemplars, and anticipating counterarguments. Table 3.5 shows steps students might take in preparing for the debate and Table 3.6 shows examples of the evidence students might compile, including arguments, counterarguments, and exemplars.

The teacher serves as judge, referee, and timekeeper. The round begins with a coin toss to determine the order of arguments. Each team presents introductory constructive arguments, rebuttals, closing arguments, and participates in two crossfire exchanges. The winning debate team is determined by the teacher/judge. Table 3.7 includes a sample debate format and detailed debate directions.

Assessment

- Following the class debate, direct each student to write a four-paragraph essay. In paragraph one, students establish which side of the debate they support, regardless of their team assignment. Students introduce the primary argument for their position and define their key counterargument against the opposing

Table 3.5 Preparation for debate

Step	Description of Tasks
1	Gather background information; read reputable sources concerning the topic; take notes on key points and evidence; cite sources.
2	Brainstorm a list of reasons your argument is true.
3	Narrow the list of reasons to the top three or four that best support your position; these will become your constructive argument.
4	Brainstorm a list of reasons your argument is false.
5	Narrow the list to the three or four most problematic obstacles to your position and generate plausible counterarguments; these will become your rebuttals and will likely be used as talking points during the crossfires.
6	Brainstorm a list of reasons your opponent's argument is false.
7	Narrow the list of arguments to the top three or four that best refute your opponent's position; these will become your challenges and will likely be used during the crossfires.
8	Collect exemplars to highlight and support your position; these include musical examples, written materials, quotes from experts, recordings, etc.
9	Assign tasks and roles; prepare for each portion of the debate; practice delivery of speeches and discourse, focusing on clarity, persuasiveness, and time management.

Table 3.6 Sample of student-compiled evidence

Medium	Argument	Evidence
Music	Emotional impact	• The emotional impact of music can be immediate and instinctual. • Music has the power to connect emotionally with listeners and evoke a wide range of emotions, from joy and excitement to sadness and nostalgia. • Music is effective for conveying mood or atmosphere.
	Universal language	• The appeal of music transcends cultural and linguistic barriers, making it accessible to people of different backgrounds, cultures, and ages. • Music can convey narrative and storytelling elements through lyrics, melodies, and musical motifs, allowing for the communication of themes, messages, and perspectives. • Music is a universal language that transcends cultural and linguistic barriers, making it accessible to people of different backgrounds and ages.
	Elements	• Style, sound, melody, rhythm, harmony, lyrics, dynamics, structure, instrumentation, and musical motifs allow for the communication of themes, messages, and perspectives.
	Non-verbal expression	• Music often bypasses the need for language. • Instrumental music, in particular, can convey emotions without relying on lyrics, allowing for a more abstract and open-ended interpretation of emotions. • Music often employs symbolic and metaphorical elements, such as musical motifs, themes, and imagery, which can convey abstract ideas and concepts in a non-verbal manner.

Table 3.6 Continued

Medium	Argument	Evidence
	Historical context; cultural significance	• Music can communicate historical and cultural context. • Music serves as a form of cultural expression and identity, conveying cultural values, traditions, and histories through musical styles, genres, and lyrics.
	Individual preference and interpretation	• Preference for specific musical genres and styles is subjective. • Musical preference is dependent on factors such as cultural background and personal experiences. • People may interpret the same piece of music differently based on their own associations and emotional experiences.
Writing	Memory and association	• Music can enhance memory and association, making it effective for conveying information through mnemonic devices, jingles, and musical cues. • In many cases, the effectiveness of communication depends on the alignment between the medium and the message. For example, complex scientific concepts may be more effectively communicated through written explanations, while cultural traditions and emotional experiences may be better conveyed through music.
	Clarity and Specificity	• Writing allows for precise and clear communication, making it ideal for conveying detailed instructions, technical concepts, and complex information. • The direct expression of ideas through language enables individuals to articulate their thoughts, opinions, and arguments.
	Elements	• Many attributes of writing impact readers' perceptions, including imagery, organization, theme, point of view, word choice, and tone.
	Personal Expression	• Writing enables individuals to articulate emotions and thoughts in a personal and direct manner, fostering connections and empathy with readers. • Writing allows for clear and specific communication of emotions, facilitating the portrayal of complex emotional states.
	Contextual Understanding	• Writing can convey content within a specific context, such as personal letters, diaries, emails, and texts, providing additional layers of meaning and interpretation. • Writing can adapt to different contexts and audiences, allowing authors to tailor their message to effectively communicate ideas to specific groups or individuals.
	Accessibility and Flexibility	• Written information can be easily disseminated and accessed through various mediums, including books, articles, websites, and digital documents. • Writing can accommodate a wide range of topics and styles, from academic essays and scientific reports to creative storytelling and persuasive arguments.
	Preservation	• Writing provides a durable means of recording information, allowing it to be preserved and referenced over time.

Table 3.7 Debate format

Team	Time in minutes	Element	Details
A	4	Constructive Arguments	The opening statements in the debate should clearly establish the team's position, summarize the key arguments that support their position, and present corroborating evidence. Sample statements:
			It is our position that ..
			We will argue that there are three reasons why . . .
			First . . .
B	4		Second . . .
			Lastly . . .
			The following musical examples (or written examples or other evidence, depending on the team) support our claim. As you listen to the brief excerpt, notice the . . .
A + B	3	Crossfire I	The crossfire portions of the debate allow members of each team to clarify the arguments presented by their opponents and to question the evidence they offered. Each team strives to demonstrate flaws in their opponent's position. Both teams ask and respond to questions during this segment of the debate. Crossfire tips:
			• Balance time spent asking and responding to questions; share responsibility.
			• Strive to ask specific questions that focus the discussion and highlight core distinctions between the two sides.
			• Maintain professional, respectful conduct.
			• Listen carefully and take notes during opponent's presentations; formulate questions and potential responses.
B	3	Challenges and Rebuttals	In this portion of the debate, teams must divide their time between offense and defense.
			• Challenges offer the opportunity for teams to call their opponent's reasoning into question, dispute their claims, and cast doubt on their evidence.
A	3		• Rebuttals offer teams the chance to contradict claims made against them and to refute specific statements or allegations made by their opponents.
			• Students may again choose to use musical or textual examples to support their case during this portion of the debate.
A + B	3	Crossfire II	See Crossfire I.
A	2	Closing Comments	The final statements in the debate should synthesize the key points for the judge to take into consideration. Closing comment tips:
			• Focus on a synopsis rather than specific details.
B	2		• Emphasize the team's best arguments, counter the opposition's best arguments, and highlight the opposition's biggest weaknesses.
			• Do not introduce new evidence.

position. In paragraphs two and three, students elaborate on their arguments and counterarguments, offering specific evidence and examples for each. Paragraph four is a personal conclusion, similar to the closing comments portion of the debate, written to support their position.

Lesson 3.4: Poetic and Musical Elegies

Grade Level

High school, but may be adapted

Essential Question

How can poetry and music memorialize? How can poetry and music convey messages about the human experience of loss?

Objectives

- Students will identify and explain the purpose of an elegy in literary and musical contexts, describing the key characteristics of elegies and emphasizing their role in mourning or memorializing a literal or figurative loss.
- As a whole class and in collaborative groups, students will analyze and compare examples of well-written poetic and musical elegies, using a template to document themes of loss, the nature of emotional expression, techniques specific to each discipline, and style.
- Students will write short poetic elegies inspired by a loss or remembrance, demonstrating an understanding of tone, voice, and style in crafting an elegy that is respectful and meaningful.
- Students will identify elegiac music that aligns with the emotions they wish to convey, selecting an example with appropriate tempo, dynamics, instrumentation, harmony, and style to accompany their poetic elegies.
- Students will engage in peer review: presenting their combined poetic and musical products in small groups; discussing how they used musical and poetic elements to express their chosen themes; and giving and receiving constructive feedback.

Common Core State Standards for English Language Arts Addressed

- CCSS:R4, CCSSR6: Craft and structure
- CCSS:R9: Integration of knowledge and ideas

- CCSS:W1: Text type and purposes
- CCSS:W4, CCSS:W5, CCSS:W6: Production and distribution of writing
- CCSS:W9: Research to build and present knowledge
- CCSS:SL1, CCSS:SL3: Comprehension and collaboration
- CCSS:L3: Knowledge of language

National Core Arts Standards for Music Addressed

- MU:Cr1: Generate and conceptualize artistic ideas and work
- MU:Cr3: Refine and complete artistic work
- MU:Pr4: Select, analyze, and interpret artistic work for presentation
- MU:Re8: Interpret intent and meaning in artistic work
- MU:Re9: Apply criteria to evaluate artistic work

Materials

- Examples for class analysis
  - Video: *Barack Obama Speaks at Memorial Service for John McCain* (youtube. com/watch?v=7NxO_IyVabk)
  - Poem: "Elegy for One Billion Animals" by Brittany Corrigan (watershedreview.com/poetry/brittney-corrigan-2/)
  - Video: *Ludovico Einaudi—"Elegy for the Arctic"—Official Live (Greenpeace)* (youtube.com/watch?v=2DLnhdnSUVs)
- Additional poems
  - "Cherry Trees" by Edward Thomas
  - "Dirge Without Music" by Edna St. Vincent Millay
  - "Elegy Written in a Country Churchyard" by Thomas Gray
  - "I Roamed with Anger Out of the House" by Emmanuel George Cefai
  - "O Captain! My Captain!" by Walt Whitman
  - "To an Athlete Dying Young" by A. E. Housman
- Additional Musical Examples
  - *Adagio for Strings* by Samuel Barber
  - "Alabama" by John Coltrane
  - "Candle in the Wind" by Elton John
  - *Cantus in Memoriam* by Arvo Pärt
  - "Elegy" by Lisa Gerrard
  - *Elegy for Strings*, Op. 58 by Edward Elgar
  - *Song for Athene* by John Tavener

In this lesson, students will create and present poetic elegies, allowing them to use language to express and process emotions related to loss. Incorporating music into the presentation of their elegies capitalizes on music's unique ability to evoke memories, encourage introspection, and connect with listeners on an emotional level.

Procedure

1. Definitions and Background

First, explain the difference between a eulogy and an elegy. A eulogy is most commonly a speech that is given as part of a funeral, but it can also be a written essay. Eulogies convey grief, but their primary function is to honor the life of someone who has died by praising their character and commending their actions. Depending on the class time available, allow students the opportunity to experience a model of a eulogy by watching the video *Barack Obama Speaks at Memorial Service for John McCain* (AP Archive, 2018). Ask students to dissect the tribute, noting the respectful tone, the reverent commendations, and the specific accolades. In contrast, an elegy is an introspective expression of sorrow or grief, created to mourn the loss of someone or something, regardless of whether the loss is literal or figurative. While a eulogy consists of written or spoken prose, elegies are typically poems or musical compositions. Additionally, while eulogies are almost always created soon after someone's death by people close to the deceased, elegies can be created immediately following a loss, they can be written years after an event, or they might even be created before a loss as a warning or caution. In this lesson, students will examine a poetic elegy and a musical elegy.

In general, contemporary elegies are poets' or composers' responses to loss. Typically, poetic elegies display the following characteristics: (1) discuss the loss of someone or something; (2) express feelings of sorrow, regret, or longing; (3) utilize evocative imagery; and (4) convey a solemn or mournful tone. Musical elegies are often characterized by (1) slow, reflective tempos; (2) minor harmonies; (3) dissonances that provoke feelings of tension; and (4) dynamic swells that evoke intensity and drama.

2. Analyzing Exemplars

Analyze the characteristics of one poetic elegy and one musical elegy together as a class. The poem "Elegy for One Billion Animals" by Brittany Corrigan was written in memory of the animals that died during Australia's 2020 wildfires (Corrigan, 2024). The World Wildlife Federation (WWF) reported that the estimate is actually closer to three billion animals that were killed or displaced by that year's bushfires in Australia (see Figure 3.4). The specific breakdown includes 143 million mammals, 2.46 billion reptiles, 180 million birds, and 51 million frogs (WWF, 2020).

First ask students to read the poem in its entirety. Next, ask pairs of students to identify specific sections of the poem that exemplify the characteristics of a contemporary elegy. Table 3.8 shows possible student responses.

Watch the official live recording of the musical composition "Elegy for the Arctic" by Ludovico Einaudi (Einaudi, 2016). In the video, Einaudi performs the piano solo

Figure 3.4 Koala in Australia bush fire.
© izanbar/iStockphoto.com, ID 1200977363.

from a floating dock in the middle of the Arctic (see Figure 3.5). Again, ask pairs of students to identify specific aspects of the composition that exemplify the characteristics of a contemporary elegy (see Table 3.8).

Next, divide the class into small groups and provide each group with a poem and musical example to analyze (see materials list for ideas). Direct students to repeat the analysis process just employed by the whole class to examine each work. You might provide blank templates for students to collect and organize their findings. Invite each group to present their findings to the class, showcasing ways their poems and musical compositions exemplify the characteristics of an elegy.

3. Creating an Elegy

Tell students they will create individual elegies by writing short poems, selecting music to complement their poems, and presenting their combined poetic and musical products. Either provide students with the specific person, idea, object, or event that will be the subject of their elegy, or direct students to choose a subject with which they resonate. Possible subjects include the death of fictional character, a personal loss, or a broader issues like environmental damage or the losses caused by trauma or dislocation.

Ask students to reflect about the person or thing that will become the subject of their elegy:

- What specific qualities, traits, values, or attributes can they highlight?
- How will they acknowledge or represent grief and loss?

Figure 3.5 Icebergs on Arctic Ocean.
© Erectus/Dreamstime.com, ID 19673623.

Table 3.8 Features highlighting characteristics of elegies

Characteristics of an elegy	Poem: "Elegy for One Billion Animals"	Music: "Elegy for the Arctic"
Communicates the loss of someone or something	• The loss of Australian animals during the 2020 wildfires	• The loss of Arctic environments due to global warming
Emotional expression	• Sorrow • Regret	• Grief • Remorse • Introspection
Techniques	• Evocative imagery • Expressive vocabulary • Use of figurative language, for example, "Your black eyes like embering coals" (Corrigan, 2021) • Use of rhetorical devices, for example, "What can we do to resurrect you? What on earth can we say?" (Corrigan, 2021) • Precise names, for example, bristlebird, koala, wallaby, quokka, and honeyeater	• Minor key • Slow, flexible tempo • Descending melodic figures • Use of silence • Diminuendos at the ends of phrases • Return of opening theme is incomplete • Solo piano
Mood	• Solemn, mournful tone • Somber	• Solemn, mournful tone • Poignant

- Will their poem include words of comfort or hope?
- Will they suggest a sense of closure?

Next, invite students to brainstorm about the specific emotions, ideas, or memories the loss of their subject evokes:

- What specific vocabulary choices will help them portray a reflective tone?
- What vivid imagery can they incorporate?
- How might they include figurative language?
- What rhetorical devices might they employ?

Note: Students may need to conduct additional research to gather sufficient background information about particular experiences, concepts, historical events, cultural practices, or details about specific individuals.

Allow time for students to write, revise, and refine their poetic elegies. All poems must include:

- two to three stanzas of four or more lines each
- deliberate, thoughtful word choices
- appropriate tone
- specific vocabulary
- at least one example of figurative language
- at least one rhetorical device

As a part of the editing process, students should practice reading their elegies aloud to ensure that they flow well and capture the intended feeling; repeated practice sessions may facilitate greater poise and confidence. Students should note and record the time required to read their poems aloud.

Once students have finished writing, invite them to compile a set of musical characteristics that align with their poems and would support the specific emotions or memories they wish to convey. What music might capture the essence of the person, idea, or event that is the subject of their elegy? What music might capture the sense of grief surrounding the loss of their subject? What music would effectively accompany a reading of their elegy? Students' lists might include musical elements related to:

- melody
- harmony
- rhythm
- dynamics
- style
- instrumentation
- structure
- tempo
- lyrics

Next, students search for and select musical examples to accompany their poems, allowing them to apply their musical knowledge and understandings in a meaningful context. Invite students to utilize playlists or links on their phones, if allowed. Alternately, provide access to a set of musical choices or direct students to choose from among the pieces the class previous analyzed. The length of the musical excerpt they choose should align with the time it takes to read their elegy aloud.

4. Performance and Reflection

Finally, organize a performance showcase in which each student reads their elegy accompanied by the musical example they chose. Delivering elegies orally reinforces public speaking skills and the offers an opportunity to practice connecting emotionally with an audience. After each individual performance, facilitate a short Q and A, directing audience members to celebrate successes and inviting the presenters to reflect about their creative products.

Assessment

Assess students' understanding of the characteristics of poetic and musical elegies based on their ability to craft and present an original poetic elegy accompanied by a musical example, demonstrating their ability to effectively convey emotions through text and music.

Extension

Additional compositions to explore:

- *A Downland Suite*, II. "Elegy" by John Ireland
- *Materna Requiem*: Paradisum Interlude by Rebecca Dale
- "Fire and Rain" by James Taylor

Inventory of Ideas

The following collection of ideas contains additional lesson topics, specific teaching strategies, and recommended activities.

1. Explore ways authors and composers utilize the devices of exaggeration and embellishment for emphasis or effect. These techniques can draw attention to specific events or characters, convey intense emotional states, emphasize ideas, or add humor. For example, the Book of Kells is a Celtic illuminated manuscript created in a Scottish or Irish monastery around AD 800. The added embellishments and complex decorations emphasize themes in the text, which is written in Latin (see Figure 3.6). Musically, embellishments to melodies are a defining characteristic of Irish and Scottish folk music. These include quick single upper and lower grace

notes, ornaments involving double grace notes added above or below a pitch, smooth glides between notes, triplets with three pitches played in the space of one beat, and combinations of these elements. Listen to the traditional Irish reel "Maud Millar," performed on accordion by Colm Gannon at youtube.com/watch?v=m6eKrI_MmII to hear a variety of these embellishments.

Consider the archetype of the fish tale as representative of stories that embellish the truth. The term "fish tale" comes from the popular opinion that anglers always

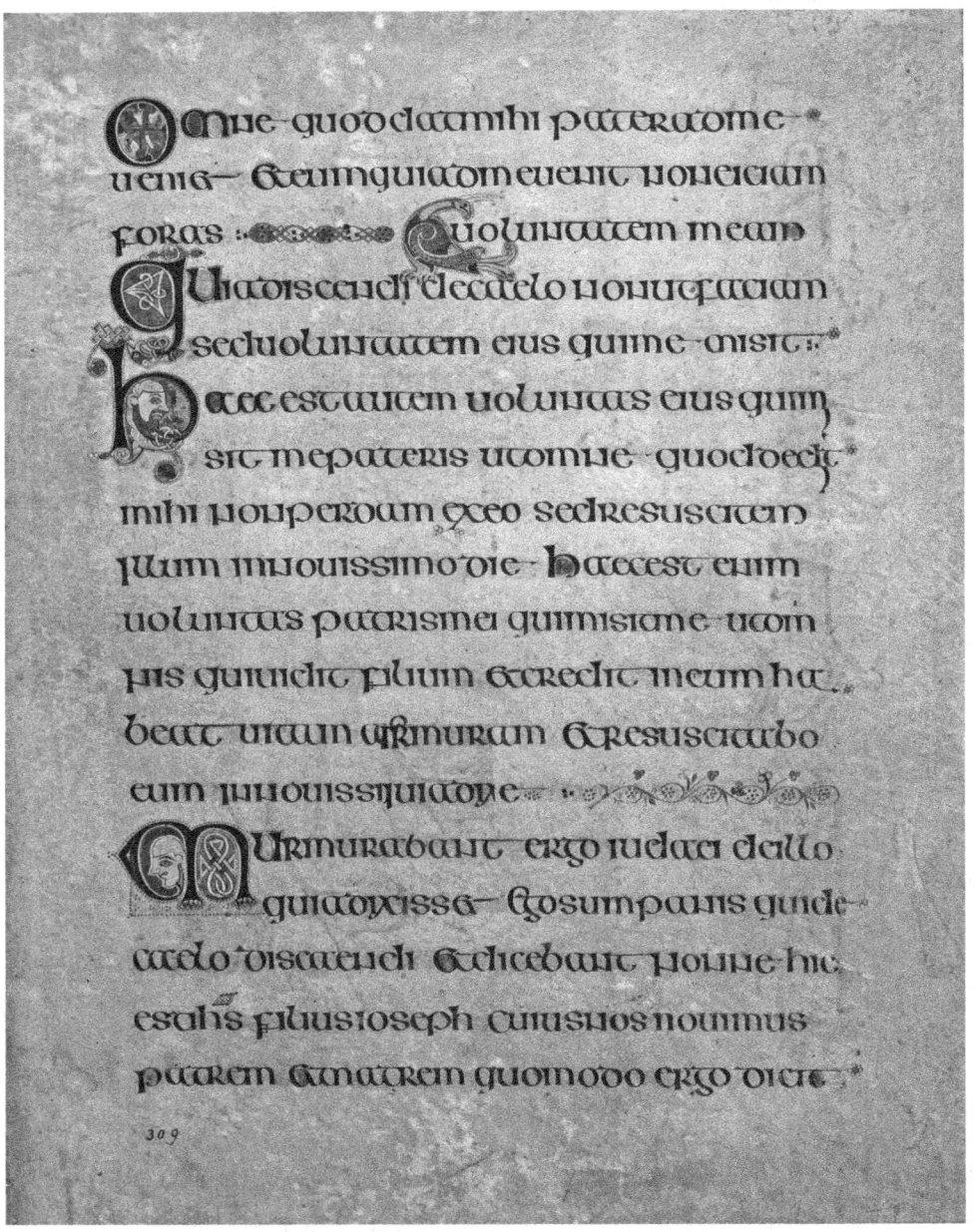

Figure 3.6 Illuminated manuscript page from the *Book of Kells.*
Public Domain/The Library of Trinity College Dublin/Wikimedia.

embellish the size of the fish they catch, and especially the size of those fish that got away, guaranteeing that their accounts cannot be confirmed. Exaggeration postcards, also known as tall tale post cards, were common in the first half of the twentieth century in North America. Figure 3.7 is an example of a tall tale postcard sent in 1953 from Stone Lake, Wisconsin. The text on the reverse side reads, "Hi Mom! We are having a great time. So far fishing has been good. Kelly caught the one on front. Mine will be shipped on a flat car. Love, Ray" (see Figure 3.8).

To continue with the fish tale theme, examine musical embellishment in the fourth movement of Franz Schubert's Piano Quintet in A major, D. 667, nicknamed "The Trout Quintet." To prepare, listen to Schubert's song "Die Forelle" and read an English translation of the lyrics. This song became the basis for the fourth movement of the Trout Quintet. Schubert reinvented his earlier piece by embellishing and exaggerating the melody in a series of variations that feature elaborate ornamentation, dramatic contrasts, and variations in tempo. As an extension, many other fish-themed songs are available to explore. These include "Fishin' in the Dark" by the Nitty Gritty Dirt Band, "Just Fishin'" by Trace Adkins, and "Fish Tale for Flute and Guitar" by Osvaldo Gloijov. Finally, invite students to write their own postcard (or blog post) utilizing exaggeration and embellishment as a deliberate aesthetic device.

2. When studying various texts, take the opportunity to also listen to and perform musical examples with identical titles. Simultaneously delving into books and music with matching titles allows students to engage in comparative analysis, evaluating the ways various themes and viewpoints are represented in different mediums. The list presented in Table 3.9 is intended as a starting point and inspiration.

Figure 3.7 Postcard of Dickinson's Store, Stone Lake, Wisconsin, 1953.
Image courtesy of author.

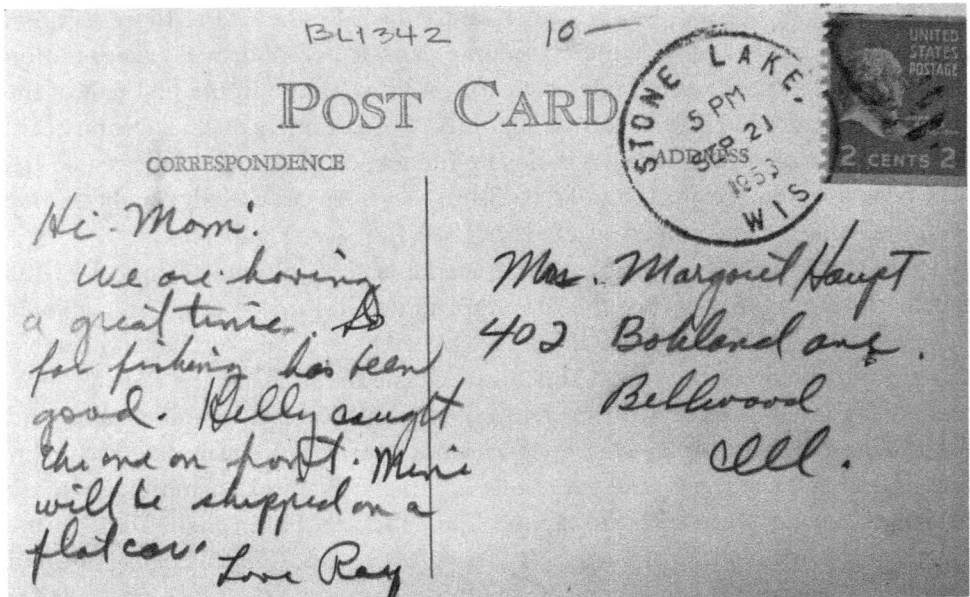

Figure 3.8 Reverse side of postcard of Dickinson's Store, Stone Lake, Wisconsin, 1953. Image courtesy of author.

3. Allow students to draw connections between the live delivery of speeches and songs. In both language arts and music, a presenter must perform with proficiency, confidence, and imagination. They utilize effective pronunciation, inflection, dynamics, and eye contact, and they maintain a relaxed, upright posture. Perhaps most important, their delivery is accurate and well-rehearsed. Throughout the school year, as students have opportunities in language arts class to individually present their work, read aloud, or participate in a speech unit, reinforce students' presentation skills with informal musical performances. Invite small groups of students to select short songs, locate karaoke-style accompaniments, rehearse together, and perform for the class. Singing and speaking in front of peers can be intimidating, and strategies to manage performance anxiety are similar in both disciplines. Most important is lots of practice, including breaking a presentation into manageable segments, studying and rehearsing complex or difficult passages, and rehearsing what to do if mistakes occur, such as continuing with poise and keeping errors to yourself. Successful preparation for a live presentation often includes relaxation techniques such as deep breathing, visualizing success, and positive self-talk. These presentations offer opportunities for students to engage as respectful, empathetic audience members, as well.

4. In musical examples with lyrics, word painting is frequently utilized by composers to emphasize the connection between music and language. Word painting occurs when specific aspects of the music mimic or reflect specific words in the text. Two obvious examples are the high note that aligns with the word "high" in

Table 3.9 Literature and music with identical titles

Literature	Music
1984 by George Orwell	"1984" by David Bowie
2112 by Ayn Rand	"2112" by Rush
Alone by Edgar Allan Poe	"Alone" by Green Carnation
Anthem by Ayn Rand	"Anthem" by Rush
Las Batallas en el Desierto by José Emilio Pacheco	"Las Batallas" by Café Tacuba
Bernice Bobs Her Hair by F. Scott Fitzgerald	"Bernice Bobs Her Hair" by The Divine Comedy
Blue Castle by Lucy Maud Montgomery	"Blue Castle" by Glen Velez
Call of the Wild by Jack London	"Call of the Wild" by Chris LeDoux
Don Quixote by Miguel de Cervantes	"Don Quixote" by Gordon Lightfoot
The Catcher in the Rye by J. D. Salinger	"The Catcher in the Rye" by The Dandy Warhols
The Faerie Queene by Edmund Spenser	*The Fairy Queen* by Henry Purcell
I, Robot by Isaac Asimov	"I, Robot" by the Alan Parsons Project
Lord of the Flies by William Golding	"Lord of the Flies" by The X Factor
The Machine Stops by E. M. Forster	"The Machine Stops" by Hawkwind
Martin Eden by Jack London	"Martin Eden" by Billie Hughes
Matilda by Roald Dahl	"Matilda" by Harry Styles
My Ántonia by Willa Cather	"My Antonia" by Emmylou Harris and Dave Matthews
Prince Caspian by C. S. Lewis	"Prince Caspian" by Phish
Richard Cory by Edwin Arlington Robinson	"Richard Cory" by Paul Simon
The River by Flannery O'Connor	"The River" by P. J. Harvey
Romeo and Juliet by William Shakespeare	"Romeo and Juliet" by Dire Straits
Wonder by Rachel Vail	"Wonder" by R. J. Palacio
Wuthering Heights by Emily Brontë	"Wuthering Heights" by Kate Bush

John Denver's song "Rocky Mountain High," and the sudden silence in the middle of the phrase, "Stop; hammer time" in the song "U Can't Touch This" by M. C. Hammer. The choral tradition is especially rich with examples of word painting, but examples can be found across genres and time periods. Direct students to identify examples of word painting in songs of their choice and share their findings with the class.

5. A common strategy in ELA is to study books alongside their movie adaptations. An imaginative way to take that strategy a step further is to also consider the musical score of the film in question. Film scores encompass a wide range of musical styles, and can include instrumental pieces, songs, ambient noise, and sound effects. A film score can be created by a single composer or by a collection of various artists. Juxtaposing literature, film, and music can encourage critical thinking, foster engagement in learning, and promote comprehension among tentative readers. Table 3.10 includes a selection of books with associated movie adaptations and musical scores. Direct students to compare a written text to its film counterpart, then further assess the impact of the musical score in communicating the story. Guide pairs of students to utilize a triple Venn diagram to depict similarities and differences in the corresponding works. Specific items for comparison include:

- Presentation of characters
- Depiction of specific scenes
- Interpretation of specific themes
- Representation of setting
- Portrayal of action, conflict, or tension
- Elements depicted in one medium, but not another (e.g., plot, subplots, events, context, characters, mood, tone, sequence)

6. Throughout the school year, students encounter texts representing a wide array of formats and levels of complexity. These genres often include short stories, dramas, poems, biographies, essays, news articles, letters, memoirs, poems, and song lyrics. For any given set of lyrics, you might ask students to interpret central ideas or themes, identify supporting details, describe characters, or focus on the plot. For example, you might direct students to write a claim that answers two questions: What is the composer or lyricist trying to say through their text and what literary elements do they employ? Song recommendations for lyric analysis include:

- "Both Sides Now" by Joni Mitchell
- "High Horse" by Kasey Musgraves
- "It's Nice to Get Up in the Mornin'" by Harry Lauder
- "Lemon Tree" by Fool's Garden
- "Summer Breeze" by Seals and Crofts
- "The Weight" by Aretha Franklin
- "Wildflowers" by Tom Petty

If a song's lyrics have an easily identifiable rhyme scheme or structure, as an extension, direct students to create their own lyrics that align with the meter and format of the original. Locate a karaoke version of the song and invite students to perform their newly composed lyrics for the class.

Table 3.10 Suggested books with associated movie adaptations and musical scores

Title	Author	Book Copyright	Movie Copyright	Composer
Because of Winn Dixie	Kate DiCamillo	2000	2005	Rachel Portman
The Book Thief	Markus Zusak	2005	2013	John Williams
The Boy in the Striped Pajamas	John Boyne	2006	2008	James Horner
The Breadwinner	Deborah Ellis	2000	2017	Mychael and Jeff Danna
Bridge to Terabithia	Katherine Paterson	1977	2007	Aaron Zigman
The Chronicles of Narnia: The Lion, the Witch, and the Wardrobe	C. S. Lewis	1950	2005	Harry Gregson-Williams
Ella Enchanted	Gail Carson Levine	1997	2004	Various artists
Everything Everything	Nicola Yoon	2015	2017	Various artists
The Fault in Our Stars	John Greene	2012	2014	Various artists
Forrest Gump	Winston Groom	1986	1994	Various artists
The Giver	Lois Lowry	1993	2014	Various artists
Harry Potter and the Prisoner of Azkaban	J. K. Rowling	1999	2004	John Williams
Hidden Figures	Margot Lee Shetterly	2016	2016	Hans Zimmer, Pharrell Williams, and Benjamin Wallfisch
Holes	Louis Sachar	1998	2003	Various artists
I Am Malala/He Named Me Malala	Malala Yousafzai	2013	2015	Thomas Newman
If I Stay	Gayle Forman	2009	2014	Various artists
Just Mercy	Bryan Stevenson	2014	2019	Joel P. West
Little Women	Louisa May Alcott	1868-69	2019	Alexandre Desplat
The Lord of the Rings: The Return of the King	J. R. R. Tolkien	1954–1955	2003	Howard Shore
A Series of Unfortunate Events: The Bad Beginning	Lemony Snicket	1999	2004	Thomas Newman
Wonder	R. J. Palacio	2012	2017	Marcelo Zarvos
The Wonderful Wizard of Oz/The Wizard of Oz	L. Frank Baum, illustrated by W. W. Denslow	1900	1939	Harold Arlen, Herbert Stothart, and E. Y. Harburg

7. Another idea for exploring song lyrics as poetry involves contrasting the experience of performing or listening to lyrics with and without music. This activity highlights the significance of the musical elements of a song in communicating meaning beyond the text. Have students read and analyze a set of lyrics before listening to the song, perhaps focusing on theme, mood, structure, or literary devices. Afterward, listen to the song, guiding students to scrutinize musical elements such as melody, rhythm, harmony, style, dynamics, and instrumentation. Next, direct students to compare and contrast the two experiences asking questions such as, "What did you observe when reading the text in isolation?," "What did you perceive when hearing the text with the musical accompaniment?," and "In what ways do the text and the music reinforce, complement, or contradict each other?" Suggested songs include:

- "At Last!" by Etta James
- "Build Me Up, Buttercup" by Mike d'Abo and Tony Macaulay
- "Pennies from Heaven" by Arthur Johnston and Johnny Burke
- "September" by Earth, Wind & Fire
- "Thinking About You" by Cody Fry

8. In their research, students are likely familiar with the practice of quoting other texts to reinforce a particular point of view and support their claims. Quotations impact a work's meaning and tone, adding depth and perspective by connecting to broader contexts or serving as a tribute to the original author. When Madeleine L'Engle opened her book *A Wrinkle in Time* with the classic trope, "It was a dark and stormy night," she immediately established an atmosphere of tension, mystery, and suspense. Composers utilize the custom of quotation, as well. For example, in Lesson 3.1, Carter Pann's piece *Slalom* opens with a direct quote from Beethoven's Ninth Symphony. Encourage students to find examples of musical quotations in contemporary works and to practice inserting select quotes in their own writing or musical compositions.

9. Dialogue is a literary element that drives narratives. Written or spoken conversations contribute to the development of characters, themes, and plots. As students examine dialogue across literary genres such as short stories, novels, and screenplays, consider the role of dialogue in music, as well. The lyrics of some songs are obvious as literal conversations, as heard in "Jenny" by the New Zealand duo Flight of the Conchords or in "Anything You Can Do (I Can Do Better)" by Irving Berlin. Challenge students to also ascertain the "conversations" present in purely instrumental music, when different instruments or combinations of players interact and respond to each other melodically, rhythmically, or thematically. For example, J. S. Bach's Trio Sonata in G Major, BWV 1039: IV. Presto includes a spritely conversation between flute, violin, cello, and harpsichord. In G. F. Handel's Organ Concerto No. 5 in F Major, Op. 4, No. 5, HWV 293: II. Allegro it is easy to distinguish the tone color of the organ as it engages in a conversation with the rest of the orchestra. In

jazz, musical conversations are labeled as call-and-response. A question (the call) is played by one or more instruments and then answered (the response) by another instrument or group. This design is easily discernible in the jazz standard "Wang Wang Blues" by Henry Busse, Gussie Mueller, and Theron E. "Buster" Johnson.

10. Many people utilize music to motivate themselves. Someone might choose music with a specific purpose in mind such as boosting their mood, building excitement, conveying encouragement, or enhancing their focus, productivity, or determination. In your classroom, choose a musical example to accompany a writing task as students define and describe personal goals. Without giving any musical background or explanation, start the recording, then invite students to engage in a four-part brainstorm. First, students reflect about something that is important to them. Next, they consider their current position relative to that thing or idea. Third, they envision what they want to do or what they hope to achieve. Finally, they outline the steps they will take to achieve that objective. After the song concludes, direct pairs of students to reflect about any impact the song had on their writing. Ask students to share what they heard in the music and how they may have interpreted those elements as motivational. Musical components that may direct students' thinking include upbeat tempos evoking energy and drive, uplifting melodies, and intense dynamics and harmonies. As a concluding activity, have students sing the song together, then write their final goal statements for the future. The musical features and positive messages contained in a song's lyrics may support students as they set personal goals and may also empower them to persevere in achieving their goals as they move ahead. This goal-setting activity could be a one-time activity, perhaps with overarching goals for a new school year, or it could be a recurring activity, in which students set more frequent, small-scale goals for the week. Suggested songs for this activity include:

- "The Best Day of My Life" by American Authors
- "Brave" by Sara Bareilles
- "Giant" by Calvin Harris
- "Keep Your Head Up" by Andy Grammer
- "Try Everything" by Shakira

11. Incorporating music as a critical aspect of creative writing lessons can engage students, focus their thinking, and inspire imaginative products. For example, in Lesson 3.1, the composition *Slalom* is a writing prompt for an in-depth project that specifically focuses on plot. Smaller-scale lessons involving music as writing prompts can also be effective. The following list includes ideas for musical prompts that focus student writing on setting, character, and mood. Your directions to students could be very open-ended, with instructions such as, "vividly describe the setting that is suggested by the following musical example," "clearly depict each of the distinct characters alluded to in the music," or "effectively portray the mood that

is evoked in this excerpt." You might also choose to offer more specific constraints or requirements.

- Setting
  - "Blue Pacific" by American composer Michael Torke. The solo piano piece was written "on a cliff side overlooking the sparkling Pacific Ocean in southern Mexico" (Torke, n.d.).
  - "Walzer, Op. 70, Act 1" from *Schlagobers Ballet* by German composer Richard Strauss. The ballet takes place in a Viennese cake shop where baked goods come to life; the title of the orchestral movement translates as "whipped cream waltz."
  - *Nursery Suite* by English composer Edward Elgar. The orchestral suite includes seven short movements and was premiered in 1931; it was dedicated to England's young princesses Elizabeth and Margaret. Three contrasting movements to emphasize include "I. Awake," "III. Busy-ness," and "VII. Dreaming."
  - "Penny Lane" was written by two members of the Beatles, Paul McCartney and John Lennon, and was named after an actual street in Liverpool. This piece is an example of a piece with lyrics, allowing students to infer information about setting from both the text and the musical elements present.
  - "V-Pop" by American violinist and composer Lindsey Stirling. This upbeat piece exemplifies classical and electronic fusion.
- Character: all these pieces have multiple sections, allowing students to write about a variety of hypothetical characters
  - *If I Were King*: "Overture" by French composer Adolphe Adam.
  - *Orpheus in the Underworld*, Act II. "Galop Infernal (Can-Can)" by German-born French composer Jacques Offenbach.
  - *First Suite in E♭ for Military Band*, Op. 28, No. 1, III. March by English composer Gustav Holst.
  - *Histoires*, No. 2, "The Little White Donkey" by French composer Jacques Ibert.
  - *Horseplay*, II. "Lively" by Belize-born British composer Errolyn Waller. This avant-garde classical piece was written for a mixed ensemble of wind and string instruments and also features two percussionists and a pianist.
- Mood
  - Danzas de Panama: IV. "Cumbia y Congo" by American composer William Grant Still. This string quartet is based on a collection of folk tunes from Panama and often utilizes the instruments for percussion-type sounds.
  - "Darude" by the Finnish electronic music producer Sandstorm. This 1999 release is categorized as a trance techno song and is popular in internet meme culture.
  - *Kinderszenen*, Op. 15, "Scenes from Childhood" by German composer Robert Schumann. This work is a set of thirteen short solo piano "scenes"

with varying characteristics, making it a good choice for writing quick-fire descriptions of multiple moods.

- "Main Title" from *Jaws* by American composer and conductor John Williams. Pieces like this allow students to explore ways composers and authors create and build suspense in their works.
- "Mr. Blue Sky" by Electric Light Orchestra. In this 1977 song, the blue sky is metaphor for happy days.
- "Out of It All" by British composer Helen Jane Long. This meditative solo piano work is among Long's works that have been downloaded over one billion times.

12. Use music as the stimulus for a brainstorm session to reinforce creative word choices. Play a recorded musical example and ask groups of students to generate five nouns, five adjectives, and five verbs that describe or define the piece. As students generate their descriptions, encourage them to choose terms that could effectively convey the music to someone who had not yet heard it. Next, each group of students produces fifteen sticky notes, with one word per note. Finally, students place their notes on the white board or wall to organize a word collage, clustering like terms, discerning categories, and sharing rationales to support their choices. Repeat the activity with a variety of music, especially noting patterns and outliers in responses. Alternately, explore word choice through song lyrics by asking students to isolate and categorize all the instances a composer utilizes specific devices within a given song. Given the printed text, they might circle all the adjectives, highlight all the similes, document each instance of symbolism, and so forth.

13. To foster student ownership and promote student choice, augment writing projects with multimedia components. Selecting or creating music to convey information, shape viewpoints, or inspire action demonstrates students' musical proficiency and highlights their varied experiences. These student projects could include:

- Selecting appropriate musical examples to accompany presentations
- Compiling playlists that include "theme songs" for each character in a literary work
- Creating presentations that integrate text, graphics, and music, allowing students to share individual research on a specific topic
- Producing a music video to accompany an existing or original song

14. To practice summarizing main ideas, ask students to write a twelve-word narrative based on the primary themes they hear in a piece of music. Alternately, they could generate a new title for a song, characterizing the piece's central idea, or devise a newspaper headline that encapsulates a musical example's main message. You could also provide students with the titles of five unfamiliar works, then randomly play the pieces and ask students to connect the names with each composition based on the musical evidence they hear in each example.

15. Compare various composers' points of view as they approach similar themes or topics and emphasize different ideas or interpretations. How does each composer's unique perspective, including their background, their compositional style, and their musical vocabulary, impact the music they create? You might opt to have students delve into serious or consequential issues that have been explored from multiple perspectives, but even mundane topics can be interesting to examine. For example, juxtapose the following songs with cats as their subject:

- "Gatinha Manhosa," a 1966 song in Portuguese by Brazilian composer Erasmo Carlos
- "Kitten on the Keys," a 1921 piano solo by American Zez Confrey
- "The Waltzing Cat," a 1950 orchestral composition by American Leroy Anderson that features meows, snarls, and a dog bark
- "Xylophone Cat," a 2023 collaboration between South African composer David Scott (The Kiffness) and his cat, Cala. The lyrics include the following line, "Let this be a lesson to everyone; you never know what your pet really wants; this cat . . . just needs a xylophone" (Scott, 2023)

4

Music and Social Studies

Introduction

Music should be studied alongside the time period and culture in which it was created. Through the study of history, students can examine the fundamental ideas and feelings of a time period and then discern ways those ideas and feelings influenced or inspired the music of that time. Likewise, students can examine music that was created at a certain point in history and consider how those pieces influenced people living at the time. Music not only reflects the time during which it was created but also influences the way listeners think or behave.

The study of multicultural music prepares students to become global citizens and reflects the diversity of our schools, communities, and world. Accessible travel, developments in media and technology, and changes in classroom makeup are creating greater opportunities for interaction between various cultural groups. When students from different cultures explore each other's music, they gain musical understandings and learn about one another as people. Music and social studies share a common focus on broad views of history and culture that embrace a panorama of various identities, beliefs, traditions, and practices; these diverse expressions can fuel curiosity while encouraging deeper knowledge and respect. Diversity, rather than homogeneity, characterizes our world and should characterize our curricular content as well.

Integrating music and social studies may promote student interest and engagement, encouraging vivid experiences with beliefs, values, and traditions. Incorporating music can be an effective way to initially hook and then continue to hold students' attention in social studies lessons. This might be attributed to music's capacity for capturing students' emotions in ways that written or spoken words cannot (Reimer, 2003). Music also gives students a richer representation of the past, reflecting the more cultural, personal, and expressive side of history, as well as portraying the hopes, dreams, and accomplishments of people from within a specific culture, community, or time. Lessons that integrate music and social studies have the potential to enrich students' understanding in both disciplines. Students who explore the historical and cultural background of a specific piece of music are better equipped to perform, listen to, and reflect about that piece.

Integrating Music Across the Secondary Curriculum. Kristin Harney, Oxford University Press. © Oxford University Press 2026.
DOI: 10.1093/9780197822036.003.0004

The chapter 4 lessons and the lesson ideas included in the chapter 4 inventory of ideas draw on a variety of musical material, including folk songs, ballads, popular music, works from the classical repertoire, and pieces representative of multiple cultures. Students will not only experience and examine musical examples but also apply and connect their understandings to specific social studies concepts, including describing the political, economic, and social constructs of cultural groups from varying times and places; drawing conclusions about the causes and consequences of events and developments; and examining the way people transmit beliefs and values (National Council for the Social Studies [NCSS], 2010). Music can provide a safe avenue for exploring an almost unlimited array of social studies topics including immigration, citizenship, taxation, surveillance, civil rights, racism, income inequality, poverty, homelessness, sexual orientation, gender identity, gender equality, natural disasters, global warming, overpopulation, disease, terrorism, bullying, and animal rights. It is not possible to address all these worthwhile topics in this chapter, although many of the ideas are incorporated in the chapter 4 lessons and inventory of ideas. The integration of music and social studies also leads students to connect with the people of various cultures and times—their lives, their actions, and their reasons for making music. Chapter 4 provides secondary teachers with compelling lessons and activities that encourage substantial interaction with social studies and music content and have the potential to enrich students' musical, historical, and cultural understandings in profound and lasting ways.

Common Links Between Music and Social Studies

Natural links and connections between music and social studies go beyond casual experiences, presentations of factual information, or disconnected encounters. Enduring ideas that can be explored in music and social studies include:

Cause and effect
Change
Choice
Context
Cooperation
Diversity
Identity
Interaction
Interdependence
Perspective
Power

Relationships
Resources
Similarities and differences
Structure
Tension and release

National Standards

The chapter 4 lessons and inventory of ideas are aligned with the National Core Arts Standards for Music, the National Curriculum Standards for Social Studies (NCSSS), and the College, Career, and Civic Life Framework for Social Studies State Standards (C3). Two distinct sets of standards for social studies (NCSSS and C3) are included because of the different purposes they serve. Although they are called "standards," the NCSSS are more "themes" that are meant to be broad and content-based, rather than standards per se (National Council for the Social Studies [NCSS], 2010). The C3 Framework Standards, on the other hand, were developed to support state-level standards revision and are pedagogically and skill-driven. C3 Framework Standards are now used much more often than the NCSSS (National Council for the Social Studies [NCSS], 2013).

Interdisciplinary connections between social studies and music are implicit in the 2014 National Core Arts Standards for Music. For example, to meet music Anchor Standard 11, students are expected to "relate artistic ideas and works with societal, cultural, and historical context to deepen understanding" (National Coalition for Core Arts Standards, 2015). Similarly, the 2010 NCSSS and C3 Framework Standards naturally connect with music. For example, to address the first NCSSS theme, Culture, it is expected that "through experience, observation, and reflection, students will identify elements of culture as well as similarities and differences among cultural groups across time and place" (National Council for the Social Studies [NCSS], 2010). The following boxes specify the standards that are addressed in the chapter 4 lessons and inventory of ideas:

- Box 4.1, National Curriculum Standards for Social Studies (NCSSS)
- Box 4.2, College, Career, and Civic Life Framework for Social Studies State Standards (C3)
- Box 4.3, National Core Arts Standards for Music

Box 4.4 offers a framework for structuring chapter 4 lessons and activities.

Box 4.1 National Curriculum Standards for Social Studies Themes included in Chapter 4 Lessons (L) and Inventory of Ideas (I)

1. Culture	Social studies programs should include experiences that provide for the study of culture and cultural diversity.	L 4.1 L 4.3 I 1 I 6 I 9 I 11
2. Time, Continuity, and Change	Social studies programs should include experiences that provide for the study of the past and its legacy.	L 4.1 L 4.4 I 3 I 5 I 7 I 8
3. People, Places, and Environments	Social studies programs should include experiences that provide for the study of people, places, and environments.	L 4.2 L 4.3 I 1 I 4 I 8
4. Individual Development and Identity	Social studies programs should include experiences that provide for the study of individual development and identity.	L 4.3 I 1 I 5 I 6 I 7 I 10 I 11
5. Individuals, Groups, and Institutions	Social studies programs should include experiences that provide for the study of interactions among individuals, groups, and institutions.	L 4.1 L 4.4 I 1 I 6 I 9 I 11
6. Power, Authority, and Governance	Social studies programs should include experiences that provide for the study of how people create, interact with, and change structures of power, authority, and governance.	L 4.3 L 4.4 I 3 I 5 I 6 I 10
7. Production, Distribution, and Consumption	Social studies programs should include experiences that provide for the study of how people organize for the production, distribution, and consumption of goods and services.	L 4.1 I 4 I 7 I 12
8. Science, Technology, and Society	Social studies programs should include experiences that provide for the study of relationships among science, technology, and society.	L 4.1 L 4.2 I 2 I 4 I 7

9. Global Connections	Social studies programs should include experiences that provide for the study of global connections and interdependence.	L 4.1 L 4.2 I 3 I 12
10. Civic Ideals and Practices	Social studies programs should include experiences that provide for the study of the ideals, principles, and practices of citizenship in a democratic republic.	L 4.3 L 4.4 I 1 I 5 I 10

National Council for the Social Studies (NCSS), *National Curriculum Standards for Social Studies: A Framework for Teaching, Learning, and Assessment* (Silver Spring, MD: NCSS, 2010).

Box 4.2 College, Career, and Civic Life Framework for Social Studies State Standards (C3) included in Chapter 4 Lessons (L) and Inventory of Ideas (I)

Dimension 1: Questions and Inquiries	Constructing Compelling Questions Constructing Supporting Questions Determining Helpful Sources	L 4.3 I 1 I 3 I 8 I 11
Dimension 2: Civics	Civic and Political Institutions Participation and Deliberation Processes, Rules, and Laws	L 4.2 L 4.4 I 5 I 6 I 10
Dimension 2: Economics	Economic Decision Making Exchange and Markets The National Economy The Global Economy	L 4.1 I 4 I 6 I 12
Dimension 2: Geography	Geographic Representations Human-Environment Interaction Human Population: Spatial Patterns and Movements Global Interconnections	L 4.1 L 4.2 I 4 I 6
Dimension 2: History	Change, Continuity, and Context Perspectives Historical Sources and Evidence Causation and Argumentation	L 4.3 I 2 I 5 I 6 I 8
Dimension 3: Sources and Evidence	Gathering and Evaluating Sources Developing Claims and Using Evidence	L 4.2 I 1 I 5 I 8 I 9

Dimension 4: Conclusions and Action	Communicating Conclusions	L 4.3
	Critiquing Conclusions	L 4.4
	Taking Informed Action	I 2
		I 5
		I 6
		I 9
		I 10

National Council for the Social Studies (NCSS), *The College, Career, and Civic Life (C3) Framework for Social Studies State Standards: Guidance for Enhancing the Rigor of K–12 Civics, Economics, Geography, and History* (Silver Spring, MD: NCSS, 2013).

Box 4.3 National Core Arts Standards for Music Included in Chapter 4 Lessons (L) and Inventory of Ideas (I)

MU:Cr1 (Create)	Generate and conceptualize artistic ideas and work	L 4.1
		L 4.4
		I 4
		I 6
		I 10
MU:Cr2 (Create)	Organize and develop artistic ideas and work	L 4.2
		I 3
		I 7
		I 9
MU:Cr3 (Create)	Refine and complete artistic work	L 4.2
		L 4.4
		I 7
		I 9
MU:Pr4 (Perform)	Select, analyze, and interpret artistic work for presentation	L 4.1
		L 4.4
		I 1
		I 5
		I 6
		I 10
MU:Pr5 (Perform)	Develop and refine artistic techniques and work for presentation	L 4.2
		L 4.3
		I 2
		I 5
		I 9
		I 11
MU:Pr6 (Perform)	Convey meaning through the presentation of artistic work	L 4.1
		L 4.3
		I 1
		I 6
		I 8
		I 12

MU:Re7 (Respond)	Perceive and analyze artistic work	L 4.1 L 4.2 L 4.3 I 3 I 4 I 7 I 12
MU:Re8 (Respond)	Interpret intent and meaning in artistic work	L 4.2 L 4.3 I 3 I 5 I 8 I 11
MU:Re9 (Respond)	Apply criteria to evaluate artistic work	L 4.3 L 4.4 I 2 I 5 I 10
MU:Cn10 (Connect)	Synthesize and relate knowledge and personal experiences to make art	L 4.2 L 4.4 I 1 I 4 I 6 I 9 I 10 I 11
MU:Cn11 (Connect)	Relate artistic ideas and works with societal, cultural, and historical context to deepen understanding	L 4.1 L 4.3 L 4.4 I 2 I 3 I 7 I 8 I 12

Box 4.4 Framework for Chapter 4 Lessons and Ideas

This chapter is designed to support middle school and high school educators as they integrate music and social studies. The four detailed, full-length lesson plans are independent and not organized as a progressive series.

- Lesson 4.1: Musical Synthesis and the Silk Road
  - While this lesson is rooted in historical content, the influence of cultural exchange, economics, and geography on societies is a relevant topic today, as well. I love Yo-Yo Ma's Silk Road Ensemble, so that was an easy choice for inclusion in this lesson. Additionally,

"Heart and Soul" is a piece with which many students may be familiar and is an easy tune to pick out in an unfamiliar arrangement. A fun side note for me is that my niece, Elizabeth Harney, plays the Chinese pipa, an instrument featured in this lesson.

- Lesson 4.2: Creating and Interpreting Maps: Visual Representations of Geographic and Musical Landmarks
  - The ability to accurately interpret maps is a useful but vanishing skill. I love the natural connection between using maps as tools to enhance our understanding and analysis of geographic and musical features.
- Lesson 4.3: "Song of the Refugee" and the Story of One Hmong Immigrant, Sying Yang
  - I started my teaching career in 1993 at Weaver Elementary in Maplewood, Minnesota, a suburb of St. Paul with a large Hmong population. I was unfamiliar with Hmong culture, and this lesson grew from a collaboration between me and the fifth grade team.
- Lesson 4.4: Reflective Thinking: Using the *What, So What, Now What* Model to Examine Ways People Create, Interact with, and Change Structures of Power
  - The *What, So What, Now What* model provides a structured and engaging way for students to critically analyze and reflect upon complex social and political dynamics. I especially appreciate the model for its focus on positive action and change, prompting students to respond to or transform existing power structures. Exploring the role of music in movements for social change is a natural fit for this critical reflection. So many times, a musical example has served as my introduction to a specific challenge or crisis. That was the case for the 1966 Gurindji Strike, the example I chose for this lesson.

The chapter ends with an inventory of ideas detailing twelve additional lesson topics, specific teaching strategies, and recommended activities. The lessons and activities may be fully taught by individual subject area (social studies or music) teachers; however, ideally, the plans will facilitate partnerships and collaboration between social studies teachers and music specialists. All lessons and activities have been reviewed by practicing teachers, and most have been field-tested in middle school and high school classrooms. Most of the lessons will need to be spread over two or more class periods. Chapter 4 lessons are adaptable to a variety of grade levels and are intended as tools for you to meet your students' needs. You and your students bring your own knowledge and experiences to these encounters, and you are invited and encouraged to apply those skills and understandings. I hope you are inspired to locate additional works to explore, including musical examples students are likely to encounter in their lives beyond school (e.g., readily recognizable musical works) and those that are less likely to be encountered (e.g., contemporary works that have not yet received widespread recognition, works for specialized groups or audiences, or works that are rooted in specific geographic regions). See additional guidelines for selecting repertoire in chapter 1. All the images included in this chapter are printed in black and white. Consider accessing full-color images online when displaying photographs, artwork, and other graphics for students, especially when lesson content directly references aspects related to a work's color. Please adjust, adapt, or expand these lessons and ideas to work best for you and for your students. Seek out teachers with whom you can collaborate and utilize the range of ideas and examples as starting points to facilitate your creativity and inspire innovative curriculum making.

Lesson 4.1: Musical Synthesis and the Silk Road

Grade Level

High school, but may be adapted

Essential Questions

How are societies influenced by geography and economics? In what ways did cultural exchange impact music during the time of the Silk Road, and what impact does cultural exchange have today?

Objectives

- Students will explain the historical significance of the Silk Road, describing the importance of the Silk Road as a network for trade, cultural exchange, and diplomatic relations between Asia, the Middle East, and Europe.
- Students will explain how the Silk Road facilitated cultural diffusion through the spread of religions, language, music, art, and technological innovations and connect the influence of the Silk Road to modern global trade networks and contemporary examples of cross-cultural exchange.
- Students will listen to a performance of the Chinese pipa and discuss its cultural significance, musical characteristics, and unique playing techniques using domain-specific language.
- Students will perform the piano duet "Heart and Soul" and compare it to a recording of "Heart and Soul" by the Silk Road Ensemble, noting specific musical elements that indicate a merging of musical styles.

National Curriculum Standards for Social Studies Addressed

- NCSSS 1: Culture: Social studies programs should include experiences that provide for the study of culture and cultural diversity.
- NCSSS 2: Time, Continuity, and Change: Social studies programs should include experiences that provide for the study of the past and its legacy.
- NCSSS 5: Individuals, Groups, and Institutions: Social studies programs should include experiences that provide for the study of interactions among individuals, groups, and institutions.
- NCSSS 7: Production, Distribution, and Consumption: Social studies programs should include experiences that provide for the study of how people organize for the production, distribution, and consumption of goods and services.

- NCSSS 8: Science, Technology, and Society: Social studies programs should include experiences that provide for the study of relationships among science, technology, and society.
- NCSSS 9: Global Connections: Social studies programs should include experiences that provide for the study of global connections and interdependence.

C3 Framework for Social Studies State Standards Addressed

- C3 Dimension 2: Economics
- C3 Dimension 2: Geography

National Core Arts Standards for Music Addressed

- MU:Cr1: Generate and conceptualize artistic ideas and work
- MU:Pr4: Select, analyze, and interpret artistic work for presentation
- MU:Pr6: Convey meaning through the presentation of artistic work
- MU:Re7: Perceive and analyze artistic work
- MU:Cn11: Relate artistic ideas and works with societal, cultural, and historical context to deepen understanding

Materials

- Images
  - Photo showing Dunhuang Cave 16 (Figure 4.1)
  - Sogdian whirl with large pipa (Figure 4.2)
  - Ming dynasty Chinese pipa (Figure 4.3)
- Video examples
  - *Wu Man—"White Snow in Spring," Declassified: Ben Folds Presents, The Kennedy Center* (youtube.com/watch?v=1Z-NLqbb8xA)
  - *Silkroad Ensemble, Yo-Yo Ma—Heart and Soul ft. Lisa Fischer, Gregory Porter* (youtube.com/watch?v=i3Z6LHtxN3U&t=10s)
  - *The Music of Strangers: Yo-Yo Ma and the Silk Road Ensemble* (https://www.silkroad.org/tmos)

Procedure

Background information: The Silk Road was a complex array of trade routes that linked the East and the West (stretching from modern-day China to the eastern shores of the Mediterranean Sea). It arose around 130 BCE and facilitated the exchange of goods such as silk, spices, tea, and textiles. Beyond the trading of goods, however, the Silk Road was a cultural pathway for the exchange of ideas, beliefs, and practices. These influences streamed in both directions and shaped cultural traditions in the regions through which the Silk Road passed. We see evidence of this cultural exchange in the Muang caves, a group of hundreds of temples carved into the sandstone cliffs near Dunhuang, a religious and cultural intersection along the Silk Road in the Chinese province of Gansu (see Figure 4.1). Murals and statues found within the caves highlight the spreading of Buddhism; numerous images demonstrate the fusion of Indian and Chinese musical traditions. For example, a mural found in cave 112 shows a Sogdian dancer in the center of the image holding a pipa, a four-string Chinese instrument. In the lower right-hand corner of the image, a seated member of the orchestra holds a smaller pipa (see Figure 4.2). Musicians traveling along the Silk Road with the four-string Chinese pipa "brought not only a new sound, but also new repertoires and musical theory" (Moore, 2003). Figure 4.3 shows a Chinese pipa from the late sixteenth to early seventeenth century. The instrument got its name because of the way it is played, with a forward stroke ("p'i") followed by a backward stroke ("p'a").

Listen to and watch pipa player Wu Man in the video *Wu Man—"White Snow in Spring," Declassified: Ben Folds Presents, The Kennedy Center* (Kennedy Center, 2020). Note the repeated melody notes, the pentatonic scale, the wide range of dynamics,

Figure 4.1 Dunhuang Cave 16 and entrance to Cave 17, the "Library Cave."
Public Domain/Aurel Stein/Wikimedia.

Figure 4.2 Sogdian whirl with large pipa.
Public Domain/Wikimedia.

and the vertical orientation of the pipa in this energetic performance. Focus on Wu Man's hands during close-up shots to examine the forward and backward plucking motion she employs. Perhaps play a short excerpt at a slower playback speed to more easily discern the movement of her fingers.

Next, ask students if they are familiar with the popular piano duet "Heart and Soul." In classrooms with access to a piano or keyboard, invite pairs of students to perform the piece for the class. In classrooms without a piano, students could record themselves performing the song and later share that in class. Alternately, locate recordings of the piano duet online.

After hearing student examples of "Heart and Soul," introduce the Silk Road Ensemble, an eclectic collection of musicians from different regions along the Silk Road established by cellist Yo-Yo Ma. Members of the ensemble aspire to create music honoring the spirit of the exchanges that historically took place along Silk Road routes. For their sixth album, *Sing Me Home*, released in 2016, musicians in the ensemble collaboratively created new arrangements of works with special meaning to individual members of the group. Listen to their performance of "Heart and Soul" on the video *Silkroad Ensemble, Yo-Yo Ma—Heart and Soul ft. Lisa Fischer, Gregory Porter* (Ma, 2016). The arrangement opens with an extended instrumental introduction during which the original "Heart and Soul" tune and accompaniment may not

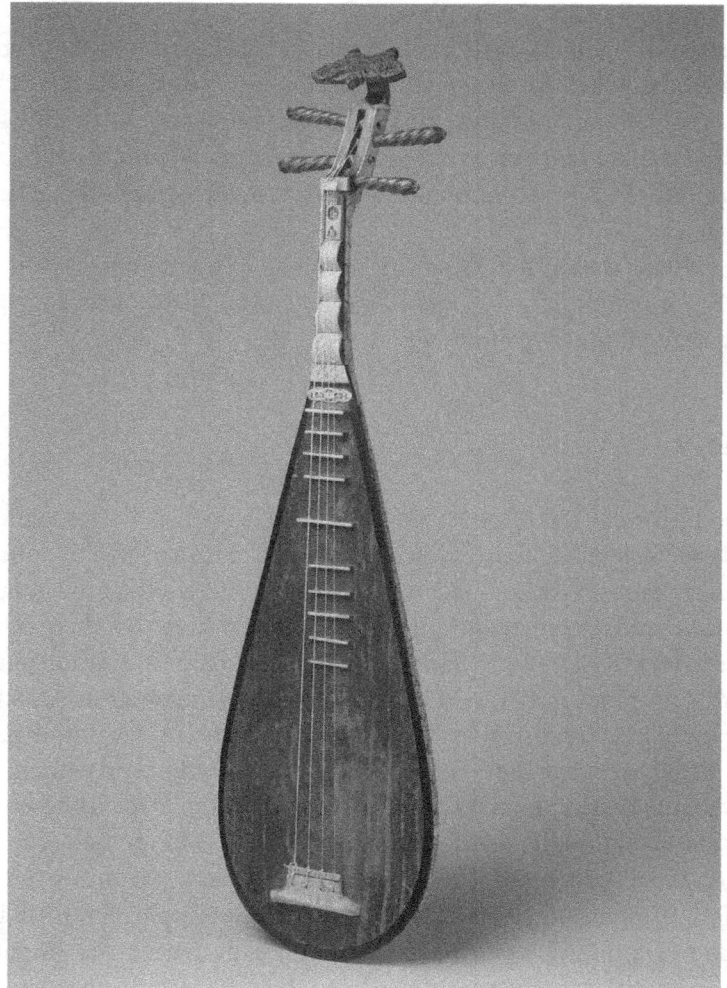

Figure 4.3 Ming dynasty Chinese pipa.
Public domain/Metropolitan Museum of Art/Bequest of Mary Stillman Harkness.

be recognizable until a more obvious nod to the piano duet accompaniment registers. The vocalists then join in, with clear references to the melody, harmony, and structure of Hoagy Carmichael's original "Heart and Soul," with its AABA form. That construction is emulated in this arrangement, followed by a playful instrumental interlude. The piece then concludes with a reprise of the final B and A sections.

After listening to the Silk Road Ensemble's arrangement of "Heart and Soul," initiate a think-pair-share session to guide a brief class discussion. Use prompts such as

- How easy was it for you to identify the main "Heart and Soul" melody?
- What instruments were you able to perceive?
- Were any instruments unfamiliar to you?

- Did you spot Wu Man playing the pipa?
- What musical elements distinguished this arrangement from the original?
- How does the Silk Road Ensemble's work demonstrate a cultural exchange that reflects the economic, cultural, and/or geographic aspects of the Silk Road?
- How do these examples bring the historical Silk Road to life today?
- Why is music effective at communicating history and geography that is far removed?

If time allows, watch the Grammy-nominated documentary *The Music of Strangers: Yo-Yo Ma and the Silk Road Ensemble* (Ma, 2015) or listen to additional tracks from their album *Sing Me Home*.

Assessment

Just as the historical Silk Road routes brought together Eastern and Western traditions and fostered a rich cultural synthesis, the merging of musical styles continues to inspire musicians today. To examine the contemporary relationship between music and globalization, direct students to draw on their own musical preferences to identify a musical work that might be classified as fusion or a synthesis of styles. You could also provide a list of pre-selected songs from which students could choose. For each musical example, ask students to utilize online resources to trace the cultural exchange that was necessary for its creation and to identify distinct musical elements that support its classification as fusion. Depending on the music they select, students might investigate geographic, social, or political influences. They could explore the economic or technological impacts on music production and consumption. Students might also explore ways their example of musical fusion falls short in terms of communicating complex diverse experiences. Ask students to document their findings using graphic organizers, then share their conclusions in small groups, playing short excerpts of their songs to support their ideas.

Lesson 4.2: Creating and Interpreting Maps: Visual Representations of Geographic and Musical Landmarks

Grade Level

Middle school, but may be adapted

Essential Question

How can maps enhance our understanding and analysis of geographic and musical features?

Objectives

- Students will identify and interpret the essential components of maps, demonstrating their ability to visualize and decipher complex geographic and musical features.
- Students will create and share geographic maps that demonstrate adequate preparatory research, utilize various visual symbols, and accurately portray essential map elements.
- Students will collaboratively analyze musical examples, classifying the structure of the composition and identifying relationships between the structure and various musical elements.
- Students will create and share musical listening maps that demonstrate precise musical analysis, utilize various visual symbols to convey complex ideas, and accurately portray essential map elements.

National Curriculum Standards for Social Studies Addressed

- NCSSS 3: People, Places, and Environments: Social studies programs should include experiences that provide for the study of people, places, and environments.
- NCSSS 8: Science, Technology, and Society: Social studies programs should include experiences that provide for the study of relationships among science, technology, and society.
- NCSSS 9: Global Connections: Social studies programs should include experiences that provide for the study of global connections and interdependence.

C3 Framework for Social Studies State Standards Addressed

- C3 Dimension 2: Civics
- C3 Dimension 2: Geography
- C3 Dimension 3: Evaluating sources and using evidence

National Core Arts Standards for Music Addressed

- MU:Cr2: Organize and develop artistic ideas and work
- MU:Cr3: Refine and complete artistic work
- MU:Pr5: Develop and refine artistic techniques and work for presentation
- MU:Re7: Perceive and analyze artistic work
- MU:Re8: Interpret intent and meaning in artistic work

- MU:Cn10: Synthesize and relate knowledge and personal experiences to make art

Materials

- Images
  - Topographic map of Chios and Psara islands, Aegean Sea, Greece (Figure 4.4)
  - Listening map of first eight measures of "Les baricades mistérieuses" by François Couperin (Figure 4.5)
  - Opening of "Les baricades mistérieuses" by François Couperin (Figure 4.6)
  - *Bell Illuminations* by Augusta Read Thomas (Figure 4.7)
  - Examples of different maps
- Supplies for creating maps
  - Blank paper or large poster board
  - Pencils and erasers
  - Colored markers/pens/crayons
  - Rulers
  - Templates for map features
- Optional: Digital tools such as Google Maps, Map Maker, ArcGIS, or StoryMaps
- Video example
  - *The Mysterious Barricades, arranged by Alma Deutscher* (youtube.com/watch?v=Weauc3fVSFM)
- Musical examples
  - Pre-selected song choices or option for students to locate examples

Procedure

Conventionally, maps are defined as symbolic representations of one or more characteristics of a place, displaying specific features in terms of their relative size and position on a flat surface. The map shown in Figure 4.4 displays cities, roads, mountain ranges, and bodies of water. Additionally, it includes a bar scale in kilometers and miles, latitude and longitude grid lines, an inset map to provide context, and two map legends. Besides reference maps like Figure 4.4, thematic maps are also commonplace. As their name suggests, thematic maps emphasize a specific theme or topic, such as population, temperature, or language.

Pass out supplies and direct students to create geographic maps in collaborative groups, aligning the guidelines to their previous experience with interpreting and creating maps. Consider offering general outlines and/or allowing students to use digital tools. Directions might include: (1) selecting a real-world location

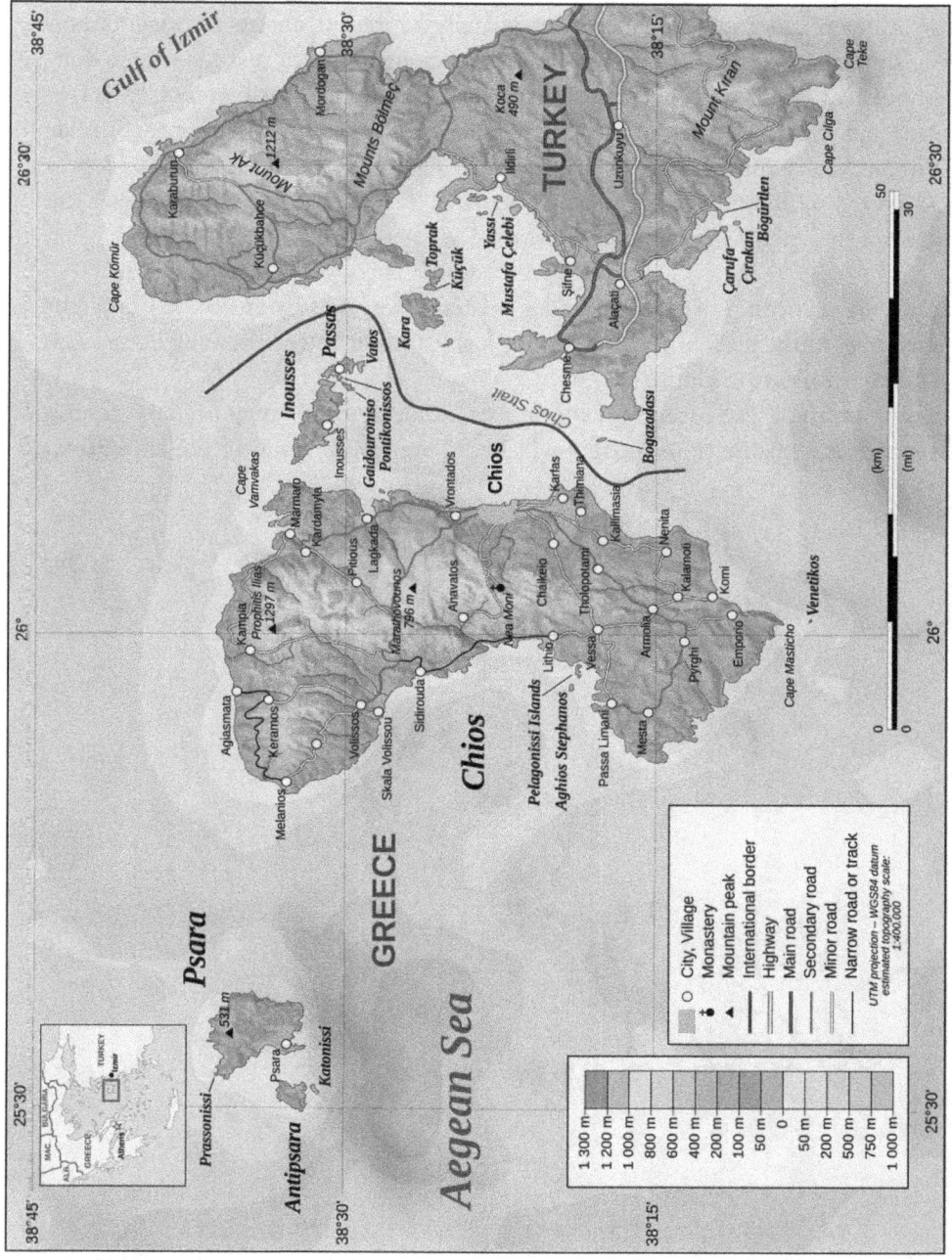

Figure 4.4 Topographic map of Chios and Psara islands, Aegean Sea, Greece.
Eric Gaba/Wikimedia Commons, Creative Commons Attribution-Share Alike 4.0 International.

to represent; (2) deciding which features to include; (3) sketching a rough draft; (4) adding geographic and manmade features; (5) inserting labels and keys; and (6) sharing maps with peers, explaining key features and discussing the accuracy of their visual representations.

Just as reference and thematic maps visually represent abstract concepts and relationships using symbols, listening maps are an engaging, accessible way to document musical events and their relationship to each other. "Music mapping" is frequently employed in elementary general music, with results that may appear similar to Figure 4.5, a listening map that utilizes unconventional music symbols to represent the opening melody of François Couperin's "Les baricades mistérieuses." The full score of the opening is shown in Figure 4.6.

- Locate a recording of "Les baricades mistérieuses" and listen to the first eight measures of the piece three times: once just listening, once following Figure 4.5, and once following Figure 4.6.
- Compare the three listening experiences. Some students may prefer listening without any distractions, others will likely prefer interpreting the traditional

Figure 4.5 Listening map of first eight measures of "Les barricades mystérieuses" by François Couperin.
Image courtesy of author.

Figure 4.6 Opening of "Les barricades mystérieuses" by François Couperin.
Public Domain image courtesy of IMSLP.

score, and for some, the non-standard visual representation might serve as a guide for their listening. Invite students to share their perceptions.

- Next, consider a contemporary arrangement of Couperin's piece, devised by Alma Deutscher when she was sixteen years old. Her YouTube performance *The Mysterious Barricades, arranged by Alma Deutscher* breaks the piece into five voice parts and includes a visual map showing the pitch contour of each vocal line (Deutscher, 2021). How does the listening map add to your understanding of the composition's structure?

While listening maps are beneficial in elementary general music, they are also effective tools for secondary students and are even utilized by professional composers such as Augusta Read Thomas (see Figure 4.7).

In preparation for creating original listening maps, engage secondary students in a variety of preliminary activities including analyzing and interpreting existing listening maps, reassembling printed sections of maps in the correct order, and completing unfinished listening map templates by filling in missing sections

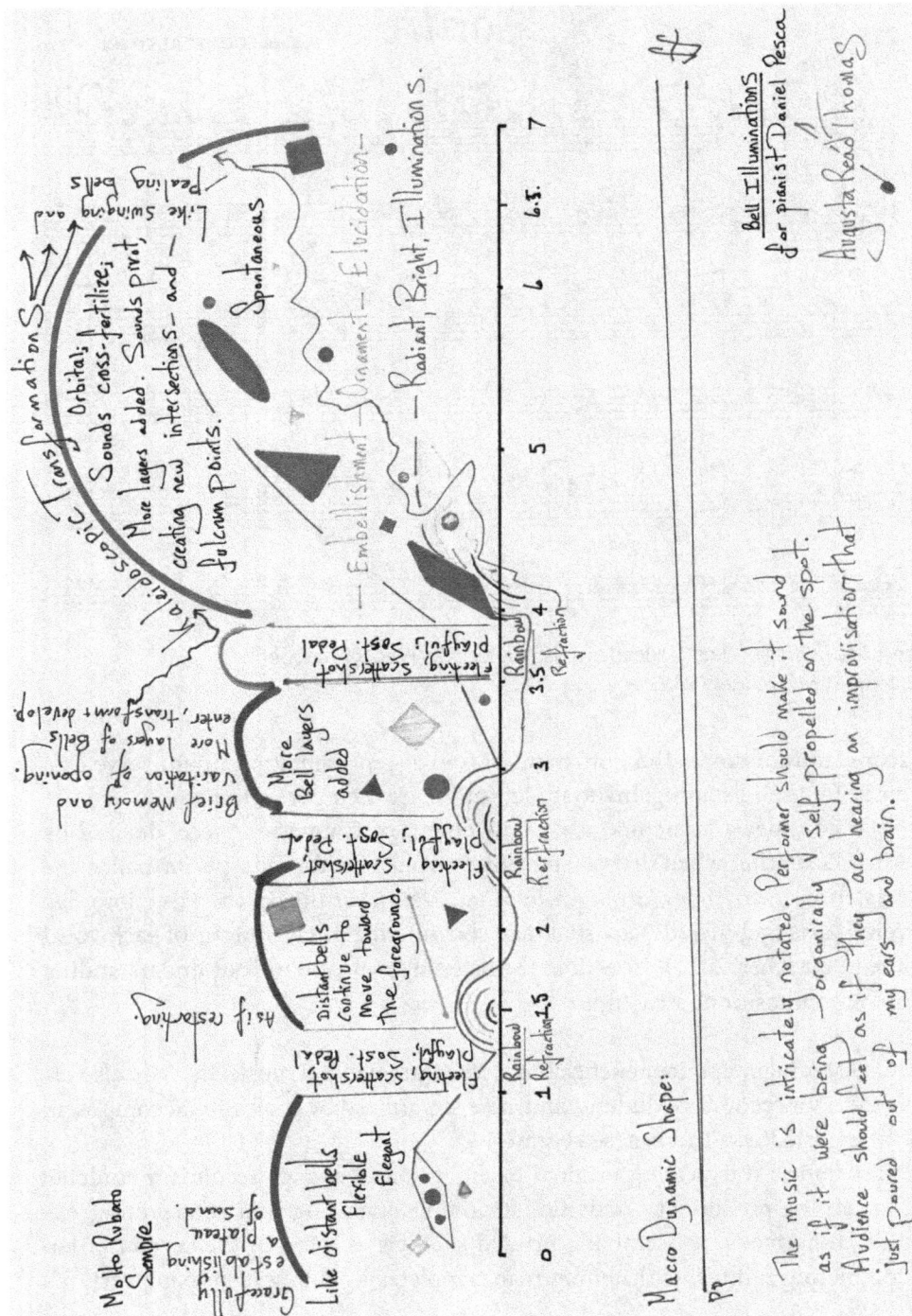

Figure 4.7 "Bell Illuminations" by Augusta Read Thomas, 2020: Symbolic map of form as drawn by the composer. Image courtesy of composer.

or adding fine details. Students should be comfortable aurally analyzing musical examples and proficient at reading, interpreting, and creating traditional maps.

Prior to creating individual listening maps, provide opportunities for students to collaboratively create visual representations of musical examples, encouraging co-operation and allowing them to consider multiple perspectives.

- Divide students into groups and assign musical examples. For simplicity, you might have the whole class work on a common song. You could also allow groups students to choose from a pre-selected set of songs with a common theme, for example, "Memphis, Tennessee" by Chuck Berry, "Memphis Soul Stew" by King Curtis, and "Walking in Memphis" by Marc Cohn.
- Direct students to first work together to analyze their song's large-scale design. They should listen to their piece all the way through as many times as needed to determine the overall structure, noting how the song breaks down into large chunks or sections and listening for contrasting segments or portions that re-peat. If the example has lyrics, they might give clues to the form, as well. For students having trouble discerning the form of their piece, suggest that they label the "beginning, middle, and end" of the music. Steer them to visualize how the sections come together to construct the whole.
- Next, guide students to scrutinize the instrumentation in their song. What spe-cific instruments or voices can they identify? Is the instrumentation consistent throughout the entire piece? Would they describe the texture of the work as thick, thin, or variable? During subsequent repeated listenings, focus students' attention on additional features of the music such as melodic themes, rhythmic characteristics, dynamics, tempo, style or genre, and text, if present.

When creating maps, cartographers must determine what information to present, what details to include, and how to arrange the content. To help emphasize this reality, consider incorporating several examples of "subjective" maps. Research suggests that people often interpret maps as facts; however, all maps are created with certain data selected and other data excluded. The same is true for creating listening maps; not every aspect of a piece can be included, and students must systematically simplify the musical content by eliminating unneeded details.

Using the results of their collaborative investigations, each student will create an original listening map that must convey information about the following musical elements:

- Formal structure: a simple and clear representation of the form or design of their piece; a visual model depicting significant events such as repeated or contrasting sections of music.
- Instrumentation and texture: an illustration of the tone colors (instrumenta-tion) and layers (texture) of their piece; students might choose a different color

for each instrument and trace the presence of each instrument throughout the piece; students might also choose to represent texture separately from instrumentation, perhaps utilizing different densities of lines.

- In addition to formal structure, instrumentation, and texture, students must choose two additional musical elements to map, tying back to the concepts they analyzed in their groups. These may include melodic themes, rhythmic characteristics, dynamics, tempo, style or genre, and text. For example, students might use a rising line to represent an ascending melody or a swelling dynamic level; they might differentiate between various rhythmic articulations by varying the length or quality of the lines they portray.

Before putting pencil to paper, some students may benefit from kinesthetically "drawing" the music in the air. Invite students to repeatedly experience and explore the music by humming, tapping, or gesturing along with a recording. This repetition may assist students in creatively representing their ideas. Next, students need to consider the map symbols they will use for the project and determine how they will represent the various gestures they've demonstrated with symbols. Regarding specific layouts, some students' maps might be drawn and read from left to right, while others might travel in a back-and-forth pattern. Still others might follow a concentric spiral or travel from top to bottom. Students should plan to create several written drafts, experimenting with various symbols, colors, and styles.

As students create their final drafts, remind them to take care to produce a legible, orderly map with clear attention to detail. In addition to the required musical elements, students' maps must contain the following basic features:

- Title: the main label for the map; likely includes the title of the music and composer, such as *A Map of The Carpenters' "I'm on Top of the World"*
- Map symbols: the letters, characters, shapes, lines, or colors that graphically represent various aspects of the music
- Map legend: a key to all the map symbols included
- Credits: a citation for the musical example and the map creator's name

Assessment

- Following the completion of their listening maps, invite students to share their map by tracing their diagram in time with the music as it plays. You could have two to three students present simultaneously with maps that portray identical examples. Informally assess the alignment of students' visual representations with the musical elements present in each piece.
- Collect students' geographic and musical maps and assess each based on the inclusion of essential map elements, accurate portrayal of fundamental components, and attention to detail.

- Collect exit ticket responses. Invite students to respond to various prompts such as:
  - What was the most challenging part of creating maps for this lesson?
  - What are the clearest connections between geographic and musical maps?
  - How did you use your creativity in designing and constructing your maps?
  - Why do geographical maps of the same place or musical maps of the same piece look different?
  - Why are maps constructed to emphasize different features or include different areas of focus?
  - What are the motivations of different mapmakers?

Extensions

- Explore digital mapping by having students use online mapping tools or software (like Google Maps, Map Maker, ArcGIS, or StoryMaps) to create digital versions of their maps.
- Map the geography of a specific region, then map a musical example that originates from that area.
- Select a song such as Johnny Cash's "I've Been Everywhere." Create a geographic map of all the locations mentioned in the lyrics and a listening map of all the musical components.

Lesson 4.3: "Song of the Refugee" and the Story of One Hmong Immigrant, Sying Yang

Grade Level: Middle school, but may be adapted

Essential Question: How can stories and songs reflect themes of displacement, adaptation, cultural identity, and the immigrant experience?

Objectives

- Students will explore the history, culture, and experiences of Hmong immigrants, considering the personal story of Sying Yang, focusing on the events that led to his immigration, his journey to the United States, and his challenges adjusting to life in the United States.
- Students will listen to and analyze recordings of traditional Hmong music, identifying the emotional tone, instruments, and context of the recorded examples and discussing the historical role of music within the Hmong community, including its connection to oral traditions and the transmission of cultural knowledge.

- Students will explore the tonal nature of the Hmong language, listen to "Song of the Refugee," and discuss the significance of the implied text, observing connections between the musical and textual meanings.
- Students will identify an immigrant community and research about its traditions, values, language, and music utilizing primary and secondary sources.
- Through small group and class discussions, students will demonstrate their understanding of the relationship of the Hmong immigrant experience within the broader context of immigration in the United States.

National Curriculum Standards for Social Studies Addressed

- NCSSS 1: Culture: Social studies programs should include experiences that provide for the study of culture and cultural diversity.
- NCSSS 3: People, Places, and Environments: Social studies programs should include experiences that provide for the study of people, places, and environments.
- NCSSS 4: Individual Development and Identity: Social studies programs should include experiences that provide for the study of individual development and identity.
- NCSSS 6: Power, Authority, and Governance: Social studies programs should include experiences that provide for the study of how people create, interact with, and change structures of power, authority, and governance.
- NCSSS 10: Civic Ideals and Practices: Social studies programs should include experiences that provide for the study of the ideals, principles, and practices of citizenship in a democratic republic.

C3 Framework for Social Studies State Standards Addressed

- C3 Dimension 1: Questions and inquiries
- C3 Dimension 2: History
- C3 Dimension 4: Communicating conclusions and taking informed action

National Core Arts Standards for Music Addressed

- MU:Pr5: Develop and refine artistic techniques and work for presentation
- MU:Pr6: Convey meaning through the presentation of artistic work
- MU:Re8: Interpret intent and meaning in artistic work

- MU:Re9: Apply criteria to evaluate artistic work
- MU:Cn11: Relate artistic ideas and works with societal, cultural, and historical context to deepen understanding

Materials

- Printed excerpts from article "Minnesota's Newest Immigrants" (excerpts A through M)
- Photos and images (Figures 4.8 through 4.21)
- Map of Asia or detailed world map
- Video examples
  - *Hmong Song Poet of Kwv Txhiaj: Bee Yang* (youtube.com/watch?v=K_acojZLSU8)
  - *Hmong Songs of Memory by Victoria Vorreiter* (youtube.com/watch?v=Dmhv6QyLJFg)
- Musical example
  - "Tsi teb tsaws chaw (Song of the Refugee)" (Mua, 1995)

Procedure

First, ask a student to locate Laos on a classroom world map to identify the country where the many Hmong Americans have roots, then watch the video *Hmong Song Poet of Kwv Txhiaj: Bee Yang* (Twin Cities PBS, 2021). In the video, author Kao Kalia Yang translates her father Bee Yang's words, songs, and stories.

Next, share a narrative account of a single Hmong immigrant, Sying Yang, who came to America in the late 1970s. Ask for reasons that people from this area of the world are still immigrating today (economics, politics, safety). Show images to illustrate Sying Yang's story as members of the class take turns reading excerpts of the following account of his background, his journey, and his life in America (all excerpts taken from Seidl, 1983, pp. 20–29; permission granted by Minnesota Historical Society).

A. Sying Yang (pronounced *s'ying yahng*) can make a top in twenty minutes (see Figure 4.8). He uses a large knife that he got in Thailand. Sying learned to whittle during the long years his family spent in a refugee camp there. Now in St. Paul, he amazes his new American friends with his skill in creating a top out of a hunk of wood. Sying is Hmong. He and his people make up Minnesota's newest immigrant group (see Figure 4.9). They are here because they helped America fight in Southeast Asia. They are here because, when the war ended, they were driven from their country and had nowhere else to go.

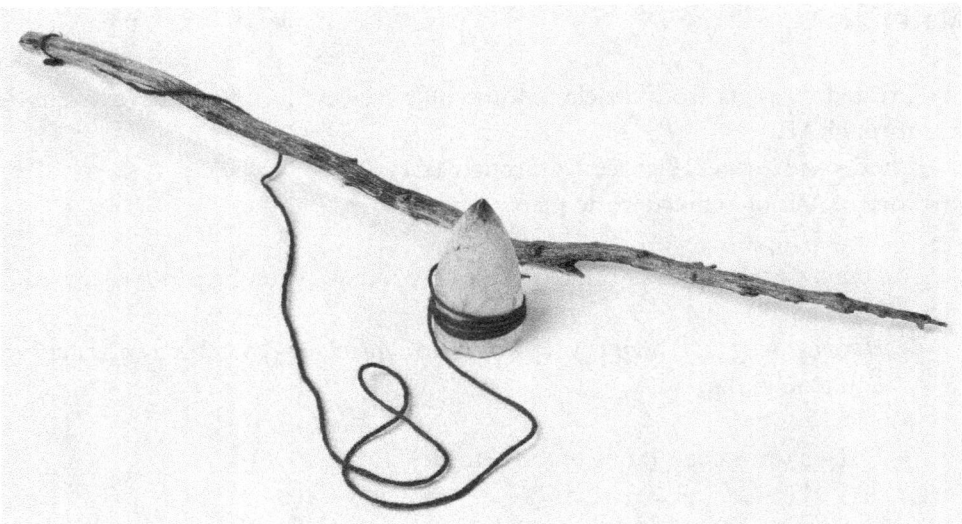

Figure 4.8   Top made by Sying Yang.
Image courtesy of the Minnesota Historical Society.

Figure 4.9   "Minnesota Welcomes You" highway sign.
Lorie Shaull/Wikimedia Commons, Creative Commons Attribution-Share Alike 2.0 Generic license.

B. The Hmong have migrated several times in their history. Thousands of years ago they moved southward from Siberia and Mongolia into China. In the nineteenth century they migrated southward again into Vietnam and finally to Laos, where they settled in mountain villages to farm the land. Sying was born in the village of Pha Khay (pah kay) in the mountains of Laos. In his village, and in others like it, Hmong people raised rice, corn, and vegetables (see Figure 4.10). Sying's family also kept animals—water buffalo to pull their plow, pigs and chickens for meat. The Hmong had farmed like this for generations, but Sying's life would be different.

Figure 4.10 Hmong farming village in mountains of Laos.
© Withgod/Dreamstime, ID 81075101.

C. During America's war in Southeast Asia in the 1960s and 1970s, the US government recruited the Hmong to fight for the Americans. Thousands of Hmong soldiers died and many more were wounded, including Sying's father (see Figure 4.11). The government had promised that when the war was over, America would help the Hmong. But when the war finally ended in 1975, American troops pulled out in a hurry. The Hmong were left to face their enemies alone.

Figure 4.11 Sying and his father.
Image courtesy of the Minnesota Historical Society.

D. Sying was only five years old when his village was attacked. "Everybody tried to run away into the forest," he recalls. The Yangs fled with only what they could carry on their backs—some clothing, a few cooking pots, rice, and an M-16 rifle. For several days they traveled through the thick forest, always on the lookout for enemy patrols. When Sying got tired, his father carried him. Eventually they reached the city of Vientiane, the capital of Laos. There, Sying's father bought passage on a boat across the Mekong River (see Figure 4.12). On the other side lay their destination—a refugee camp in Thailand. But the Mekong, a wide and rushing river, was patrolled by enemy soldiers on one side and scouted by Thai bandits on the other. The Yangs knew that crossing the river would be dangerous.

Figure 4.12 Mekong River near Vientiane.
© Nathapon Watmanee/Dreamstime, ID 28708368.

E. Sying and his family made it safely to the refugee camp. In Nong Khai (nong ky), they joined thousands of other Hmong who had fled for their lives. Although the Thai government tried to care for the homeless people, life in the camp was not easy. The Hmong were farmers, but now they had no land to farm. There was little for them to do and no place to go. To fill the long hours, the children taught each other games (see Figure 4.13). Here, Sying learned to make tops. He had plenty of time to practice until he became an expert.

Figure 4.13 Hmong refugees playing in Thai refugee camp.
Ken and Visakha Kawasaki, kawasaki@brelief.org/Wikimedia Commons, Creative Commons CC0 1.0 Universal Public Domain Dedication.

F. Sying's family lived at Nong Khai for two years. Then they were moved to another camp called Ban Vinai (bahn vee ny), where they stayed for two more years (see Figure 4.14). At Ban Vinai, Sying went to school for the first time. He studied reading and writing in the Thai language. He also learned arithmetic and a little English. But his family worried about Sying's future.

Figure 4.14 Ban Vinai refugee camp.
Ken and Visakha Kawasaki, kawasaki@brelief.org/Wikimedia Commons, Creative Commons CC0 1.0 Universal Public Domain Dedication.

G. For months the Yangs had watched other families leave the camp to resettle in America. The US government, aided by private relief agencies, was finally helping the Hmong find new homes. Sying's family began to think about moving there, too, but they were sadly torn. To Hmong people, the most important thing of all is to live among relatives (see Figure 4.15). They have a saying, "To be without family is to be lost." Sying's mother and father knew that if they went to America, they would never again see their aged relatives who chose to stay in the camp. They knew they would probably never again see Sying's oldest brother, who had been captured in Laos and sent to a prison. They knew they would cut off forever their ties to dozens of their relatives.

Figure 4.15 The Yang family in Thai refugee camp.
Image courtesy of the Minnesota Historical Society.

H. But the Yangs had relatives in America, too. Sying's uncle and his family had been sent by an agency for refugees to a place called St. Paul. He mailed back cassette tapes urging his sister's family to follow. "It is better if you come to the United States," he said. "There is more food here." He offered to help them get settled. Sying's family listened to the tapes again and again. They finally decided to go. The US government paid for their trip. Sying recalls that, during the bus ride from camp, he "cried all day long. I didn't want to come to America because I had to leave my brother Dao who took care of me when I was little." (His brother was able to join them later in St. Paul.) In Bangkok, they boarded a plane that would take them to Seattle and then on to St. Paul (see Figure 4.16). On the plane, Sying found himself surrounded by people speaking a language he didn't understand. "I couldn't talk to them because I didn't know the words. It felt like I didn't have a mouth."

Figure 4.16 View from plane above Bangkok.
© Weedezign/Dreamstime, ID 61799153.

I. In St. Paul, Sying's uncle met the family at the airport. They would stay with him for a few weeks until they found a place of their own. When Sying first saw his uncle's apartment, he was astonished. "You can cook very fast here and get water inside," he exclaimed. In Laos, Sying had lived in a house made of bamboo, with a thatched roof and a dirt floor. He had fetched water from a well and gathered firewood for cooking. Now his family would have plumbing and electricity. They would also have to adjust to a world of cars, TV sets, furnaces, and telephones (see Figure 4.17).

Figure 4.17 Sying riding a bike in St. Paul.
Image courtesy of the Minnesota Historical Society.

J. All over America the Hmong have come to live near relatives (see Figure 4.18). That is one reason the Hmong population in St. Paul grew so fast. Just as Sying moved here to join his uncle's family, thousands of other Hmong did the same. Even with help from family and friends, the Hmong find life in America very hard. They have few of the job skills needed in a modern city. And they must learn to speak a new language. Reading and writing English are even more difficult because few Hmong in Laos ever learned to read and write their own language.

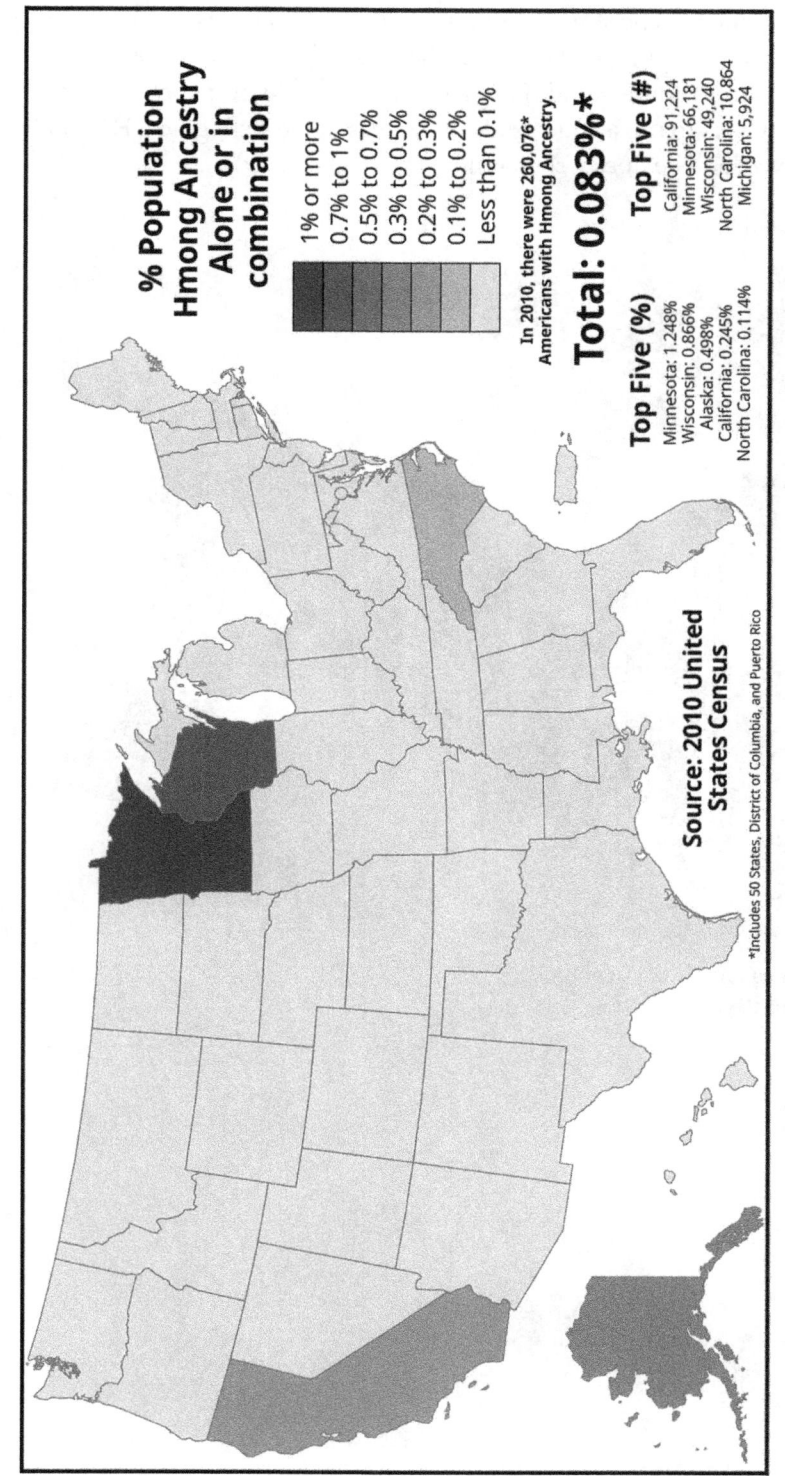

Figure 4.18 Americans with Hmong ancestry by state.

K. Sying recalls the trouble he had on his first day at school in St. Paul. Because he had gone to school for two years in Thailand, he was put in a third grade class. To test what he knew, the teacher asked him to bring her an eraser. But Sying couldn't understand. He gave her some colored pencils instead. So, he was sent back to the second grade. Now he is in the sixth grade. His English has improved, and he does well in school (see Figure 4.19).

Figure 4.19 The Yang family in America.
Image courtesy of the Minnesota Historical Society.

L. His mother is having a much harder time learning English. She attends a special class, but when she gets back home, she speaks only Hmong. Sying tries to help his parents. "I teach my father the ABCs and I teach him to write his name." Sying also watches the news on TV with his father and tries to explain the stories. He goes with his family to the social worker's office and helps translate for them. Because Sying has learned English faster than his parents, things are turned upside down for him and his family. In the traditional Hmong way of life, it is very important for children to respect their elders, follow their advice, and obey their wishes (see Figure 4.20). But in America Sying finds that he must sometimes advise his parents about new customs.

Figure 4.20 Hmong woman guides children as they dry chilis in the sun.
© Narongrit Sritana/iStock, iStock Content License Agreement.

M. Sying often has to choose between doing things the Hmong way and doing things the American way. When Sying imagines raising his own children in America, he says he will try to teach them Hmong ways. "I'll tell them Hmong stories and teach them Hmong-style cooking. I'll tell them they have to act like Hmong. That means they have to learn to do work when they are little, and they have to listen to what their parents say." He imagines that his children will dress in American clothes. "But they will have black hair so they will remember that they are Hmong." And of course, Sying will teach them the games he learned as a boy in Asia, including how to carve a perfect top" (see Figure 4.8).

Student prompt: "The story we just read gives us insights into Sying's experiences as an immigrant. Imagine you were moving to a new country; what would you bring with you?" Students' answers will most likely highlight the "stuff" they would bring. "What about things you can't see?" Encourage students to consider intangible things that might be important to them, such as traditions, customs, memories, perceptions, stories, songs, or games; connect these intangible ideas to those described by Sying Yang.

Engage students in an activity that will allow them experience Hmong music codes on a simple level. Student prompt: "I would like you to try something. I am going to hum a song for you. When I am done, I am going to ask you what the words of the song were." Hum a simple tune such as "Twinkle, Twinkle Little Star" or "Happy Birthday." When students identify the song and articulate the associated text, ask them how they were able to speak or sing the lyrics of the song when it was not sung to them. "Now I would like you to try another song." Hum a made-up tune and repeat the process. "This time when I asked you to tell the words, you could not answer. Why not?" Students will likely reply that they had not heard song before, so did not have any lyrics associated with that tune.

In Hmong culture, people learn to hear the text of a song whether words are sung or not. This is possible because of the tonal nature of the spoken Hmong language, which primarily utilizes one-syllable words; each word is based on three components, the consonant, the vowel, and the tone. There are eight different tones in the spoken Hmong language and these tones can be precisely reproduced through music (Cooper, 1996).

If time allows, watch *Hmong Songs of Memory by Victoria Vorreiter* (songsofmemory, 2016), a video showing examples of various Hmong instruments. Listen to the spike fiddle at 1:09, a leaf melody at 1:36, a mouth harp at 2:07, various flute-type woodwind instruments starting at 2:43, and the qeej (pronounced keng) starting at 4:39.

Listen to "Tsi teb tsaws chaw" (Song of the Refugee), performed on the fipple flute (see Figure 4.21) by Boua Xou Mua. There are no "lyrics" or singing on the recording; it is a solo flute performance. (Author's note: I had two of my fifth grade Hmong students listen to this recording. One was able to give me an almost word-for-word "translation," one was able to decipher just the main idea. Neither had heard the song before, and when asked, neither could articulate how they were able to interpret the text. They both simply stated that it was something they had always been able to do.) Ask a volunteer to read the text of "Song of the Refugee." The opening melody translates as:

> *Because of the country becoming unpeaceful, I have to escape to another country.*
> *To this country I leave my parents and cousins in another part of the world.*
> *I miss them so much, is there anyone who will know or not?* (Mua, year, track 12)

Discuss how the associated text of song might epitomize an immigrant's feelings about leaving Laos. How does the emotion portrayed in this musical performance align with the content of the text? How can music communicate beyond the spoken word?

Figure 4.21 Man playing Hmong reed flute.
Ken and Visakha Kawasaki, kawasaki@brelief.org/Wikimedia Commons, Creative Commons CC0 1.0 Universal Public Domain Dedication.

Invite students to identify a different immigrant community to investigate, acknowledging that students in your class may have personal histories that mirror the experience of the Hmong community in Minneapolis. Provide access to online resources to allow students to research the communities they selected. Encourage students to utilize primary and secondary sources such as oral histories, documentaries, and articles to research about traditions, values, and languages. Consider using a standard template for students to record their findings. Challenge students to locate a representative recorded musical example and document their source, as well. As a potential structure, students might create digital stories with images from their chosen immigrant community with their selected musical example as the soundtrack.

Direct students to share the data they gathered, listen to musical examples, and communicate their conclusions in small groups or pairs. Finally, in a whole class discussion, explore the relationship between the Hmong immigrant experience and the broader immigrant experience in the United States, inviting individuals to support their responses by providing documentary evidence and offering specific representative examples.

Assessment

- Informally assess students' responses and engagement during small group and class discussions:
  - Did students actively participate in the conversation?
  - Did students raise questions or respond to others' points?
  - Did students engage with other points of view in a respectful manner?
  - How well did students use evidence or examples to support their views?
- Collect students' research documentation and assess the inclusion of appropriate sources, accurate citations, and logical conclusions.

Lesson 4.4: Reflective Thinking: Using the *What, So What, Now What* Model to Examine Ways People Create, Interact with, and Change Structures of Power

Grade Level

High school, but may be adapted

Essential Questions

What role does music play in movements for social change? How can critical reflection about social issues lead to creative solutions? How does the presenting and sharing of information, images, and music influence and shape ideas, beliefs, and actions? What role should celebrities (e.g., songwriters, singers, instrumentalists) play in drawing attention to social and political issues?

Objectives

- Through independent research and class discussion, students will critically evaluate the impact of music in social and political movements, considering the role music can play in shaping or reflecting actions, advocating for change, protesting inequalities, and promoting understanding.
- Students will analyze a musical work associated with a social or political movement, identifying the specific musical elements and choices employed to transmit messages and inspire audiences.
- Students will utilize the *What, So What, Now What* model to select and investigate an issue that is meaningful to them; to observe and accurately describe the issue; to reflect on the significance of the issue; and to develop strategies for advocacy or change.
- Students will create and share multimedia presentations that demonstrate their critical reflection and provide platforms for proposing action plans that address the issues they considered.
- Students will apply their understanding of music as a means for conveying information, shaping viewpoints, and inspiring action by selecting music with musical elements that align with and support their action plan and promote their message.

National Curriculum Standards for Social Studies Addressed

- NCSSS 2: Time, Continuity, and Change: Social studies programs should include experiences that provide for the study of the past and its legacy.
- NCSSS 5: Individuals, Groups, and Institutions: Social studies programs should include experiences that provide for the study of interactions among individuals, groups, and institutions.
- NCSSS 6: Power, Authority, and Governance: Social studies programs should include experiences that provide for the study of how people create, interact with, and change structures of power, authority, and governance.
- NCSSS 10: Civic Ideals and Practices: Social studies programs should include experiences that provide for the study of the ideals, principles, and practices of citizenship in a democratic republic.

C3 Framework for Social Studies State Standards Addressed

- C3 Dimension 2: Civics
- C3 Dimension 4: Communicating conclusions and taking informed action

National Core Arts Standards for Music Addressed

- MU:Cr1: Generate and conceptualize artistic ideas and work
- MU:Cr3: Refine and complete artistic work
- MU:Pr4: Select, analyze, and interpret artistic work for presentation
- MU:Re7: Perceive and analyze artistic work
- MU:Re9: Apply criteria to evaluate artistic work
- MU:Cn10: Synthesize and relate knowledge and personal experiences to make art
- MU:Cn11: Relate artistic ideas and works with societal, cultural, and historical context to deepen understanding

Materials

- Images
  - Optional: Photograph of Vincent Lingiari (Figure 4.22)
  - The *What, So What, Now What* model (Figure 4.23)
- Student handouts
  - Copies of Table 4.1
- Access to digital tools to create multimedia projects
- Musical examples
  - Optional: "From Little Things Big Things Grow" by Kev Carmody and Paul Kelly

Procedure

Part 1

First, explore the role of music in social and political movements such as the American civil rights movement, various labor movements, or one of the many anti-war protests worldwide. Throughout history, music has been used to advocate for social change, to rally support for war efforts, and to protest violence. Additionally, music has served as a critical mechanism for promoting understanding and building solidarity. Composers use a variety of musical elements including lyrics, melodies, rhythms, and tone color to transmit messages and persuade or inspire their audiences. In some situations, music served as a platform to express ideas when other forms of communication fell short. The capacity to broadly spread awareness for social issues is one of music's strengths.

Choose one musical example for an in-depth analysis. Following close listening, direct students to use print or online reference materials to research the example's historical and cultural background, other prominent contextual features, and the impact of the piece as a means of social change, then lead a large group discussion. For pieces with text, encourage students to sing along with a recording, especially on refrains.

Consider selecting the song "From Little Things Big Things Grow" by Kev Carmody and Paul Kelly for the class discussion. This well-known Australian protest song conveys the story of Aboriginal rights activist Vincent Lingiari (see

Figure 4.22 Photograph of Vincent Lingiari.
Ian Cochrane/Flickr, Creative Commons Attribution 2.0 Generic license.

Figure 4.22), his part in the 1966 Gurindji Strike, and Indigenous Australians' struggle for land rights. Musically, the piece follows a simple verse-chorus format, with harmonica solos following most choruses and a four-chord harmony that is used throughout. The repetitive pentatonic melody (based on a five-note scale) has an almost spoken-word quality. A consistent strumming pattern in the guitar and banjo and the lack of fluctuation in dynamics reinforce the role of the music as an unpretentious backdrop for the story.

The song opens with these words: "Gather round people, I'll tell you a story; an eight-year long story of power and pride" (Kelly, 1991, track 13). The lyrics go on to imply that the initial walk-out was the "little thing" that started the rebellion and led to the "big thing" of equal rights. After eight years of struggle, Australian prime minister Gough Whitlam (called a "tall stranger" in the lyrics) symbolically returned the land to the Indigenous people, pouring a handful of sand through Lingiari's fingers. The song ends with optimism and conviction: "That was the story of Vincent Lingiari, but this is the story of something much more; how power and privilege cannot move a people who know where they stand, and they stand in the law. From little things, big things grow" (Kelly, 1991, track 13). In September 2020, fifty-four years after the Gurindji walk-off, the full claim for land rights was granted (National Museum Australia, 2023).

Alternate song suggestions include the iconic "The Times, They Are A-Changin' " by Bob Dylan and "A Change Is Gonna Come" by Sam Cooke.

Part 2
Initiate a class discussion about the *What, So What, Now What* model, a guide for critical reflective thinking (see Figure 4.23). The model was designed by educator

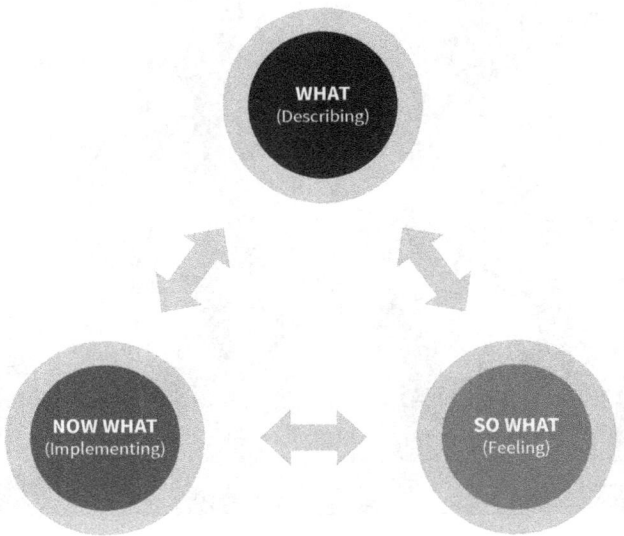

Figure 4.23 The *What, So What, Now What* model.
Adapted from Rolfe et al., 2001. Image courtesy of Annika Harney.

Terry Borton in 1970, but it gained prominence when Rolfe, Freshwater, and Jasper (2001) reframed it as a reflective tool for clinical healthcare workers.

Distribute copies of Table 4.1 and briefly describe each stage, timeframe, and focus, then prompt students to share their impressions. Choose a sample challenge or concern and work through the model as a class. This will allow students to first apply the model collaboratively before attempting it alone. After students are familiar with the template and the process, direct everyone to select a social challenge, experience, or issue that is meaningful to them. Teens can be influential agents of social change, and this student-centered project encourages them to use their strengths and interests to bring about change as they care for themselves, their communities, and the world.

Especially if you studied "From Little Things Big Things Grow" in Part 1, remind students that even small actions can have a big impact. A student's little thing might be something like donating time to the local food bank or initiating one garbageless lunch a week at school. Of course, students are capable of big things, as well, and some may wish to address large issues such as gun violence, anxiety leading to self-harm, or ableism.

Part 3

As a culmination of their research, students will create multimedia projects that demonstrate their critical reflection and provide platforms for proposing action plans that address the issues they considered. Prior to this project, students should have experience creating presentations with static slides and basic proficiency-building multimedia presentations and utilizing tools and elements such as narration, GIFs, animations, infographics, and surveys. Tailor the assignment directions to align with the digital platforms and software available at your school, to support your specific curricular goals, and to build on students' previous technology skills and understandings. For example, you might want to emphasize civic engagement by directing students to design presentations to fit expectations for a county commission meeting, state legislative hearing, or some other decision-making group.

Students' research and preparation using the *What, So What, Now What* templates will drive the creation of their multimedia presentations. The following steps could guide their work:

1. Draft an outline based on a three-part structure:
   - What headings and written content will you use to highlight each stage of the *What, So What, Now What* framework?
   - What images or graphic elements will you incorporate (e.g., photos, drawings, tables, charts)?
   - How many slides will each section contain? How will you order your slides?
2. Design the slides:
   - What overall slide design or theme will you utilize?
   - What color schemes will enhance your presentation?

Table 4.1 *What, So What, Now What* reflection template

Stage	Focus	Guiding Questions	Student Responses
WHAT?	Describing	• What is the challenge, experience, or issue? • What are the surrounding circumstances? • Are any patterns evident? • What measures or strategies, if any, have been undertaken or applied? • What objective resources inform my understanding? • What policies, laws, structures, or systems have shaped the challenge, experience, or issue? • How has the challenge, experience, or issue changed over time?	
SO WHAT?	Feeling	• What does this challenge, experience, or issue mean to me? • What does it mean to others? • How can we make sense of or draw insights from this matter? • What does this teach me about myself?	
NOW WHAT?	Implementing	• What insights have I developed and how can those inform my future actions? • What knowledge and skills can I use to respond to the situation? • What simple steps can begin right away? • What are longer-term solutions? • What personal actions, group activities, or other resources are needed to implement my ideas? • What are relevant opportunities at local, state, national, and global levels? • What are relevant legislative, executive, and/or judicial responses? • What are the next steps?	

Adapted from: G. Rolfe, D. Freshwater, and M. Jasper, *Critical Reflection for Nursing and the Helping Professions: A User's Guide.* (Palgrave Macmillan, 2001).

- What interactive elements could you add?
- What musical content will you select or create?
- Apply your understanding of music as a means for conveying information, shaping viewpoints, and inspiring action to select or create music to accompany your presentation.
- The lyrics, melody, rhythm, and mood of your piece should support or promote your message.
3. Build each slide:
   - Assemble content to clearly convey information
   - Arrange elements to emphasize points and add interest
4. Review, revise, and present
   - Proofread, edit, and condense as needed
   - Present final projects in small groups or as whole class

Assessment

- Collect students' *What, So What, Now What* reflection templates. Assess the depth and breadth of students' investigations about their selected issue. Have they accurately described and defined the issue? Have they reflected deeply about the significance of the issue? Have they developed or proposed effective, practical strategies for advocacy or change?
- As students share their multimedia presentations, assess their work based on alignment with the three-part structure of the *What, So What, Now What* framework, the design and execution of slides, the incorporation of supporting musical examples, and overall attention to detail.

Inventory of Ideas

The following collection of ideas contains additional lesson topics, specific teaching strategies, and recommended activities.

1. Initiate a "Songs and Stories" project as an introduction to ethnographic research. After students are comfortable with interview techniques (e.g., through teacher modeling and practicing with peers), direct students to select a family member or adult mentor and secure their permission to participate in the project. Reinforce the respectful representation of people and their practices as students gain hands-on experience with various aspects of ethnographic fieldwork including interviewing, making field recordings, and taking field notes. Students can utilize a common semi-structured or open-ended interview template, or each student could create unique interview prompts. As a part of each interview, students digitally record participants

Figure 4.24 Flag of the Crow Nation.
Public Domain/Wikimedia.

as they tell a favorite story and/or sing a favorite song. Provide the opportunity for students to share the information they documented, along with their personal insights about the intersection of who we are and why we tell stories and sing songs. For example, a Crow student of mine collected the traditional Crow lullaby "Little Bear Song." She reported that her great-aunt, Louella Johnson, Iilapaatbish itchish (Makes Good Friend), sings the song on the Crow Apsaalooké language learning app (Crow Nation, 2024). When describing the project, she stated, "This song has been passed down for generations, not just in my family, but all the Crows use it. It belongs here in this land; by passing it on, I'm keeping the family spirit alive" (see Figure 4.24).

2. Use music as primary source material. Song lyrics can express the literal meaning of historical events, identify individuals or communities, describe locations and occasions, and characterize consequences or outcomes. For example, examine "America" (My Country 'Tis of Thee) (see Figure 4.25) or "Aloha 'Oe," the Hawaiian folk song written by Hawaii's Queen Lili'uokalani (see Figure 4.26), the last sovereign monarch of the Hawaiian Kingdom. Students could also examine song lyrics specific to various genres in terms of their representation of social expectations and the American Dream, investigate country music texts and their portrayal of economic expectations, or explore ways various hip-hop and rap artists offer stereotypical or counternarrative representations.

3. Compare and contrast musical and written historical accounts of various events, using a Venn diagram to record insights and analyses. For example, the instrumental jazz piece "Alabama" by John Coltrane was written in 1963 in response to the Ku

Figure 4.25 Photograph of first page of "America" (My Country 'Tis of Thee).
Image courtesy of the Library of Congress, Music Division.

Figure 4.26 Queen Lili'uokalani, last ruler of the Hawaiian Kingdom.
Public Domain/Hawaii State Archives/Wikimedia Commons.

Klux Klan's bombing of the 16th Street Baptist Church in Birmingham, Alabama, that killed four African American girls and injured many others. As a written account, consider reading the transcript of the remarks given by Martin Luther King Jr., who spoke at the funeral for the girls. Coltrane reportedly incorporated the rhythms of MLK's speech patterns in his music (Feinstein, 1996).

4. People in the United States and throughout the world are both producers and consumers of goods and services. Explore the production and consumption of music as students build economic understandings. For example, if your class is studying the Industrial Revolution, discuss the mass production of musical instruments and the expansion in musical genres related to greater access to music making. Discussions of the music industry fit well with lessons focusing on access to and availability of resources, job creation, and impacts on local economies. You could also listen to, perform, and analyze songs that emphasize consumerism, materialism, wealth, or finances.

5. Many musicians have been inspired to create songs that recount history or convey sentiments surrounding past events. While songs with historical subjects often succinctly encapsulate the essence of past occurrences and demonstrate a deep understanding of their surrounding context, they are not always historically accurate and do not always get every detail correct, providing opportunities for students to critically examine accounts of events that have shaped our world. Examine songs with historical themes to verify information that is correct and to ascertain material that is untrue or even misleading. Additionally, strive to go beyond the lyrics; beyond the text of songs about past events, what does the music add to our understanding? How does singing these songs add to your understanding? Table 4.2 includes suggestions for musical exploration.

6. Discuss the ways that music can shape individual and group identities, including ethnicity, culture, age, gender, and sexuality. Composers often use music to express personal experiences, challenge stereotypes, and advocate for social justice. For example, the song "Swimming Pool" by Anna Calvi examines rigid gender boundaries. Calvi, who is gay, stated, "I think the sound is completely tied up with my identity" (Songfacts, 2024). Regarding "Swimming Pool," she added:

> I wanted to create guitar parts that sounded similar to the way the David Hockney *Swimming Pool* paintings look. Hockney painted them when there was still a lot of prejudice against being gay and yet his depictions of men are beautiful . . . without any sense of shame. I found this very powerful. I wanted to pay tribute to the idea in this song. (Songfacts, 2024)

Encourage students to locate additional examples of music that advocates for human rights or supports diversity, in any of its many forms. Invite students to share recordings or perform songs for their peers.

7. Set aside a long, narrow portion of your classroom wall for students to create a timeline related to a historical era they are studying. Have students place significant events and their corresponding dates above the line, and excerpts of song lyrics with corresponding dates below the line (see Figure 4.27). This chronological display will not only show the order of events but will also capture the relationship between music and history, highlighting instances in which music either reflected or

Table 4.2 Songs with historical themes

Song Title	Creator(s)	Topic
"April 29, 1992 (Miami)"	Sublime	Riots and violence after the Rodney King beating
"All and Everyone"	PJ Harvey	Describes the events of the Gallipoli Campaign of 1915 and 1916
"American Witch"	Rob Zombie	Salem witch trials
"The Battle of New Orleans"	Johnny Horton	The 1815 Battle of New Orleans
"Buffalo Soldier"	Bob Marley & The Wailers	African American cavalry who fought for the United States during the American Indian Wars and as part of the Spanish-American War
"Cortez the Killer"	Neil Young	Inspired by Hernán Cortés's conquest of the Aztec Empire under Moctezuma II in the sixteenth century
"Cult of Personality"	Living Colour	Propaganda in authoritarian states
"Enola Gay"	OMD Orchestral Manoeuvres in the Dark	Story of the *Enola Gay*, the plane that dropped the atomic bomb on Hiroshima
"Hurricane"	Bob Dylan	The prosecution and incarceration of Rubin "Hurricane" Carter
"Keep the Home Fires Burning"	Irving Berlin	British patriotic song from World War I about the message of hope and resilience for families on the home front
"The Longest Day"	Iron Maiden	D-Day invasion on June 6, 1944
"The Night Chicago Died"	Paper Lace	A shoot-out between the Chicago Police and gangsters tied to Al Capone
"The Night They Drove Old Dixie Down"	The Band	Describes the final days of the American Civil War from the viewpoint of one Confederate soldier
"Oliver's Army"	Elvis Costello	The English Civil War
"Pride (In the Name of Love)"	U2	Tribute to the life of Martin Luther King Jr.
"Rasputin"	Boney M	Story of Grigori Yefimovich Rasputin, an advisor to Russia's Tsar Nicholas II
"Redemption Song"	Bob Marley	Transatlantic Slave Trade
"Revolution"	The Beatles	Chairman Mao's policies in China
"Smoke on the Water"	Deep Purple	Inspired by the December 4, 1971, fire at Switzerland's Montreux Casino
"Sophiatown Is Gone"	Miriam Makeba	Opposition of the Apartheid regime in South Africa
"Sunday Bloody Sunday"	U2	Lyrics from the perspective of an observer of the Troubles in Northern Ireland
"William the Conqueror"	DMX Krew	The Norman Conquest

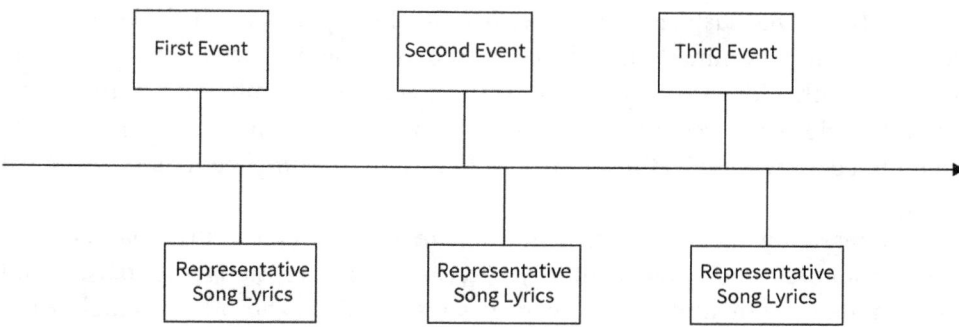

Figure 4.27 Example timeline.
Image courtesy of Annika Harney.

influenced significant historical events. You can also encourage students to make individual timelines, starting from scratch or working from a template. They might generate timelines of their lives, including both personal and world events along with excerpts of song lyrics connected to those milestones.

8. Music naturally relates to the exploration of time and place. Connect students' examination of specific regions or time periods to the music associated with that location or era. For example, how might listening to, analyzing, or performing "Charleston" by Cecil Mack inform a unit on the "Roaring 20s?" How might the Irish reel "Cooley's," performed by The Tulla Céilí Band, illuminate students' perceptions of Ireland? What performance practices or specific musical techniques exemplify various times and places? How might students classify works for which they do not know the time or place of origin?

9. Choose a song that is sung from a first-person perspective. Can a song be considered a valid primary source? What impact do personal accounts have on our understanding of events? What additional insights can listeners gain by hearing first-person accounts set to music? Depending on students' comfort and skill levels, direct them to compose original lyrics for an existing tune or create entirely new pieces based on events to which they were eyewitnesses. Alternately, guide students as they create digital scrapbooks to record their firsthand accounts of an event, with each page of their scrapbooks reinforced and intensified by a musical example of their choosing.

10. During a unit on ethics, play a musical version of the popular online game "Among Us." In the online game, ten players try to complete tasks while identifying the unethical "imposter." To play the high-energy musical game and reinforce rhythmic performance skills, project a rhythm and practice clapping it as a class. Then, choose three or four people as imposters by handing out slips of paper that read "imposter" or "teammate." Each "imposter" must establish a duplicitous way to deceive their peers, performing the rhythm incorrectly in a way that is imperceptible to others in the class. All the "teammates" must perform the rhythm

accurately to avoid suspicion. After performing the rhythm two or three times as a large group, take nominations and vote the most obvious imposter out of the group. Continue with additional rhythms until an agreed upon number of teammates remain. Conclude the game by discussing the ways various moments in the game exemplified duty-based ethics, virtue ethics, and the implications of personal choice.

11. Integrating mental health education in social studies curricula can promote awareness and understanding, decrease misconceptions and biases, and equip students with strategies to manage stress, anxiety, and other mental health challenges. Music can serve as an accessible entry point for discussions related to this challenging topic, develop a common vocabulary, and foster a sense of community. For instance, the lyrics of "Wake Me Up" by Swedish DJ Avicii state, "I tried carrying the weight of the world, but I only have two hands" (Avicii, 2013). Relatedly, the song "The Tears of a Clown" by Hank Cosby, Smokey Robinson, and Stevie Wonder includes the following phrase, "Now if I appear to be carefree, it's only to camouflage my sadness" (Robinson, 1970). Two additional songs to explore include "Fly Away" by Lenny Kravitz and "Shining Star" by Earth Wind & Fire.

12. The term "protest song" often recalls anti-war protest songs such as Bob Dylan's "Blowin' in the Wind" from 1962, Bob Seeger's "Where Have All the Flowers Gone?" from 1955 (his a cappella version is especially poignant), or Jonathan Edwards's "Sunshine Go Away" from 1971. As seen in Lesson 4.4, however, music can help galvanize people regarding a topic like workers' rights. Explore and perform two additional protest songs, each focused on harsh and dangerous working conditions. At first, "Workin' in a Coal Mine" by Allen Toussaint, performed by Lee Dorsey, sounds like an upbeat, peppy, jazz standard, but a closer look reveals the deeper message of the 1966 hit, including the following lyrics, "Down, down, down . . . oops, about to slip down," "How long can this go on?," and "Lord, I'm so tired" (Toussaint, 1971, track 6). The music of "The Chemical Worker's Song (Process Man)," a 1964 protest song by Ron Angel, performed by Great Big Sea, more closely reflects the message found in the lyrics. The stark, open vocal harmonies and pounding bodhran drum accentuate the text, which highlights the long-term effects of working in a polluted working environment and contains the following phrases: "I work and breathe among the fumes that trail across the sky," "there's poison in the air," and "every day you're in this place, you're two days nearer death" (Angel, 1964, track 10). The piece ends with a sense of resignation, with an extremely long, sustained note on the final word, "But you go" (Angel, 1964, track 10).

5
Music and Science

Introduction

Science and music are not simply bodies of knowledge; both disciplines expand our capacity for acquiring knowledge and experiencing life. In both science and music, students are encouraged to think logically and creatively, and in both disciplines, students develop conclusions and create artifacts that require rational thought and inspiration. The interaction of pitches and rhythms creates music, and an infinite variety of musical creations are possible from those building blocks; the interaction of existing evidence and imagination produces limitless new scientific discoveries. Both science and music use inquiry to solve problems and examine the mysteries of life. While science and music as unique disciplines have immeasurable value, activities that integrate music and science encourage active student engagement and offer opportunities for students to perceive connections, make observations, synthesize disparate information, formulate conclusions, and thoughtfully reflect. Integrated lessons that reinforce standards in music and science deepen students' understanding of both disciplines.

The lessons and the strategies and activities included in the chapter 5 inventory of ideas promote active engagement in learning, explore high-level concepts, draw on a wide variety of musical examples, and focus on valid connections between music and science.

Common Links between Music and Science

A common strategy for connecting music and science is to explore "big ideas" that the two disciplines have in common, utilizing the tools of each discipline to examine shared concepts. Enduring ideas that might be explored in music and science include:

Balance
Beauty
Cause and effect
Change
Classification
Cycle
Development

Integrating Music Across the Secondary Curriculum. Kristin Harney, Oxford University Press. © Oxford University Press 2026.
DOI: 10.1093/9780197822036.003.0005

Diversity
Energy
Flexibility
Force
Frequency
Habit
Hierarchy
Inquiry
Instinct
Interdependence
Intuition
Measurement
Models
Motion
Observation
Pattern
Prediction
Repetition
Stability/instability
Structure
Synergy
Systems
Transformation

National Standards

It is important for teachers to address standards in music and science when designing lessons that integrate the two disciplines. Including standards from each discipline promotes a balance between music and science and helps to avoid one subject serving the other. Regarding calls for integration, the National Core Arts Standards for Music unambiguously emphasize integration, specifically inviting students to explore ways that other disciplines connect with music. The Next Generation Science Standards (NGSS) do not explicitly promote music integration; however, broad themes included in the standards suggest many meaningful curricular connections with music. For example, NGSS Crosscutting Concepts facilitate students' exploration of science concepts across the four primary domains of Life Science, Earth and Space Science, Physical Science, and Engineering Design. Just as those broad concepts are a way of linking the domains of science, they are also useful for connecting with disciplines outside science. The NGSS were developed through a collaborative process and were released in 2013. They are broadly based on the National Academy of Science's Framework for K–12 Science Education. The following boxes specify the standards that are addressed in the chapter 5 lessons and inventory of ideas:

- Box 5.1, Next Generation Science Standards
- Box 5.2, National Core Arts Standards

Box 5.3 offers a framework for structuring chapter 5 lessons and activities.

Box 5.1 Next Generation Science Standards Included in Chapter 5 Sample Lessons (L) and Inventory of Ideas (I)

Life Science	LS1	From Molecules to Organisms: Structures and Processes	L 5.2 L 5.3 I 3 I 6 I 7 I 13 I 17
	LS2	Ecosystems: Interactions, Energy, and Dynamics	L 5.1 L 5.4 I 1 I 13 I 16
	LS3	Heredity: Inheritance and Variation of Traits	L 5.2 L 5.3 I 3 I 6 I 8 I 17
	LS4	Biological Evolution: Unity and Diversity	L 5.3 L 5.4 I 3 I 6 I 7 I 8 I 15
Earth & Space Science	ESS1	Earth's Place in the Universe	L 5.1 L 5.3 I 2 I 4 I 14
	ESS2	Earth's Systems	L 5.1 L 5.3 I 1 I 4 I 12 I 17

	ESS3	Earth and Human Activity	L 5.1 L 5.4 I 3 I 9 I 15 I 16
Physical Science	PS1	Matter and Its Interactions	L 5.1 I 2 I 5 I 10 I 12
	PS2	Motion and Stability: Forces and Interactions	L 5.2 I 5 I 10 I 13 I 14
	PS3	Energy	L 5.4 I 2 I 4 I 8 I 9 I 12
	PS4	Waves and Their Applications in Technologies for Information Transfer	L 5.4 I 9 I 11 I 12 I 13 I 14 I 17
Engineering Design Introduction	ETS1	Engineering Design	L 5.2 I 5 I 9 I 11 I 12 I 14 I 16

Next Generation Science Standards: For States, By States. NGSS Lead States, 2013, The National Academies Press.

Box 5.2 National Core Arts Standards for Music Included in Chapter 5 Lessons (L) and Inventory of Ideas (I)

MU:Cr1 (Create)	Generate and conceptualize artistic ideas and work	L 5.2 I 7 I 9 I 11 I 13 I 17

MU:Cr2 (Create)	Organize and develop artistic ideas and work	L 5.3 L 5.4 I 5 I 6 I 10 I 12 I 15
MU:Cr3 (Create)	Refine and complete artistic work	L 5.1 I 1 I 6 I 10 I 11 I 15
MU:Pr4 (Perform)	Select, analyze, and interpret artistic work for presentation	L 5.2 I 4 I 9 I 12 I 16
MU:Pr5 (Perform)	Develop and refine artistic techniques and work for presentation	L 5.1 L 5.3 I 3 I 9 I 10 I 11 I 17
MU:Pr6 (Perform)	Convey meaning through the presentation of artistic work	L 5.1 L 5.3 I 4 I 6 I 14 I 15 I 16
MU:Re7 (Respond)	Perceive and analyze artistic work	L 5.1 L 5.4 I 1 I 6 I 10 I 12 I 13 I 14
MU:Re8 (Respond)	Interpret intent and meaning in artistic work	L 5.1 L 5.3 I 3 I 4 I 5 I 7 I 14 I 16

MU:Re9 (Respond)	Apply criteria to evaluate artistic work	L 5.3 L 5.4 I 2 I 8 I 13 I 16 I 17
MU:Cn10 (Connect)	Synthesize and relate knowledge and personal experiences to make art	L 5.2 L 5.3 I 2 I 5 I 7 I 12 I 14 I 15 I 17
MU:Cn11 (Connect)	Relate artistic ideas and works with societal, cultural, and historical context to deepen understanding	L 5.2 L 5.4 I 1 I 3 I 4 I 8 I 9 I 16

Box 5.3 Framework for Chapter 5 Lessons and Ideas

This chapter is designed to support middle school and high school educators as they integrate music and science. The four detailed, full-length lesson plans are independent and not organized as a progressive series.

- Lesson 5.1: "Feels Like Summer" by Childish Gambino: The Role of Music in Environmental Awareness and Action
    - It was important to me to include a lesson exploring climate change in this chapter. Music's roles in environmental awareness are often to emotionally connect people to issues, raise awareness, and inspire action. I hope students will see how music can drive social change and feel empowered to take action themselves.
- Lesson 5.2: Biological and Psychological Relationships between Music and Memory
    - I have had firsthand experience observing dementia patients' remarkable responses to music. This lesson introduces students to the connection between music and the recall and retention of information as well as the field of music perception.

- Lesson 5.3 Life Cycles and Stages: "Merry Go Round of Life" by Joe Hisaishi
  - In science, lessons exploring the stages of development of various organisms are a common. This expressive piece offers the opportunity for students to engage in in-depth musical analysis and draw connections between musical structure and different stages of life. Special thanks to the undergraduate student who introduced me to this piece and the movie from which it is drawn.
- Lesson 5.4 AI-Generated Music: The Intersection of Technology and Creativity
  - Artificial intelligence is transforming the way we teach, learn, and assess student progress by personalizing instruction, automating administrative tasks, and providing students with adaptive tools and real-time feedback. AI is also transforming the music industry. In this lesson, students explore advantages and disadvantages of AI through the lens of AI-generated music.

The chapter ends with an inventory of ideas detailing seventeen additional lesson topics, specific teaching strategies, and recommended activities. The lessons and activities may be fully taught by individual subject area (science or music) teachers; however, ideally, the plans will facilitate partnerships and collaboration between science teachers and music specialists. All lessons and activities have been reviewed by practicing teachers, and most have been field-tested in middle school and high school classrooms. Most of the lessons will need to be spread over two or more class periods. Chapter 5 lessons are adaptable to a variety of grade levels and are intended as tools for you to meet your students' needs. You and your students bring your own knowledge and experiences to these encounters, and you are invited and encouraged to apply those skills and understandings. I hope you are inspired to locate additional works to explore, including musical examples students are likely to encounter in their lives beyond school (e.g., readily recognizable musical works) and those that are less likely to be encountered (e.g., contemporary works that have not yet received widespread recognition, works for specialized groups or audiences, or works that are rooted in specific geographic regions). See additional guidelines for selecting repertoire in chapter 1. All the images included in this chapter are printed in black and white. Consider accessing full-color images online when displaying photographs, artwork, and other graphics for students, especially when lesson content directly references aspects related to a work's color. Please adjust, adapt, or expand these lessons and ideas to work best for you and for your students. Seek out teachers with whom you can collaborate and utilize the range of ideas and examples as starting points to facilitate your creativity and inspire innovative curriculum making.

Lesson 5.1: "Feels Like Summer" by Childish Gambino: The Role of Music in Environmental Awareness and Action

Grade Level

High school, but may be adapted

Essential Questions

How can musicians draw attention to environmental issues? How might music prompt people to change their behaviors or take action?

Objectives

- Students will engage in class discussions about climate change, demonstrating their understanding of the impact of rising temperatures on ecosystems.
- Students will contrast textual components of "Feels Like Summer" with various indicators of climate change.
- Students will explain the relationship between musical components of "Feels Like Summer" and various indicators of climate change.
- Students will sing the chorus of "Feels Like Summer" in tune, with accurate rhythms and clear enunciation.
- Students will evaluate strategies musicians utilize to address environmental concerns, examining themes, lyrics, and musical elements in representative songs.
- Students will explore and identify human actions that can have a positive impact on the natural world, including climate change.

Next Generation Science Standards Addressed

- LS2: Ecosystems: Interactions, Energy, and Dynamics
- ESS1: Earth's Place in the Universe
- ESS2: Earth's Systems
- ESS3: Earth and Human Activity
- PS1: Matter and Its Interactions

National Core Arts Standards for Music Addressed

- MU:Cr3: Refine and complete artistic work
- MU:Pr5: Develop and refine artistic techniques and work for presentation
- MU:Pr6: Convey meaning through the presentation of artistic work
- MU:Re7: Perceive and analyze artistic work
- MU:Re8: Interpret intent and meaning in artistic work

Materials

- Audio recordings
  - "Feels Like Summer" by Childish Gambino
  - "Don't Go Near the Water" by The Beach Boys
  - "Calypso" by John Denver
  - "Pass It on Down" by Alabama
  - "Gaia" by James Taylor
  - "Burn the House Down" by AJR
  - "Despite Repeated Warnings" by Paul McCartney
  - "The 1975 (Visualiser)" by The 1975
- Video recording
  - *Feels Like Summer* by Childish Gambino (youtube.com/watch?v=F1B9Fx_SgI0)
- Copies of Table 5.1
- Images
  - Ten indicators of global warming (Figure 5.1)
  - Attribution of global warming to climate drivers (Figure 5.2)
  - Future emissions scenarios, including Paris climate pledges (Figure 5.3)

Procedure

Consider playing "Feels Like Summer" by Donald Glover, also known as Childish Gambino, as a backdrop to other activities in the days leading up to this lesson, to surreptitiously expose students to the song. On the day of the lesson, project the lyrics to "Feels Like Summer" and direct students to individually decode the text as they listen to the recording. Divide the class into small groups or pairs of students to allow each person to share their initial ideas, then lead a whole class discussion about the potential meanings.

- The lyrics of "Feels Like Summer" do not simply reference warm, care-free summer days; instead, Childish Gambino is commenting on global climate challenges and their correlation with human impacts. Figure 5.1 shows

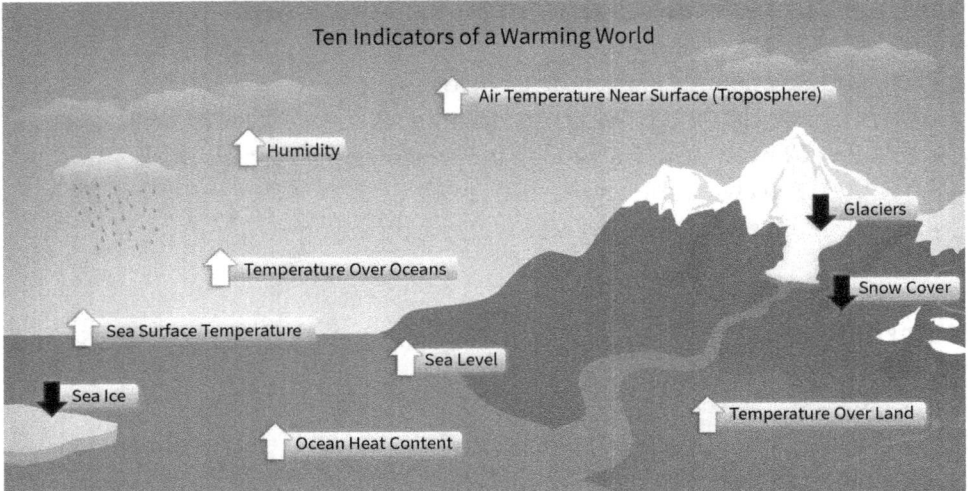

Figure 5.1 Ten indicators of global warming.
Public Domain/US National Oceanic and Atmospheric Administration: National Climatic Data Center/ Wikimedia.

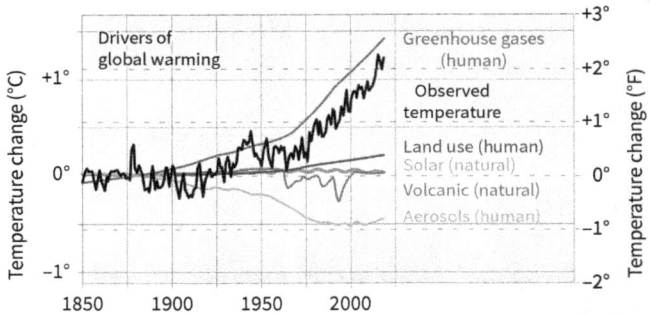

Figure 5.2 Attribution of global warming to climate drivers.
Fifth National Climate Assessment (NCA5) of the US Global Change Research Program (USGCRP)/Wikimedia, Creative Commons Attribution-Share Alike 4.0 International license.

measurable signs that signal earth's warming temperatures and Figure 5.2 shows the direct relationship between those rising temperatures and human actions related to the release of greenhouse gases.

- In the first verse of "Feels Like Summer," Childish Gambino sings, "Seven billion souls that move around the sun; rolling faster, fast and not a chance to slow down" (Childish Gambino, 2018). While there have been numerous efforts to constrain global warming, Figure 5.3 projects the impact of greenhouse gas emissions (measured in gigatonnes of carbon dioxide equivalents) on global temperatures according to various potential scenarios. The lyrics "not

Global greenhouse gas emissions and warming scenarios

- Each pathway comes with uncertainty, marked by the shading from low to high emissions under each scenario.
- Warming refers to the expected global temperature rise by 2100, relative to pre-industrial temperatures.

Annual global greenhouse gas emissions
in gigatonnes of carbon dioxide-equivalents

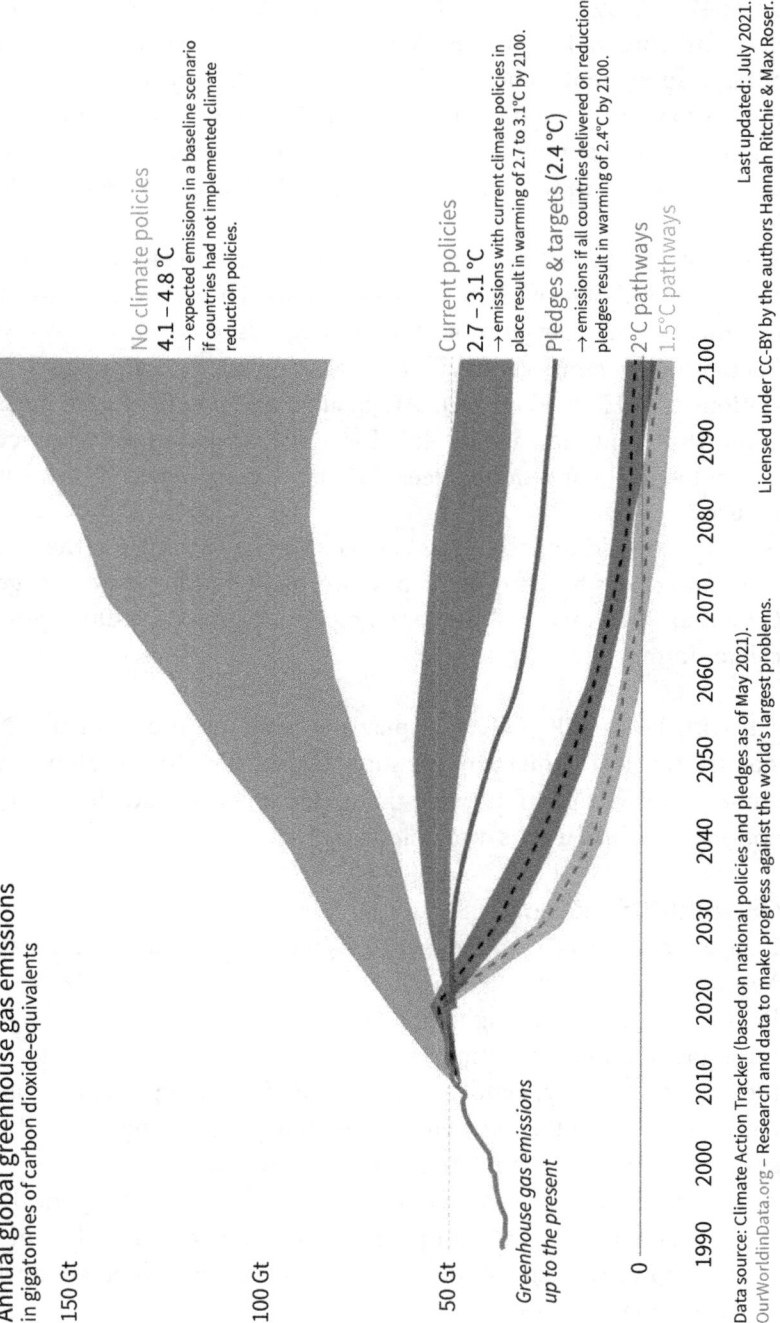

150 Gt

100 Gt

50 Gt

Greenhouse gas emissions up to the present

0

No climate policies
4.1 – 4.8 °C
→ expected emissions in a baseline scenario if countries had not implemented climate reduction policies.

Current policies
2.7 – 3.1 °C
→ emissions with current climate policies in place result in warming of 2.7 to 3.1°C by 2100.

Pledges & targets **(2.4 °C)**
→ emissions if all countries delivered on reduction pledges result in warming of 2.4°C by 2100.

2°C pathways
1.5°C pathways

1990 2000 2010 2020 2030 2040 2050 2060 2070 2080 2090 2100

Data source: Climate Action Tracker (based on national policies and pledges as of May 2021).
OurWorldinData.org – Research and data to make progress against the world's largest problems.

Last updated: July 2021.
Licensed under CC-BY by the authors Hannah Ritchie & Max Roser.

Figure 5.3 Future emissions scenarios, including Paris climate pledges.
Hannah Ritchie and Max Roser/Wikimedia, Creative Commons Attribution 4.0 International license.

a chance to slow down" (Childish Gambino, 2018) may refer to these types of predictions. For example, following currently implemented climate strategies (labeled "current policies" in Figure 5.3) is projected to lead to earth's warming by 2.5–2.9° C by the year 2100 (relative to pre-industrial temperatures); a scenario in which all countries meet their pledged targets set within the Paris climate agreement (labeled "pledges and targets" in Figure 5.3) is predicted to lead to an estimated warming of 2.1° C; and even an extremely exigent reduction in global greenhouse gas emissions (labeled 1.5° C in Figure 5.3) is expected to result in earth's warming by 1.5° C by the year 2100 (Ritchie & Roser, 2022).

- Verse two of "Feels Like Summer" includes the phrase "Every day gets hotter than the one before" (Childish Gambino, 2018). While this statement is technically an exaggeration that disregards day-to-day and year-to-year fluctuations in temperature, there is strong consensus among scientific organizations (i.e., HadCRUT, NOAAGlobalTemp, GISTEMP, and Berkeley Earth) about the rapid increase in global average temperatures when compared to pre-industrial conditions (see "observed temperature" measurements in Figure 5.2).

- Among the additional references to global warming in the text, Childish Gambino closes his song with these words, "Oh, I hope we change" (Childish Gambino, 2018), seemingly expressing optimism for the future amid an urgent call for immediate action.

Next, with lyrics still projected, play the song again and instruct students to focus on the musical elements of the song. Direct them to sing along on the chorus each time it occurs. Again, provide the opportunity for individuals to share their perceptions, then lead a class discussion.

- Genre: R&B/funk/soul
- Instrumentation: acoustic and electric guitars; synthesizer; percussion; vocals
- Mood: positive, relaxed, tropical feel
- Rhythm: syncopated eight-beat rhythmic accompaniment figure repeats throughout; unhurried tempo
- Melody: minor key; tendency to repeat descending stepwise and skipwise patterns; phrases often end with descending pitches; single voiced melody with additional vocal harmonies that add depth to sound
- Additional effects: many vocal calls and sound effects interspersed throughout; a brief pause in the accompaniment rhythm immediately following the text "no sound" captures listeners' attention; melody sung up an octave during the final verse heightens tension
- A seeming disconnect between seriousness of lyrics and lighthearted musical content; approachable sound may serve as an accessible channel to more widely share the underlying message

If time allows, consider watching the music video that accompanies "Feels Like Summer." The animated cartoon shows Gambino strolling through a neighborhood and encountering a multitude of modern African American figures such as Michelle Obama hugging a crying Kanye West, Will Smith washing his car, and Oprah Winfrey braiding Lil Uzi Vert's hair. While the animation and the text might seem to be disconnected, Childish Gambino may have been critiquing the focus in American media on celebrity culture rather than on global climate issues (Myhre, 2023).

Set up seven listening stations around the room and divide students into groups. Just as the class examined "Feels Like Summer," at each station, students will listen, analyze, and record their perceptions and observations (see Table 5.1). Depending on time, groups may not visit every station.

Regroup and lead final whole-class discussion:

- What themes are common among the songs?
- Which songs have the most explicit environmental messages? The least overt messages? How does that affect their impact?
- What similarities and differences might relate to the year each song was created?
- Why might composers use their music as a platform for environmental activism? What challenges might they encounter?

Assessment

- Collect students' Listening Station Templates and check responses for accuracy and completeness.
- Informally assess students' performance of the chorus of "Feels Like Summer" for in-tune, rhythmically accurate singing, and clear enunciation.

Extensions

- Invite students to identify a current environmental issue and create their own awareness chant or song.
- Not all music connected to environmental activism has lyrics. Explore two instrumental pieces that promote action and awareness. "I Giorni" by Ludovico Einaudi features a violin melody with piano and string accompaniment. Einaudi composed "I Giorni" after hearing a twelfth-century folk song from Mali that described people's mourning after the killing of a hippopotamus (Classic FM, 2024). "Farewell to Stromness" by Peter Maxwell Davies was written for solo piano. The piece is from a collection of works Davies composed to protest against a uranium mine that was proposed on the Orkney Islands where he lived (Dixon, n.d.).

Table 5.1 Listening station template: Songs of environmental activism

Station	Musical Example	Main Idea/Theme	Specific Lyrics	Musical Elements
1	"Don't Go Near the Water" (1971) by The Beach Boys			
2	"Calypso" (1975) by John Denver			
3	"Pass It on Down" (1990) by Alabama			
4	"Gaia" (1997) by James Taylor			
5	"Burn the House Down" (2017) by AJR			
6	"Despite Repeated Warnings" (2018) by Paul McCartney			
7	"The 1975 (Visualiser)" (2019) by The 1975			

Lesson 5.2: Biological and Psychological Relationships between Music and Memory

Grade Level

Middle school, but may be adapted

Essential Questions

How does music connect to memory? What behavioral or cognitive factors impact musical memories?

Objectives

- Students will explore the reliability of their musical memories, comparing their perceptions following initial and repeated exposure.
- Students will review and consider various biological and psychological factors that impact musical memory through video presentations and class discussion.
- Students will share musical memories with a partner, collect direct observations, and generate inquiry-based reports that demonstrate the interpretation of cognitive, behavioral, and emotional meanings.

Next Generation Science Standards Addressed

- LS1: From Molecules to Organisms: Structures and Processes
- LS3: Heredity: Inheritance and Variation of Traits
- PS2: Motion and Stability: Forces and Interactions
- ETS1: Engineering Design

National Core Arts Standards for Music Addressed

- MU:Cr1: Generate and conceptualize artistic ideas and work
- MU:Pr4: Select, analyze, and interpret artistic work for presentation
- MU:Cn10: Synthesize and relate knowledge and personal experiences to make art
- MU:Cn11: Relate artistic ideas and works with societal, cultural, and historical contexts to deepen understanding

Materials

- Audio recordings
  - Four contrasting thirty-second musical excerpts
- Video recordings
  - *Bobby McFerrin Hacks your Brain with music; Video on TED.com* (youtube. com/watch?v=E2yAddhsLlg)
  - *Nova Short: Inside Oliver Sacks's Brain* (youtube.com/watch?v=wc6m0Uyis-8)
  - *Alive Inside: A Story of Music and Memory [2014] Documentary* (youtube. com/watch?v=x9IHUPamCB4)
- Projected image
  - Figure 5.4 Robert Plutchik's Wheel of Emotions

Procedure

Open with a quickfire observation game as a warm-up activity. Play four separate thirty-second musical excerpts, then assess the accuracy with which students can recall various musical details from each piece. Choose examples that exhibit varied characteristics and represent different styles. Play them one after the other with no interceding discussion. After the fourth excerpt concludes, engage students in an interactive discussion. As students answer questions about their listening experience, keep a record of responses on the board. You might solicit information related to enjoyment of the musical examples, specific musical content that stood out, or excerpts that were more memorable than others. Ask students their thoughts about why we don't remember all music equally well and what factors or features might account for differences in memorability. You might also ask for volunteers to sing, hum, or tap out any portions of the music they can recall.

Next, watch two short videos. First, in the short Ted Talk video *Bobby McFerrin Hacks Your Brain with Music*, McFerrin elicits singing on specific pitches by an audience (SpadoCons, 2010). Next, neuroscientists use fMRI (functional magnetic resonance imaging) to compare Dr. Oliver Sacks's brain activity with his emotional reactions to the music of Bach and Beethoven in the video *Inside Oliver Sacks's Brain* (NOVA PBS Official, 2009).

Utilize the think-pair-share model to continue the class discussion, asking students to comment on the biological and psychological processes that might account for people's responses in the video clips and to brainstorm strategies that might enhance musical memory. Student responses might include:

- Musical training
- Experience with specific genre/style
- Conscious effort to focus on musical elements such as melody, rhythm, harmony, dynamics, structure, or instrumentation

- Attaching meaning to sounds such as creating an accompanying narrative or associating visual memories
- Repeated exposure
- Directed study about a piece of music including reading program notes, reviews, commentary, and lyrics; studying musical scores or maps; and examining historical or cultural context
- Listening context: live performance vs. recording; multitasking vs. focused; specific location and company

Armed with various strategies to employ, inform students that you will replay the four thirty-second excerpts from the quickfire at the beginning of the lesson. Challenge them to concentrate on textual and musical elements of each piece and to identify five features of each piece that they didn't remember after their initial exposure. Allow students to report their observations and compare their results. Does the opportunity to listen again and double check their initial perceptions highlight any limitations of their memories?

If it hasn't yet come up in the class discussion, introduce the science of music perception, the study of musical behavior and experience. Psychologists and neurologists who study music perception examine ways people create, process, interpret, and respond to music. Recently, insights about encoding and retrieving musical content have led to positive outcomes for Alzheimer's patients (Margulis, 2018). Watch the first twelve minutes of the award-winning documentary film *Alive Inside: A Story of Music and Memory* (or longer, if time allows) featuring social worker Dan Cohen's work with dementia patients and their incredible responses to music, showing the potential benefits for individuals living with cognitive and physical challenges, and highlighting the compelling connection between music and memory (EncourageTV, 2021).

As seen in the *Alive Inside* clip, long-term memories involving music can elicit emotional responses. Reinforce that connection by directing students to retrieve and share a music-evoked autobiographical memory using the following steps:

- Select a musical example with special meaning from your past
- Locate a recording of the song online
- Locate lyrics (if applicable)
- Write down a memory evoked by the song
- Identify at least one emotion evoked by the song (see Figure 5.4)
- Share musical memories, associated emotions, and recorded examples with a partner
- Take notes to record information pertaining to your partner's presentation

Assessment

- Evaluate students' verbal explanations of biological and psychological influences, checking for accurate information and demonstrated understanding that music can impact people's perceptions of specific times, places, and occasions.

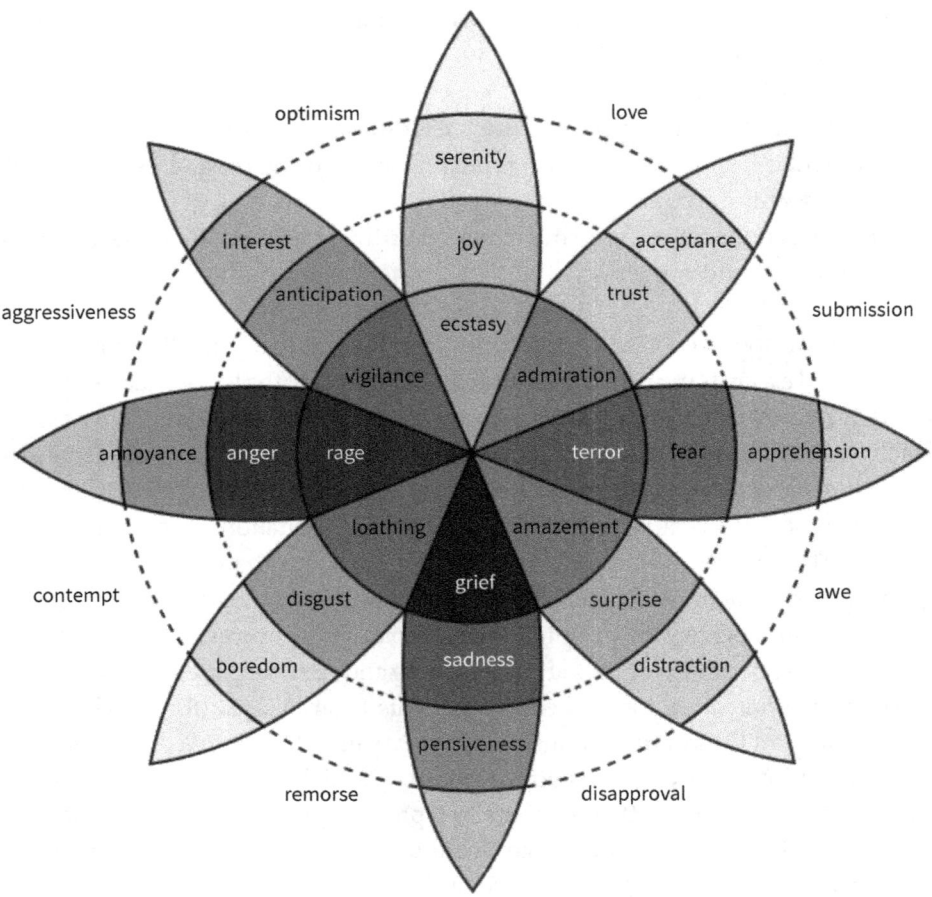

Figure 5.4 Robert Plutchik's Wheel of Emotions.
Public Domain/Machine Elf 1735/Wikimedia.

- Direct students to generate inquiry-based reports interpreting data collected during the partner activity. Students will answer the following questions in formal written reports that clearly reference their direct observations:
  - What musical memory did your partner share?
  - What emotion(s) did your partner verbally express? What emotion(s) did you observe in your partner? Why might these differ or align?
  - What emotion(s) did the presentation evoke for you? How might you explain your reaction?
  - How were cognitive, behavioral, and emotional meanings connected in this presentation?

Extensions

- Promote additional exploration of the science of music perception. Students might research topics such as music therapy, the relationship between music and emotional regulation, the impact of music on blood pressure, and so forth.
- Ask students to design and implement experiments in which they measure physiological responses to music such as heart and respiration rates.

Lesson 5.3: Life Cycles and Stages: "Merry Go Round of Life" by Joe Hisaishi

Note: The musical aspects of this lesson could also work with science lessons that focus on cycles of nature and the alignment of seasons with the tilt of earth's axis and rotation around the sun.

Grade Level

Middle school, but may be adapted

Essential Question

How can music depict the human life cycle or portray a human life?

Objectives

- Students will analyze and accurately describe stage-related developmental events or experiences that occur during a human's lifespan.
- Students will aurally distinguish and collaboratively label the musical structures and elements of the song "Merry Go Round of Life," drawing connections between different sections of the music and different stages of life.
- Students will identify personal stages of development, select and share corresponding musical examples, and depict connections using correct musical and scientific terminology.

Next Generation Science Standards Addressed

- LS1: From Molecules to Organisms: Structures and Processes
- LS3: Heredity: Inheritance and Variation of Traits
- LS4: Biological Evolution: Unity and Diversity
- ESS1: Earth's Place in the Universe
- ESS2: Earth's Systems

National Core Arts Standards for Music Addressed

- MU:Cr2: Organize and develop artistic ideas and work
- MU:Pr5: Develop and refine artistic techniques and work for presentation
- MU:Pr6: Convey meaning through the presentation of artistic work
- MU:Re8: Interpret intent and meaning in artistic work
- MU:Re9: Apply criteria to evaluate artistic work
- MU:Cn10: Synthesize and relate knowledge and personal experiences to make art

Materials

- Music example
  - audio recording of "The Merry Go Round of Life" or locate the video recording *Merry Go Round of Life—Howl's Moving Castle (Joe Hisaishi)* (youtube.com/watch?v=HMGetv40FkI)
- Images
  - Life cycle of a frog; life cycle of a carnation (Figure 5.5)
  - Structure, Elements, and Stages template (Table 5.2)

Procedure

The stages of development for a given organism are often portrayed as a life cycle (see Figure 5.5, a scientific drawing from 1752, which depicts the stages of development of a frog and of a carnation). The basic stages in the mammalian life cycle, which includes the human life cycle, are: (1) fertilized egg; (2) infancy; (3) childhood; (4) adolescence; and (5) adulthood. Of course, depending on the grade level and focus, your class may go into much greater specificity. In biological life cycles, the same series of stages repeat in cyclic manner (i.e., an egg develops into an adult that produces another egg, and so on) and the conventional end stage aligns with reproduction. More all-encompassing, ontogeny is the study of all the developmental events that occur

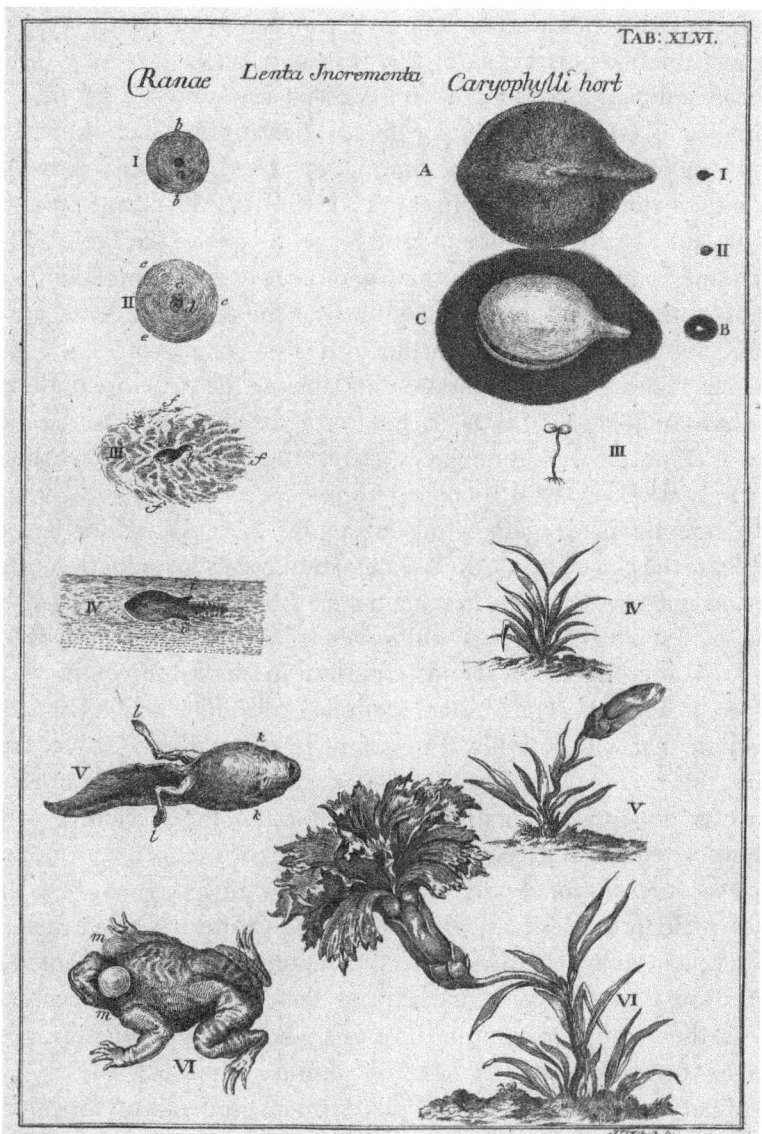

Figure 5.5 Life cycle of a frog; life cycle of a carnation.
Public Domain/Johann Swammerdamm/Wellcome Collection.

across an organism's whole lifetime. With that perspective, ask students to generate a list of all the stage-related (or age-related) developmental events or experiences that might occur during a human's lifespan. Encourage them to think creatively and to speculate about occurrences that fall outside traditional scientific classifications.

Ask students to recall a time when they listened to a piece of instrumental music that seemed to tell a story. Accept a variety of student responses and encourage a class discussion. Introduce the piece "The Merry Go Round of Life" by Joe Hisaishi.

The piece is the main theme from the movie *Howl's Moving Castle*, a Japanese animated fantasy film that portrays aging as a positive process.

First, locate a digital recording of "The Merry Go Round of Life" that displays a moving timestamp (see Materials). For the first hearing, ask each student to simply focus on the big picture and note the time stamp at specific points in the recording that align with obvious musical changes (i.e., 0:00, 0:50, 2:33, 2:58, 3:20, and 4:04).

Project a blank Structure, Elements, and Stages template (see Table 5.2). Go back and listen to the points students identified and come to consensus about which time stamps should be included in the breakdown of the piece. Students' answers will likely match closely with the times included the first column of Table 5.3, included here for teacher reference. In preparation for labeling the structure of the piece (the second column of Table 5.2), ask students to sing or hum along to the melodies at 0:11 and at 1:32, noting their differences. Define the melody at 0:11 as the A Theme and the melody at 1:32 as the B Theme.

Listen to the entire piece again, filling out column 2 as a class while the piece plays. For example, as the piece begins, the teacher could write "introduction" across from 0:00 on the second row. Once the first main melody begins at 0:11, the teacher might ask, "What section is this?" or "How will we label this melody?" then write "A Theme" in the third row after the class responds. Continue in this fashion for the entire piece.

At this point, column three, Musical Material, will still be blank. Discuss the type of information that will be utilized to complete that column. Direct students to listen again, this time paying attention to finer details and perhaps noting musical components such as instrumentation, density of sound, the development of melodic themes, tempo, dynamics, style, or sections that are distinguished by mounting tension or a sense of resolution. Softly singing or humming along may help students to characterize melodic elements; quietly performing a pattern in triple meter (e.g., pat tap tap, pat tap tap) may help them detect variations in tempo. Students can record their impressions and ideas as the music plays. Solicit individual comments, results, and analysis, then complete column three as a whole class. Student responses may align with the content included in the third column of Table 5.3.

For the final time listening to the piece, invite students to consider possible connections between different sections of the music and different stages of life. How might this piece outline the story of someone's entire life? How might specific musical components of this piece impact our perception of the various events in a human lifespan? Do any of the sections suggest biological stages such as infancy or adolescence? Do any sections evoke broader sentiments such as innocence, wisdom, or acceptance? Again, ask students to record their perceptions individually, then complete the table as a class.

Finally, ask students to apply their understanding of "The Merry Go Round of Life" to their own lives by making a list of the stages of life they have personally experienced, noting key events and experiences. Students will then select musical examples that correspond to or depict at least three of the stages or events from their lists and share their results in groups of three or four.

Table 5.2 Blank structure, elements, and stages template

Time Stamp	Structure	Musical Material	Associated Stage of Life

Table 5.3 Structure, elements, and stages template: "Merry Go Round of Life"

Time Stamp	Structure	Musical Material	Associated Stage of Life
0:00	Introduction	Solo piano	
0:11	A Theme I	Solo piano; plaintive waltz; reflective quality, perhaps suggesting an elderly person reminiscing about their youth	
0:38	Transition	Addition of upper strings	
0:50	A Theme II	Strings; more emphasized "oom pah pah" waltz accompaniment	
1:32	B Theme	Strings and piano; more variability to the sound; falling melodic motive (1:52 & 1:57)	
2:09	A Theme III	Fuller, richer sound; louder dynamic; more dense instrumentation	
2:33	Introduction Reprise	Expansion of introductory material	
2:58	A Theme IV	Piano alone, then strings added; bouncy, light-hearted character; emphatic chords accompany downbeats only (no longer the "oom pah pah" accompaniment); faster tempo	
3:20	B Theme	Starts much slower; smooth, wistful quality, gradually increasing in intensity and tempo; falling melodic motive again (3:44 & 3:49); ends with ritardando	
4:04	A Theme V	Dramatic; additional melodic and rhythmic flourishes; ends with dramatic restatement of the final portion of the phrase (4:45)	
4:53	Coda	What starts as "regular" coda or closing seems to aurally break down (4:59), pause (5:02), then resolve (5:03)	

Assessment

- Collect and review student-generated descriptions of the stages in the mammalian life cycle and developmental events that occur across an organism's whole lifetime.
- Informally evaluate students' aural analysis of the musical properties of "The Merry Go Round of Life." Note students' accuracy in describing and interpreting evidence using correct musical and scientific terminology.
- Direct students to complete short 3-2-1 written reflections. For each song they selected to depict a stage of life, they will write:
  - 3 descriptive words or phrases
  - 2 ways it connects to the life stage they discerned
  - 1 idea that illustrates their identity

Lesson 5.4: AI-Generated Music: The Intersection of Technology and Creativity

Grade Level

High school, but may be adapted

Essential Questions

What are likely advantages associated with AI-generated music? What are potential disadvantages or problems?

Objectives

- Students will examine the lyrics of the song "Still Alive" and evaluate the implied consequences of relationships between humans and artificial intelligence.
- Students will review excerpts of the Beethoven's AI-generated Tenth Symphony, examine the creative process and techniques involved, and evaluate the quality of the resulting musical product.
- Students will debate the value of AI-generated musical products to society, ranking various scenarios and products, defending their positions, and explaining the logic they employed.

Next Generation Science Standards Addressed

- LS2: Ecosystems: Interactions, Energy, and Dynamics
- LS4: Biological Evolution: Unity and Diversity
- ESS3: Earth and Human Activity
- PS3: Energy
- PS4: Waves and their Applications in Technologies for Information Transfer

National Core Arts Standards for Music Addressed

- MU:Cr2: Organize and develop artistic ideas and work
- MU:Re7: Perceive and analyze artistic work
- MU:Re9: Apply criteria to evaluate artistic work
- MU:Cn11: Relate artistic ideas and works with societal, cultural, and historical contexts to deepen understanding

Materials

- Audio recordings
  - "Still Alive" by Jonathan Coulton
- Radio broadcast
  - *Team uses AI to complete Beethoven's unfinished masterpiece* (www.npr.org/2021/10/02/1042742330)
- Video recording
  - *Livestream Q&A: 4 October 2022* (youtube.com/watch?v=JohkrV2Jt1E)

Procedure

1. Listen to the song "Still Alive" by Jonathan Coulton, a piece created for the ending credits of the video game *Portal*. The narrator in the song is GLaDOS (Genetic Lifeform and Disk Operating System), a somewhat passive-aggressive AI supercomputer with a robotic, synthesized singing voice (see Figure 5.6). In the video game, it appears that destroying the computer has defeated GLaDOS, but she returns to sing in a somewhat disengaged monotone that she is "not even angry" (Coulton, 2007). Instead, she intimates that she is continuing her research directives, "I'm doing science and I'm still alive," and recognizes that she will outlive her human enemies, "When you're dying, I'll still be alive. And when you're dead, I will be still alive" (Coulton, 2007). How might this song serve as a commentary on the relationship between humans and technology? What ethical issues does it suggest?

2. Ludwig van Beethoven (see Figure 5.7) is well known for composing nine symphonies, but he left behind rough sketches for a tenth. In 1827, just eight days before he died, he wrote a letter offering to compose a new work for the Philharmonic Society of London. In the letter, he referenced "a new symphony, which lies already sketched in my desk" (Cooper, 1985, p. 17).

Listen to a 2021 recorded radio broadcast, "Team Uses AI to Complete Beethoven's Unfinished Masterpiece," from the public media organization Minnesota Public Radio (yourclassical.org, 2021). In the report, Viennese composer Walter Werzowa and Ahmed Elgammal, the director of the Art and AI Laboratory at Rutgers University, discuss their process utilizing artificial intelligence to transform Beethoven's sketches into a completed symphony. Excerpts of the completed work can be heard in the report, as well.

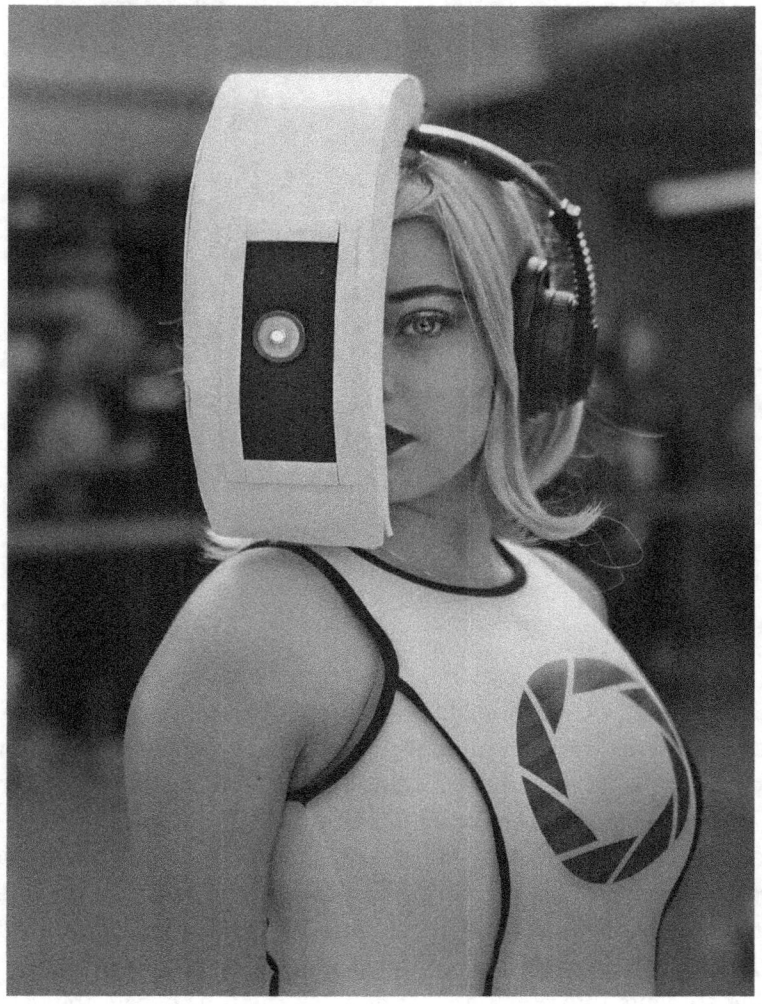

Figure 5.6 2015 New York Comic Con participant masquerading as GLaDOS.
Claudio Marinangeli/Wikimedia, Creative Commons Attribution 2.0 Generic license.

Figure 5.7 Sculpture of Ludwig van Beethoven by Hugo Hagen.
Image courtesy of W. J. Baker/Library of Congress.

For another perspective, watch an excerpt (23:45–26:48) from *Livestream Q&A: 4 October 2022* (Andreyev, 2022) with Canadian composer Samuel Andreyev. He references Werwoza and Elgammal's derived tenth symphony in his discussion of the interaction of AI and music, calling it a "shoddy mashup of fragments . . . mixed in with little pieces of the sketches" (Andreyev, 2022).

Are students confident that AI-created music is of the same quality as human composed music today? How certain are they that this will occur in the future? How much of music composition is rooted in human nature that is unreproducible by AI and how much can be learned and replicated by AI?

3. Divide students into small groups and ask them to debate the value of AI-generated musical products to society. Does AI solve specific musical problems

humans face? Do AI-generated musical products meet specific human needs? Direct students to consider various scenarios and products associated with AI music and work collaboratively to put them in order from least problematic to most problematic, then defend their positions and explain the logic they employed.

- An AI-generated jazz or orchestral arrangement of an existing pop song
- A composer utilizing AI generated melodies or harmonies as the starting point for new pieces
- An AI-enhanced assessment app that listens to musical performances and documents errors
- A producer utilizing AI-generated sound effects in a recorded track
- A live performance in which musicians collaborate with AI
- Personalized or customized playlists compiled by AI
- An AI app with piano accompaniments that complement and follow a soloist's performance
- AI suggestions for new artists, albums, or genres based on captured listening data
- AI models that generate new compositions copying the style and musical elements of selected training data
- Background music in a video game adapted by AI to align with a player's actions
- AI-generated recordings that eliminate the need for human musicians
- Utilizing AI tools to automatically transcribe audio examples as written music

Assessment

- Direct students to complete short written reflections that reference at least two specific aspects of the lesson content and address the following prompt: Are AI-generated musical products useful tools, supplements to human creativity, replacements for human expression, or some combination? Why?
- Observe students as they rank various scenarios and products associated with AI music. Informally evaluate their rationales and their descriptions of the logic they employed in making their rankings.

Inventory of Ideas

The following collection of ideas contains additional lesson topics, specific teaching strategies, and recommended activities.

1. When studying layering in earth science, concurrently investigate layering in music. For example, the ocean is often classified into five distinct layers: (1) epipelagial, the surface or sunlight zone where most marine animals live and plants carry out photosynthesis; (2) mesopelagial, the twilight zone without enough light for photosynthesis which appears pitch black to human eyes; (3) bathypelagial,

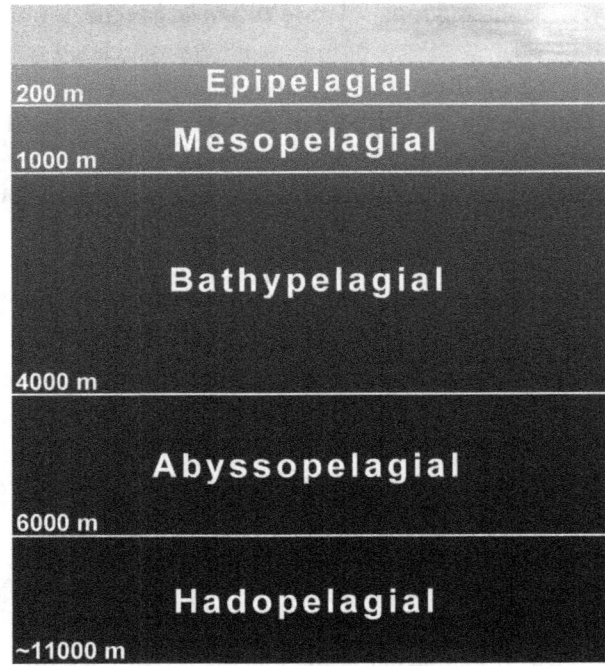

Figure 5.8 Layers of the ocean.
Public Domain/TomCatX/Wikimedia.

the midnight zone with total darkness because no sunlight can penetrate; (4) abyssopelagial, the abyssal zone with almost freezing temperatures and immense pressures; and (5) hadolpelagial, the hadal or trench zone in the deepest trenches that extend beyond the abyssal zone (see Figure 5.8).

Watch Linnea Olsson, a Swedish cellist and composer, performing her piece "The Ocean" for a live audience on the video *Linnea Olsson—The Ocean (live at Le Cafe de la Danse)* found at vimeo.com/32277288. The work, written for solo cello, relies on technology to create its layered effects. During the performance, Olsson plays her cello and sequentially records musical fragments using a loop pedal. Each recorded fragment is continuously repeated, allowing for the addition of melodic layers and sound effects. The result is a rich, multi-layered composition, created by a single player on a single instrument. For a more in-depth description of musical layering and ideas for creating layered compositions, see Lesson 2.3.

2. What differences are there in the way scientists and musicians measure time? In science, your students might examine time from the perspectives of thermodynamics or general relativity; they might study conventional representations of time, ordered in seconds, hours, days, months, or years; they might calculate the passage of time, duration of events, or estimate intervals; or perhaps they might focus on

measuring and interpreting astronomical, atomic, biological, chemical, electronic, geological, or mechanical clocks.

Musicians often think about time in terms of the time signature of a piece of music. Time signatures (see Figure 5.9) portray information about two aspects of musical time. The upper number represents the number of beats contained in each measure, and the lower number tells what length of note gets the steady beat. The time signatures in Figure 5.9 indicate three, four, and six beats per measure, respectively; in the first two examples, the quarter note gets the beat, and in the final example, the eighth note gets the beat.

The tempo of a song indicates how slow or fast it is performed and is written in terms of beats per minute (BPM). If you know the time signature, the number of measures, and the tempo of a given piece, your students will be able to estimate the total duration of the piece. Estimate a song's total time based on these data points, then listen to a performance of the piece and measure its duration with a stopwatch. Why might students' estimates only approximate the actual performance time? (Performers might not precisely follow the tempo marking; performers might incorporate subtle variations in the tempo; extra verses might be added; certain sections might get cut from the original score, etc.) Consider selecting a musical composition with a thematic focus on measuring time, the passing of time, or some other aspect of time for this activity. Suggested pieces include:

- "Does Anybody Really Know What Time It Is" by Chicago
- "Le Tic-Toc-Choc" by François Couperin
- "Sunshine, Go Away Today" by Jonathan Edwards
- Symphony No. 101, Movement II, "The Clock," by Haydn
- "The Times, They Are A-Changin'" by Bob Dylan
- "Time" from *Inception* by Hans Zimmer
- "Times Like These" by Jack Johnson
- "Wake Me Up" by Aviici

3. During a unit on bees (see Figure 5.10), you might focus on the crucial role bees play in pollination, their complex social structure, ways bees communicate complex information, or their unique flight mechanics and agility. The characteristics and behaviors of bees have inspired diverse musical examples. Some composers have emulated the rhythmic, humming quality of a bee's buzz in their music, some have been inspired by bees' animated perpetual motion, and some have endeavored to use music as a platform to promote the preservation and protection of bee habitats and populations.

Figure 5.9 Time signatures for 3/4, 4/4, and 6/8.
Image courtesy of author.

A classic (even cliché) bee composition is "Flight of the Bumblebee" by Nikolai Rimsky-Korsakov, a buzzing, frenzied instrumental portrayal of a bee in flight. Invite students to play, sing, or hum along with Rimsky-Korsakov's opening melodic phrase, a tune which has been directly quoted or adapted by many composers. A small sample includes:

- "Bumblebee" by Blechreiz
- "Bumblebee Stomp" by The Tornadoes
- "Bumble Bee Twist (The Wasp)" by The Ventures
- "Flight 76: Flight of the Bumblebee" by Walter Murphy

Many more composers have created bee-related pieces that are not derivatives of "Flight of the Bumblebee," but share some common characteristics. Examples include:

- "The Bee" by François Schubert
- "Bees" by Caribou instrumental
- "Save the Bees" by British folk band Lau
- "Honeybee Hill" by Alan Gogoll

The song "Bumblebee," released by ABBA in 2021, emphasizes the importance of bees as essential species: "A world without him; I dread to think what that would

Figure 5.10 The common worker bee.
williami5/Wikimedia, Creative Commons Attribution 2.0 Generic.

be" (ABBA, 2021, track 8). The lyrics explore themes of environmental conservation and the fragility of ecosystems, but also express a sense of wonder and amazement. Together with the lyrics, the melody and accompaniment of "Bumblebee" convey both concern and optimism regarding environmental stewardship, the plight of bees, and the impact of their decline on the natural world.

Additional resources to explore include the National Park Service lesson plan database (nps.gov), the Voice of the Hive website, a blog-type collection of first-hand accounts of beekeeping (voiceofthehive.com), and The Bee Cause Project's resource library that includes lesson plans, teacher guides, and grant information (thebeecause.org).

4. There are many songs and musical examples that focus on scientific topics and subjects. Of course, students should sing and listen to these pieces, but rather than *only* sing or listen, challenge students to examine conceptual connections such as observation, interaction, energy, structure, function, development, or change as well. Some possible songs to explore:

- "A Biologist's Mother's Day Song" by Cadamole
- "Charles Darwin's Evolution Song" by BBC's Horrible Histories
- "Chemical Calisthenics" by Blackalicious (use "radio edit" version to avoid explicit language)
- "CRISPR-Cas9" (parody of "Mr. Sandman") by Tim Blais
- "Echolocation" by LITE
- "Einstein Do It" by Ugly Duckling
- "Entropy" by Bad Religion
- "Humans" by Spose (use "radio edit" version to avoid explicit language)
- "Lab Rules" (parody of "New Rules") by Mitchell Moffit and Gregory Brown
- "NaCl" by Kate and Anna McGarrigle
- "No GMO" by Paul Izak and Seeds of Love
- "Science Is Real" by They Might Be Giants
- "The Scientific Method" by Andrew & Polly, featuring Mista Cookie Jar
- "Solid State" by Jonathan Coulton
- "Sunshine" by Jonathan Coulton
- "Uranium Fever" by Elton Britt
- "With My Own Two Hands" by Ben Harper

5. Middle school and high school science students often study basic chemistry concepts like the structure of matter, chemical properties, and the periodic table. At its most basic, the periodic table of elements displays chemical elements organized by their atomic number, the number of protons in an atomic nucleus. The elements are further arranged in periods (rows), groups (columns), and blocks that characterize the number of electron shells, chemical behavior, and properties of elements. Additionally, diagonal relationships indicate similar properties between various elements. Together, all these patterns are known as periodic trends. The periodic

table of the elements shown in Figure 5.11 displays each element's atomic number, symbol, name, and atomic weight. As a memorization tool, follow along with the periodic table while listening to, then singing "The Elements" by Tom Lehrer, a parody of a tune from Gilbert and Sullivan's *The Pirates of Penzance*. As it was written in 1959, the lyrics only include elements up through Nobelium. Challenge students to sing the entire song a cappella from memory. For extra credit or for fun, invite students to complete the song with all known elements.

Extend the idea of visually displaying relationships among elements to music. Direct small groups of students to systematically arrange various musical elements on a blank periodic template (see Figure 5.12). They might choose to classify terms related to dynamics, tempo, articulations, pitches, meter, clef, or other musical notation. Alternately, they might classify musical instruments, genres, or composers. Regardless of the categories they select, each individual square on their table must include a symbol (e.g., one or two letters, a musical symbol, a common abbreviation) that represents that musical element as well as the element's common name. Charge students with identifying relationships between various musical elements and conveying those relationships by their placement on the table. Colors may help highlight related blocks of elements as well as vertical, horizontal, and diagonal relationships.

6. Pose the question, "Is musicianship an instinct or a developed skill?" Use a quickfire Think-Pair-Share to solicit students' viewpoints. First students quickly "think" of their own positions, then "pair" with a partner to communicate their points of view, and finally "share" perceptions with the whole class. Accept all responses and encourage friendly debate on the topic. Utilize the song "Atomic Dog" by George Clinton to review the difference between instinctual and learned behaviors. The upbeat, electric funk song describes the predicament in which dogs find themselves when their instincts kick in. Lyrics from a dog's point of view, such as "Why must I feel like that? Why must I chase the cat?" (Clinton, 1982, track 6), highlight the idea of irresistible urges or innate behaviors that are beyond rational thought. Various sorts of dogs are included in the text, including rhythmic dogs, harmonic dogs, house dogs, street dogs, dancing dogs, and atomic dogs (Clinton, 1982, track 6), emphasizing that even amid the diverse expressions of "dog" possible in nature, there are similarities in the shared instincts that drive them. Direct small groups of students to create and perform additional verses to the song "Atomic Dog," incorporating lyrics that highlight learned behaviors rather than instincts.

7. Use a musical game to launch a discussion about cognitive flexibility. Cognitive flexibility, or flexible thinking, is exhibited when students adapt to unexpected changes, are receptive to new experiences, or are open to learning new ideas. Cognitive flexibility is associated with enhanced problem-solving skills, heightened empathy toward others, and creativity. In contrast, rigid or inflexible thinkers are resistant to change and may struggle to switch between tasks, adjust to new situations, or incorporate new information. On opposite sides of the classroom, post two different statements: "I am open to this experience" and "I am opposed to this

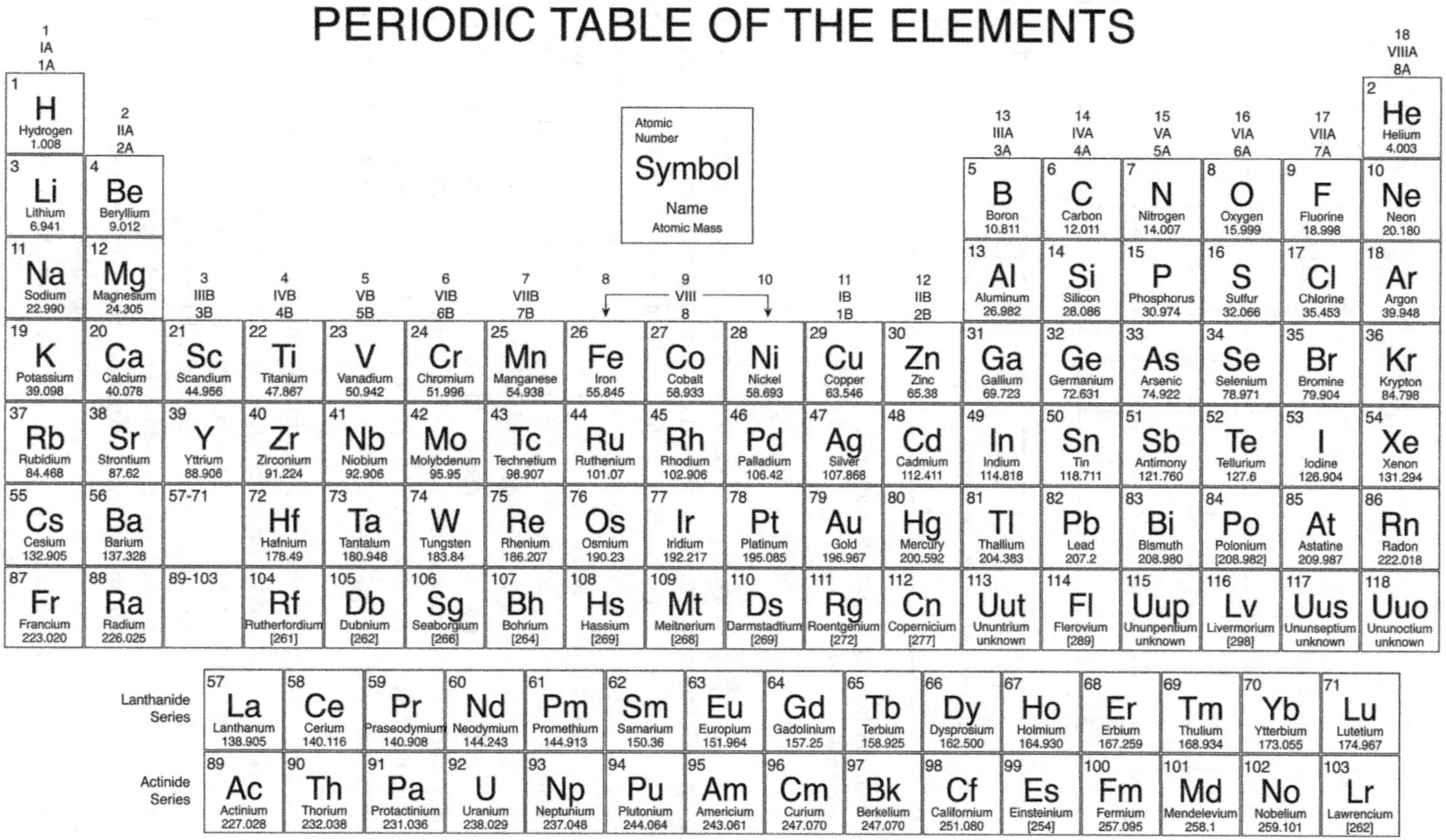

PERIODIC TABLE OF THE ELEMENTS

Figure 5.11 Periodic table of the elements.

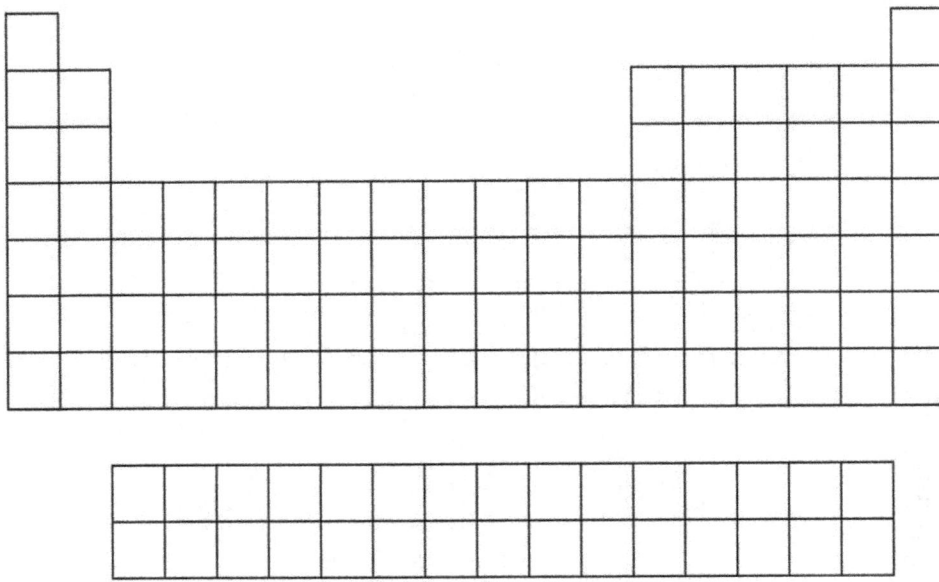

Figure 5.12 Periodic table of musical elements.
Image courtesy of Annika Harney.

experience." Say, "I will play excerpts from a variety of musical examples. Your job is to listen and silently move to the side of the room that most closely aligns with your perception of the experience. Play a wide variety of musical examples in thirty-second bursts (e.g., blues, classical, country, folk, hip-hop, jazz, metal, punk, rap, rock, salsa, ska) and allow students to move to one side or the other. Periodically, stop the music and ask one student from each side to explain their thinking. If one side is empty, ask the whole class to theorize why that might be. Play as many rounds as desired. Conclude with a whole class discussion about the experience. Direct students to consider the impact of various aspects of the music such as lyrics, tempo, instrumentation, melody, and style. Additionally, consider the role of things like familiarity, peer pressure, mood, age, and culture in their openness to different musical examples.

8. The concept of artistic evolution shares many similarities with evolution in nature; an emerging musical style can be equated to a new variant within an organic population. Both musical and biologic transformations might involve mutations, adaptations, or combinations of existent variations. To highlight this idea, explore the musical evolution of a single composer over the course of their career. The award-winning American composer and conductor John Williams (see Figure 5.13) is a prolific composer, creating some of the most popular and well-recognized film scores in history, including scores for *Jaws*, *Star Wars* films, *Superman* films, *Indiana Jones* films, *E.T.: The Extra Terrestrial*, *Home Alone* films, *Hook*, *Jurassic Park* films, *Schindler's List*, and *Harry Potter* films. In addition to his movie music, he has

composed numerous concertos, other orchestral works, chamber works, and music for television.

Over the course of Williams's seven-decade musical career, his style evolved significantly; an aural examination of his works reveals this evolution. Investigate the transformation in his musical style by comparing short excerpts from his first film composition, *You Are Welcome,* created in 1952 for the Newfoundland tourist information office, and his most recent film score, *Indiana Jones and the Dial of Destiny,* released in 2023.

Although his musical development is evident, there are also aspects of his style that have remained consistent across his compositional style. We see this in evolution in nature, as well. Some characteristics are extinguished over time, and others remain stable, even within novel organisms. Listen to excerpts from Williams's first

Figure 5.13 John Williams with the Boston Pops Orchestra.
Chris Devers/Flickr/Wikimedia Commons, Creative Commons Attribution-Share Alike 2.0 Generic license.

feature film composition, *Daddy-O* (1958) and label the predominant style as jazz. When first considering this work, it might seem completely disconnected from his later style; however, traces of Williams's early jazz influences are evident in many of his later compositions. Listen for evidence that Williams revisited his jazz roots in pieces such as "Cantina Band" from *Star Wars: A New Hope* (1977) and "The Knight Bus" from *Harry Potter and the Prisoner of Azkaban* (2004). Other musical ideas present in *Daddy-O* were also reworked in later compositions. For example, the opening of the track "Fighting Again" from *Daddy-O* sounds remarkably like "Main Title" of *Star Wars: A New Hope* at the 1:40 minute mark.

9. Explore the intersection of music and technology. Remind students that all "technology" doesn't involve computers or the internet. Consider the necessary technologies for the development of various musical instruments throughout history. For example, theorize about the tools and skills needed to make the Aurignacian (Upper Paleolithic) bone flute (see Figure 5.14), which was created between 39,000 and 43,000 years ago and found in the mountains of southern Germany in the early 2000s. What advances in technology were essential for constructing handmade wooden recorders in the 1600s (see Figure 5.15), the fragile white crystal transverse flute created in 1813 (see Figure 5.16), or modern mass-produced concert flutes and piccolos (see Figure 5.17)? Invite students to bring and demonstrate various instruments.

You might also explore the origins of recording technology and sound reproduction, discuss current topics related to acoustical engineering, audio production, and electronic composition, or analyze the relationship between digital music technology and increased accessibility and affordability of music for the general public. For additional music-technology connections, see Lesson 2.4.

10. In science, raw materials can be transformed into novel finished products. A compound is a new substance whose components were bonded with chemical reactions and a mixture is a blend of substances that were not chemically bonded. In the song "Lesson 6: The Lecture" by Jurassic 5 (MacFadden, 1997), raw materials are transformed into a finished product. The piece is an amalgam of rhythms, background accompaniments, and sound effects drawn from over forty jazz, soul, and rock tracks superimposed with cuts of lyrics extracted from hip-hop recordings and spoken fragments from historic instructional records. Determine if the piece could best be classified as a compound or a mixture.

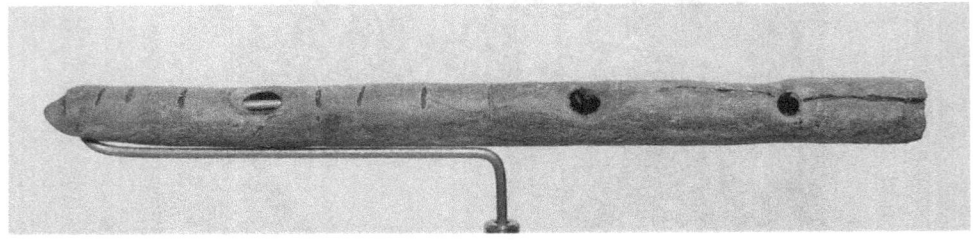

Figure 5.14 Bone flute from the Upper Paleolithic period.
José-Manuel Benito/Wikimedia, Creative Commons Attribution-Share Alike 2.5 Generic license.

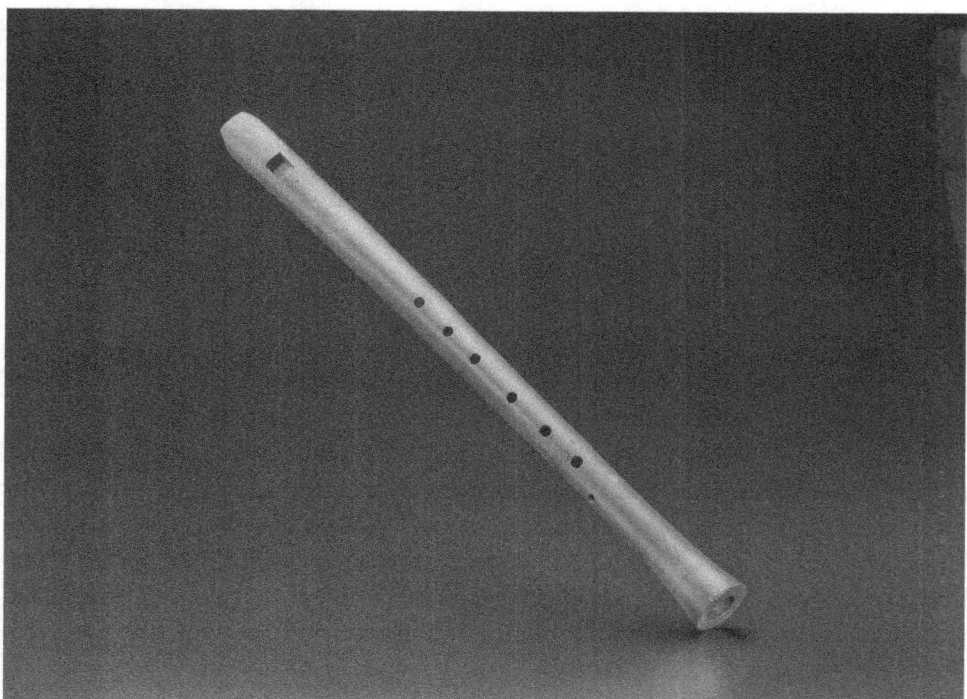

Figure 5.15 Handmade wooden recorder.
Image courtesy of The Metropolitan Museum of Art. Purchase, Amati Gifts, 2010.

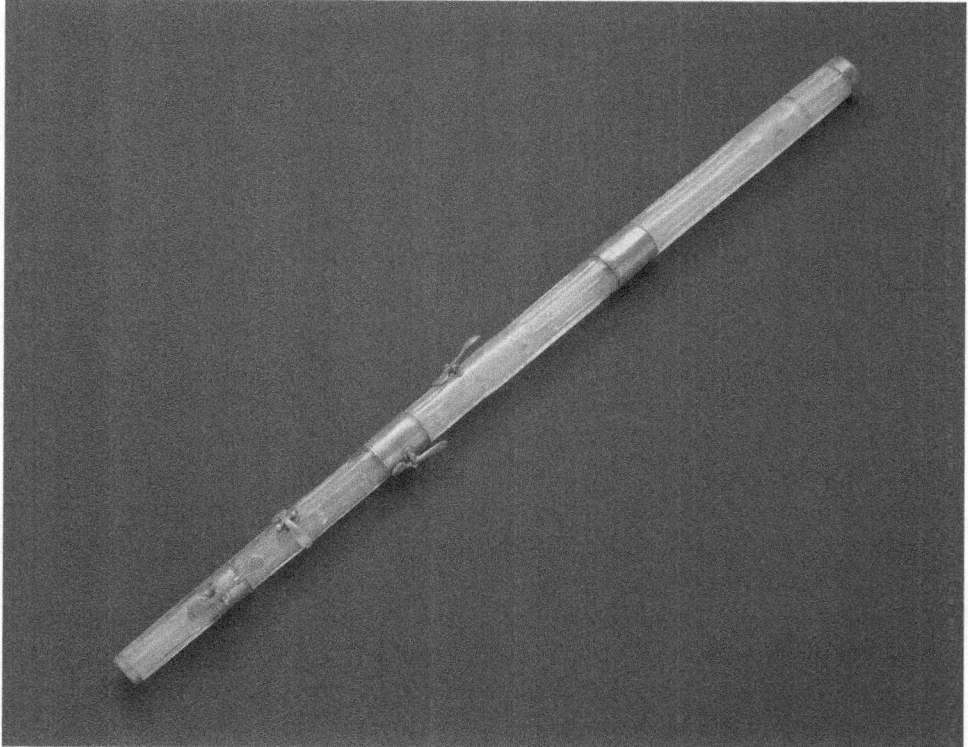

Figure 5.16 Crystal transverse flute.
Image courtesy of The Metropolitan Museum of Art, The Crosby Brown Collection of Musical Instruments, 1889.

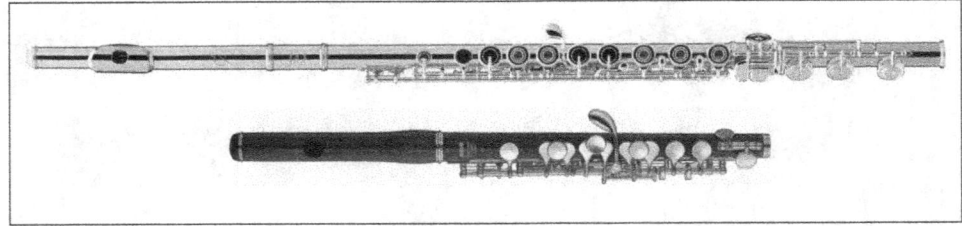

Figure 5.17 Modern mass-produced concert flute and piccolo.
Buffet Crampon and Yamaha/Wikimedia, Creative Commons Attribution-Share Alike 4.0 International.

Interestingly, two of the quotes that make up the "lyrics" of "Lesson 6: The Lecture" provide clues about its makeup. A narrator recites the following scientific definitions: "Compound: A substance composed of two or more elements, chemically combined in definite proportions by weight," and "Mixtures: Two or more substances that are not chemically united" (Jurassic 5, 1997, track 4). Invite students to compose a new musical work by digitally combining clips from two or more recorded examples. Students might incorporate fragments sequentially, simultaneously, or use some combination of methods. Which approach produces the most satisfying musical results?

11. Ask students to imagine and describe the most eccentric or extreme musical instrument they can. For example, see the 1867 portrayal of the piganino, an imaginary keyboard instrument that "plays" pigs arranged by size (Figure 5.18). Next, guide students as they follow the steps in the engineering design process to create a practical, credible instrument. Their process may look something like the following:

1. Identify a problem or need: Create an instrument that makes a sound by vibrating, that can play more than one pitch, and that can be played at more than one dynamic level.
2. Gather background information and research existing solutions: Review characteristics of instruments with which they're familiar or explore online resources for inspiration.
3. Brainstorm solutions and choose the most suitable idea: Talk with a partner to generate ideas and to narrow in on potential designs.
4. Sketch and explain the design: Draw and label a plan for the new instrument; describe it to a partner using correct terminology related to vibration, dynamics, and pitch.
5. Make and test a physical model: Use classroom supplies or bring materials from home to build a musical instrument; decorate if desired; play the instrument to test its functionality and suitability.
6. Review and share results: Play the instrument for peers; describe the ways it meets the identified problem and demonstrate that they can produce a sound by vibrating, can change the pitch of their instrument, and can change the dynamic level of their instrument.

Figure 5.18 Cover illustration for musical manuscript of "La piganino."
Public Domain/Wikimedia.

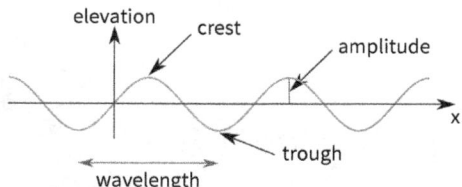

Figure 5.19 Components of a sine wave.
Kraaiennest/Wikimedia, Creative Commons Attribution-Share Alike 3.0 Unported.

7. Redesign to improve solution: Suggest improvements to the design and continue the process.

12. Explore the relationship between amplitude and volume and the relationship between frequency and pitch with hands-on activities. The height of a wave
crest (or depth of a wave trough) represents the amplitude of that wave; the amplitude of a sound wave determines its volume. Louder sounds are characterized by
larger amplitudes and softer sounds are characterized by smaller amplitudes (see
Figure 5.19). Wavelength refers to the distance between two consecutive points
(crest to crest or trough to trough) on a given wave. The number of wavelengths

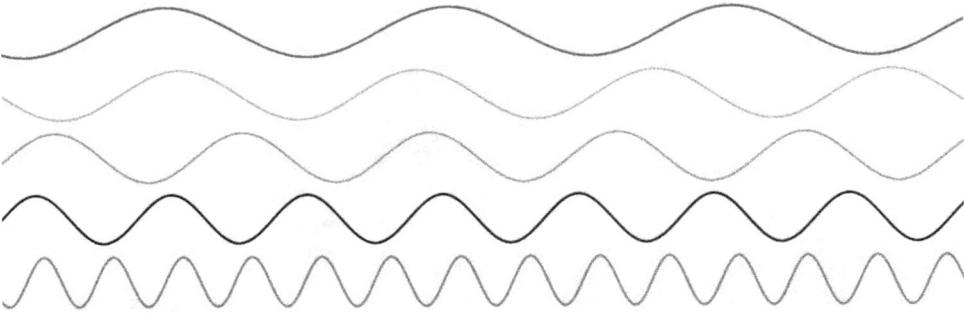

Figure 5.20 Sine waves of several frequencies.
Public Domain/LucasVB/Wikimedia.

Figure 5.21 Shattered wine glass.
Steven Duong/Flickr/Creative Commons licenses-NoDerivs 2.0/.

that pass a given point in a specific amount of time is expressed as the frequency of the wave; the frequency of a sound wave determines its pitch. Higher sounds are characterized by faster frequencies and lower sounds are characterized by slower frequencies (see Figure 5.20).

Capture your students' interest with a demonstration that illustrates both frequency and amplitude: break a glass with your voice (see Figure 5.21). You will need a crystal wine glass, a straw or small strip of paper, and eye protection for you and your students. Find the resonant frequency of the glass by tapping it with your fingernail and listening for the resulting pitch. This is the frequency at which the glass naturally vibrates. Place the straw or paper strip into the glass and hold the glass directly in front of your mouth, then sing at the frequency you identified. The straw will begin to visibly vibrate when you sing and hold the correct pitch. Demonstrate that soft singing (smaller amplitude) at the correct frequency will not break the glass. Demonstrate that loud singing (larger amplitude) at an incorrect frequency (wrong pitch) will not break the glass. Finally, sustain a sound at the correct frequency and a high volume; your glass should shatter. Watch two short clips (1:42–2:42 and 5:38–6:38) of the slow-motion video "Shattering a Wine Glass with Sound" that depict this process (youtube.com/watch?v=X3uKmTdgmQg).

Hands-on activities for students include:

- Measuring sound wave frequencies and amplitudes with a frequency spectrum analyzer. These devices work by using a microphone to convert the sound wave into an electrical signal; many spectrum analysis apps are available free of charge.
- Using differently sized tuning forks or different thicknesses and sizes of rubber bands to visualize sound waves and explore the direct correlation between frequency and pitch.
- Building a speaker with copper wire and magnets (exploratorium.edu).
- Building a phonograph with a needle, tape, and paper (gystc.org/diy-record-player/).
- Tuning a set of glasses to specific frequencies by varying the amount of water in each; exploring the impact of different shapes, sizes, and thicknesses of glasses (see Lesson 6.4 for additional ideas).
- Constructing two balloon amplifiers to compare whether carbon dioxide or nitrogen and oxygen act as better amplifiers of sound (sciencebuddies.org).
- Making a spoon gong (penshurstschool.org.uk) to demonstrate that a solid object such as string can conduct sound waves.
- Building a Chladni plate with an empty plastic container, aluminum foil, and salt (lsc.org). Alternately, investigating sound waves with an existing Chladni metal plate, a violin bow, and sand (sciencedemonstrations.fas.harvard.edu).

13. Explore auditory physiology, hearing loss, and practices related to hearing health. First, investigate the anatomy of the ear (see Figure 5.22) and the complex steps that transform sound waves to electrical signals that are then carried to the brain by the auditory nerve. Depending on grade level, you might also classify various degrees of hearing loss or differentiate between various attributes of hearing loss such as unilateral/bilateral, symmetrical/asymmetrical, progressive/sudden onset, and congenital/acquired.

Guide students through an activity that simulates the experience of hearing loss such as The National Institute for Occupational Safety and Health free Hearing Loss

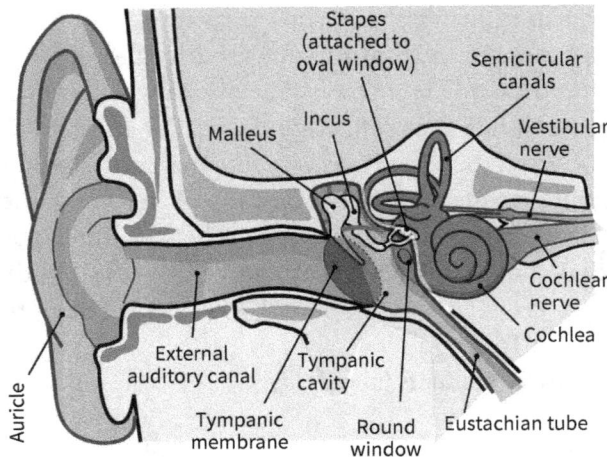

Figure 5.22 Illustration of human ear anatomy.
Lars Chittka; Axel Brockmann/Wikimedia, Creative Commons Attribution 2.5 Generic license.

Simulator (cdc.gov/niosh) or an online simulator such as the unfair spelling test demonstration (youtube.com/watch?v=l29yLTM3gFw).

Noise-induced hearing loss occurs after exposure to harmful sounds in one's environment. Sounds can be damaging when they are too loud, even for very short periods, or when they are moderately loud over extended periods. How loud is too loud? If you need to raise your voice to be heard by people in close proximity, the sound is probably damaging your hearing, but we can also precisely measure volume to determine safe levels. Sound is measured in units called decibels (dB). Measurements that register at or below 70 dB are generally considered safe, measurements at or above 85 dB are likely to damage your hearing over time, and a single loud sound at or above 120 dB can cause immediate hearing damage. Table 5.4 displays the average volume in dB of everyday sounds.

Download The National Institute for Occupational Safety and Health (NIOSH) free sound level meter app (cdc.gov/niosh/noise/about/app.html) or another smartphone app that measures dB. Measure noise levels in various parts of the school, such as a science room, a music room, a gym class, a hallway between classes, and the cafeteria during lunchtime. Consider working with students, teachers, and administration to decrease sound levels in the noisiest areas. Assign students the task of measuring and recording dB levels for environments beyond the school, as well. They might assess sound levels inside vehicles with music playing at varying volumes, at sporting events, at concerts, or in various workplaces.

Listening to loud music is a common cause of hearing damage. Invite students with headphones or earbuds to bring their devices to class. Experiment with various methods for checking volume:

Table 5.4 Average volume in dB of everyday sounds

Sounds in the environment	Average volume (dB)
Breathing	10
Whispering	30
Refrigerator	40
Dishwasher	45–65
Conversation	65–80
Lawnmower	85–100
Movie theatre	70–104
Motorcycle	80–110
Sporting events	94–110
Headphones	96–110
Rock concert	95–115
Sirens	110–129
Fireworks	140–160

Information from US Department of Health and Human Services, National Institute on Deafness and Other Communication Disorders (https://www.nidcd.nih.gov/news/2020/do-you-know-how-loud-too-loud).

- Switch on headphones and briefly listen at your preferred volume; without adjusting sound levels, remove headphones and hold directly in front of you with outstretched arm; music that is clearly audible at this distance is likely too loud.
- Switch on headphones and briefly listen at your preferred volume; check the volume setting; adjustments below the 50% mark are likely safe, settings above 66% may be harmful.
- Switch on headphones and listen at your preferred volume; ask a partner sitting beside you to focus on your music. If it is clearly audible, it is likely playing at unsafe levels.

Review strategies to protect hearing and prevent noise-induced hearing loss:

- Promote awareness of potentially harmful noise levels; identify and measure sound levels around you.
- Reduce noise levels; listen to music at lower volume; check if your device supports volume setting limits.
- Wear earplugs or use other hearing protection in loud environments.

- Increase your distance from the source of loud sounds.
- Advocate for reducing noise levels; support noise regulations.
- Regularly test your hearing; encourage hearing tests at school.
- Watch for signs of hearing damage such as clicking, ringing, or buzzing in the ears; the perception that sounds are muffled; or an escalating need to increase volume levels.

14. Secondary school science students often conduct experiments to gain experience using the inquiry process to solve problems. Procedures typically involve forming hypotheses, designing studies, collecting data, making observations, analyzing results, drawing conclusions, creating graphs to systematize and present findings, and writing lab reports. When a unit in science is focused more on the research process than on a specific product, consider selecting musical topics for investigation. Possible experiments in music include studies related to:

- the perception of pitch, dynamics, and timbre
- the perception of rhythm, tempo, harmony, and form
- the perception of style or genre
- the relationship between style or genre and emotional response
- the influence of music on recall or memory
- the influence of music on concentration
- the relationship between music and quality of sleep
- the relationship between musical preference and various demographic factors

15. What makes a catchy jingle? Explore the science behind using music as a marketing tool. Direct students to locate a recording of a musical example that was designed to influence consumers' decisions about specific goods or information. Analyze the recordings to determine what musical elements are consistent among the examples students find. Invite students to create and perform short jingles designed to persuade customers to purchase an imaginary product.

16. Modify the popular "See-Think-Wonder" routine as "Hear-Think-Wonder." Use this routine at the beginning of a unit to encourage curiosity about a new topic and to engage students in the inquiry process by encouraging them to make systematic observations and convey precise analyses of musical examples. Choose a song that connects to your theme or focus and play it for the class. Before facilitating a group discussion, direct students to document their thinking in writing. First, invite students to record in-depth observations about exactly what they are hearing. Allow multiple hearings and ask them to record what they know they have heard, not what they think they may have heard. Invite students to sing along, then ask if actively engaging with the music caused them to hear anything new. Next, instruct students to describe what they think about what they heard, asking clarifying questions to move

students from unsupported opinions toward evidence-based responses. You might ask questions such as, "What else is going on at this point in the music?" or "What do you hear that makes you respond that way?" Finally, guide students as they convey aspects of the music that may still be confusing to them. Informally collect students' responses and assemble them in analogous categories to encourage consideration and discussion.

17. Explore soundscapes by collecting and analyzing field recordings of different environments. Use audio recording equipment to capture sounds, then categorize each example according to the sound sources present: (1) geophony, sounds associated with natural events such as wind or rain; (2) anthropophony, sounds related to human actions; or (3) biophony, sounds generated by animals. To more deeply investigate one aspect of biophony, utilize Cornell University's free smartphone app Merlin Bird ID, available through the Cornell Lab of Ornithology (merlin. allaboutbirds.org). This field guide and identification app classifies birds using machine-learning technology to recognize species based on spectrograms that visually represent the pitch and pattern of each bird song or call. Merlin Bird ID is currently able to accurately identify over 1,000 different species of birds, including the western tanager (see Figure 5.23). When students tap the record button on their smartphones within the Merlin Bird ID app, Sound ID listens for audible bird songs

Figure 5.23 Western tanager.
Pacific Southwest Region US Fish and Wildlife Service/Wikimedia, Creative Commons Attribution 2.0 Generic license.

and calls, then suggests likely matches in real time. Students can then compare the songs they hear with recorded examples of suggested species to confirm the identification. Merlin Bird ID is based on participatory science, and students' field work can help add new species and expand the recording library. Invite students to mimic the bird songs they collect by singing, whistling, or using available instruments. How are the sounds birds use for communication related to human-generated music?

6

Music and Mathematics

Introduction

The disciplines of music and mathematics provide students with tools to understand the world around them and promote the development of strong reasoning skills, encouraging students to think in rational, logical ways to solve problems and evaluate information. Drawing connections between music and math can also reinforce a more creative, intuitive approach to solving problems. Ideally, students' experiences in school show them that mathematical reasoning, measuring, counting, and calculating are natural things people do every day. Similarly, every student should have experiences acknowledging the fundamental importance of music in their lives.

Math is indispensable to music; musicians use numbers and patterns every day. Likewise, music enhances math, promoting interest and enjoyment, offering real-life scenarios for applying skills, and encouraging disciplined, focused concentration. Beyond these low-level connections, however, there are many opportunities to explore fundamental concepts that music and math share. For example, music and math both utilize symbols to represent abstract ideas. Making sense of symbols can sometimes be confusing to students. In music, looking and listening for patterns, shapes, repetition, contrast, and other structural elements helps students label what they experience in a concrete way. Musical analysis can be the key to unlocking some of the mystery surrounding music. When students feel they can approach music from the perspective of an "insider," it can be very empowering. Similarly, math can feel like a mystery to some students. Connecting the idea of symbolic representation in music and symbolic representation in math can help students better grasp the concept in both disciplines.

The lessons and the strategies and activities included in the chapter 6 inventory of ideas encourage students to think critically and creatively, engage in inquiry-based problem solving, collaborate with peers, and make meaningful, real-life connections between music and math.

Common Links Between Music and Mathematics

A student may have procedural understandings in math and music, but integrating the two disciplines may help students solidify conceptual understandings in both. For example, a math student might know the procedures for adding fractions. A music student might know that to determine meter they listen for the steady

Integrating Music Across the Secondary Curriculum. Kristin Harney, Oxford University Press. © Oxford University Press 2026. DOI: 10.1093/9780197822036.003.0006

beat, discern the strong beat, then count beat groups. Knowing the procedures does not equate to deep understanding, though. "Simplification" is a concept that can be explored in music and mathematics that connects the two previous examples. Highlighting these types of higher-level connections and providing opportunities for students to explore complex concepts in math and music help them to construct and understand those concepts in both concentrated and multi-layered ways, ultimately benefiting the whole child. Enduring ideas that can be explored in both disciplines include:

Balance
Complexity
Counting
Function
Levels
Line
Measurement
Part/whole
Pattern
Proportion
Range
Ratio
Regularity
Relationships
Repetition
Rules
Same/different
Shape
Simplicity
Structure
Subdivision
Symbol
Symmetry
Trend
Unit

National Standards

Structuring integrated lessons that meet standards in music and math promotes a balance between musical and mathematical skills and concepts. The National Core Arts Standards (NCAS) for Music unambiguously call for students to integrate learning in music and other disciplines, with two of the eleven anchor standards labeled as "connecting" standards. The Common Core State Standards (CCSS) for

Mathematics do not specify interdisciplinary connections with music, but there are numerous meaningful connections that can be made.

The CCSS for Mathematics focus on topics and key ideas, conceptual understandings, and sequentially organized principles (National Governors Association Center for Best Practices, Council of Chief State School Officers, 2010b). For example, ideas connected to interpreting numbers and displaying data are found in the detailed cluster standards of every grade from sixth to twelfth. The overarching CCSS domain associated with these ideas is CCSS.Math.Content.SP: Statistics and Probability. To simplify labeling across grade levels and to allow teachers to adapt lessons and activities to their needs, the standards listed here are the CCSS domain standards.

The following boxes specify the standards that are addressed in the chapter 6 lessons and inventory of ideas:

- Box 6.1, Common Core State Standards for Mathematics: Mathematical Practices
- Box 6.2, Common Core State Standards for Mathematics: Mathematical Content
- Box 6.3, National Core Arts Standards for Music

Box 6.4 offers a framework for structuring chapter 6 lessons and activities.

Box 6.1 Common Core State Standards for Mathematics (Mathematical Practices) Included in Chapter 6 Lessons (L) and Inventory of Ideas (I)

Mathematical Practices

CCSS.Math.Practice.1	Make sense of problems and persevere in solving them	L 6.2 L 6.3 I 4 I 6 I 9
CCSS.Math.Practice.2	Reason abstractly and quantitatively	L 6.2 L 6.4 I 2 I 3 I 6
CCSS.Math.Practice.3	Construct viable arguments and critique the reasoning of others	L 6.3 L 6.4 I 3 I 5 I 6

CCSS.Math.Practice.4	Model with mathematics	L 6.1 L 6.2 I 1 I 5 I 9
CCSS.Math.Practice.5	Use appropriate tools strategically	L 6.2 L 6.3 I 1 I 3 I 7
CCSS.Math.Practice.6	Attend to precision	L 6.1 L 6.4 I 3 I 5 I 7
CCSS.Math.Practice.7	Look for and make use of structure	L 6.1 L 6.4 I 2 I 4 I 9
CCSS.Math.Practice.8	Look for and express regularity in repeated reasoning	L 6.2 L 6.3 I 3 I 4 I 6

Box 6.2 Common Core State Standards for Mathematics (Mathematical Content) Included in Chapter 6 Lessons (L) and Inventory of Ideas (I)

CCSS.Math.Content.RP	Ratios and Proportional Relationships	L 6.3 I 2 I 7 I 9
CCSS.Math.Content.NS	The Number System	L 6.2 I 1 I 2 I 8

CCSS.Math.Content.EE	Expressions and Equations	L 6.3
		I 2
		I 3
		I 7
CCSS.Math.Content.F	Functions	L 6.2
	Functions describe situations where	L 6.3
	one quantity determines another	I 6
		I 7
		I 8
CCSS.Math.Content.G	Geometry	L 6.1
		L 6.2
		I 2
		I 4
		I 5
		I 9
CCSS.Math.Content.SP	Statistics and Probability	L 6.1
		L 6.2
		L 6.3
		I 3
		I 6
		I 9
CCSS.Math.Content.N	Number and Quantity	L 6.1
		L 6.4
		I 1
		I 4
		I 8
CCSS.Math.Content.A	Algebra	L 6.1
		L 6.4
		I 3
		I 4
		I 5
		I 8
CCSS.Math.Content.M	Modeling	L 6.4
		I 1
		I 5
		I 9

Box 6.3 National Core Arts Standards for Music Included in Chapter 3 Sample Lessons (L) and Inventory of Ideas (I)

MU:Cr1 (Create)	Generate and conceptualize artistic ideas and work	L 6.1 L 6.3 I 4 I 6 I 7
MU:Cr2 (Create)	Organize and develop artistic ideas and work	L 6.2 L 6.4 I 1 I 5 I 8
MU:Cr3 (Create)	Refine and complete artistic work	L 6.2 L 6.4 I 5 I 7 I 8
MU:Pr4 (Perform)	Select, analyze, and interpret artistic work for presentation	L 6.1 L 6.3 I 2 I 6 I 9
MU:Pr5 (Perform)	Develop and refine artistic techniques and work for presentation	L 6.1 L 6.2 L 6.4 I 2 I 5 I 8
MU:Pr6 (Perform)	Convey meaning through the presentation of artistic work	L 6.2 L 6.4 I 3 I7 I 8
MU:Re7 (Respond)	Perceive and analyze artistic work	L 6.1 L 6.3 I 1 I 3 I9
MU:Re8 (Respond)	Interpret intent and meaning in artistic work	L 6.1 L 6.4 I 1 I 4 I 6
MU:Re9 (Respond)	Apply criteria to evaluate artistic work	L 6.2 L 6.3 I 2 I 4 I 9

MU:Cn10 (Connect)	Synthesize and relate knowledge and personal experiences to make art	L 6.3 I 3 I 5 I 7
MU:Cn11 (Connect)	Relate artistic ideas and works with societal, cultural, and historical context to deepen understanding	L 6.1 I 1 I 4 I 6 I 9

Box 6.4 Framework for Chapter 6 Lessons and Ideas

This chapter is designed to support middle school and high school educators as they integrate music and mathematics. The four detailed, full-length lesson plans are independent and not organized as a progressive series.

- Lesson 6.1: Fractals and Self-similarity in Music and Math: J. S. Bach's *14 Canons*
  - I absolutely love this piece and the story behind it, as well. The mathematical connections to Bach's music are well documented, and this piece is no different. I've incorporated lots of video and visual examples in this lesson to encourage active participation and engage learners.
- Lesson 6.2: Applying Probability Distributions and Stochastic Processes to Musical Composition
  - Creating a piece of music from scratch can be intimidating, even for experienced musicians. This lesson invites students to apply models of chance, allowing them to create music using a non-threatening, fun, and engaging approach to composition.
- Lesson 6.3: Developing, Conducting, and Analyzing Musical Surveys
  - The skills involved in conducting survey research apply to various fields and will serve students well. Situating the survey in musical content not only reinforces students hands-on experience with research methods but deepens their understanding of the ways music impacts individuals and communities. I got the idea for this lesson after talking with my own children who both teach at the high school level. While mean, median, and mode are often introduced in elementary school, those concepts still need to be reviewed and reinforced at the middle school and high school levels.
- Lesson 6.4: Exploring Ratios, Frequency, and Structure with Jack Johnson's "Better Together"
  - Creating musical instruments is a frequent activity in elementary school; I wanted to bring this lesson firmly into secondary-level territory. Students will use ratios, frequencies, and aural skills to design and construct instruments, then create and

perform music. I'm thankful to one of my undergraduate students for introducing me to this song. See chapter 5, inventory of ideas number 11, for additional ideas about creating instruments.

The chapter ends with an inventory of ideas detailing nine additional lesson topics, specific teaching strategies, and recommended activities. The lessons and activities may be fully taught by individual subject area (math or music) teachers; however, ideally, the plans will facilitate partnerships and collaboration between math teachers and music specialists. All lessons and activities have been reviewed by practicing teachers, and most have been field-tested in middle school and high school classrooms. Most of the lessons will need to be spread over two or more class periods. Chapter 6 lessons are adaptable to a variety of grade levels and are intended as tools for you to meet your students' needs. You and your students bring your own knowledge and experiences to these encounters, and you are invited and encouraged to apply those skills and understandings. I hope you are inspired to locate additional works to explore, including musical examples students are likely to encounter in their lives beyond school (e.g., readily recognizable musical works) and those that are less likely to be encountered (e.g., contemporary works that have not yet received widespread recognition, works for specialized groups or audiences, or works that are rooted in specific geographic regions). See additional guidelines for selecting repertoire in chapter 1. All the images included in this chapter are printed in black and white. Consider accessing full-color images online when displaying photographs, artwork, and other graphics for students, especially when lesson content directly references aspects related to a work's color. Please adjust, adapt, or expand these lessons and ideas to work best for you and for your students. Seek out teachers with whom you can collaborate and utilize the range of ideas and examples as starting points to facilitate your creativity and inspire innovative curriculum making.

Lesson 6.1: Fractals and Self-similarity in Music and Math: J. S. Bach's *14 Canons*

Grade Level

High school, but may be adapted

Essential Question

How do repetition and self-similarity in fractals enhance our understanding of complex structures in mathematics and music?

Objectives

- Students will accurately define fractals, explain their key properties, and describe representative examples in mathematics.
- Students will visually and aurally identify examples of fractals in music, correctly connecting their structural properties to the mathematical concepts of self-similarity and scale.
- Students will accurately isolate and sing the theme on which a musical fractal is based, then differentiate and accurately perform four rhythmic fractal variants.
- Students will explore and generate Sierpiński triangles, applying their knowledge of geometric tools, mathematical rules, and random processes.
- Students will summarize, represent, and interpret data depicting fractals in math and music, recognizing characteristics present in examples from both disciplines.

Common Core State Standards for Mathematics Addressed

- CCSS.Math.Practice.4: Model with mathematics
- CCSS.Math.Practice.6: Attend to precision
- CCSS.Math.Practice.7: Look for and make use of structure
- CCSS.Math.Content.G: Geometry
- CCSS.Math.Content.SP: Statistics and Probability
- CCSS.Math.Content.N: Number and Quantity
- CCSS.Math.Content.A: Algebra

National Core Arts Standards for Music Addressed

- MU:Cr1: Generate and conceptualize artistic ideas and work
- MU:Pr4: Select, analyze, and interpret artistic work for presentation
- MU:Pr5: Develop and refine artistic techniques and work for presentation
- MU:Re7: Perceive and analyze artistic work
- MU:Re8: Interpret intent and meaning in artistic work
- MU:Cn11: Relate artistic ideas and works with societal, cultural, and historical context to deepen understanding

Materials

- Video examples in lesson order
  1. *J. S. Bach "14 Canons"—BWV 1087* (youtube.com/watch?v=V4NFn4iGJIc)

2. *Mandelbrot Zoom Sequence* (youtube.com/watch?v=b005iHf8Z3g)
3. *Koch Snow Flake Animation* (youtube.com/watch?v=r6_dZHOHs4k)
4. *Sierpiński Triangle Zoom In* (youtube.com/watch?v=wXBJfaZ2LvU)
5. *Animated Julia Set* (youtube.com/watch?v=8O1y7FiNa6k)
6. *BWV 1087—14 Canons* (youtu.be/6h6AabkLvEE?si=pquh6AFNWiihlReu)
7. *J. S. Bach—14 Canons BWV 1087* (youtube.com/watch?v=8FEJHvq4-_g)
8. *Bach, Goldberg Canon à 4 per Augmentationem et Diminutionem (BWV 1087)* (youtube.com/watch?v=3liLG2RpCSc)
9. *Man Demonstrates the Sierpinski Triangle in Mathematical Visual* (youtube.com/watch?v=Fgu5-3ihVVI)
10. *14 Canons/J. S. Bach* (youtube.com/watch?v=mdI7UM7Xubw)
11. *Bach: "14 Canons" Visualization* (youtube.com/watch?v=rqrZ9aeyQQc)

• Copies of images (Figures 6.1 through 6.6)

Procedure

To introduce the lesson, view video example one, the video animation *J. S. Bach "14 Canons"—BWV 1087* (Harpsichord Drawing, 2022), which visually portrays the musical transformations in the work.

Review fractals in mathematics with students: In math, fractals are complex geometric shapes or patterns that exhibit self-similarity by replicating at progressively smaller scales. Fractals display identical or analogous designs whether you zoom in or zoom out on the figure; no matter the scale, the shapes or patterns of the fractal resemble the overall shape. Figure 6.1 displays a simple fractal structure. A square is first divided into quadrants. Next, the upper right-hand quadrant becomes a 1/4-scale replica of the whole, and this pattern repeats for six iterations.

Consider inviting students to perform mathematical calculations associated with various fractals. For example, students might use fractions and deductive reasoning to determine what percentage of Figure 6.1 is black. Solution: because the top-right quadrant of the original square is a 1/4-scale duplicate of the original, the scaling will not alter the overall ratio of black:white and the recursive square will always have the same color proportions as the original. Therefore, no matter how many iterations of the pattern there are, the overall ratio of black:white will remain constant. There are three non-recursive squares in the original image; two of those are white squares and one is a black square, so 1/3 of the image is black.

As a class, view animations of various mathematical fractals.

• Video example two: *Mandelbrot Zoom Sequence* (Mathigon, 2020)
• Video example three: *Koch Snow Flake Animation* (Gubicza, 2020)
• Video example four: *Sierpiński Triangle Zoom In* (SongsBackwards, 2014)
• Video example five: *Animated Julia Set* (Arneauxtje, 2015)

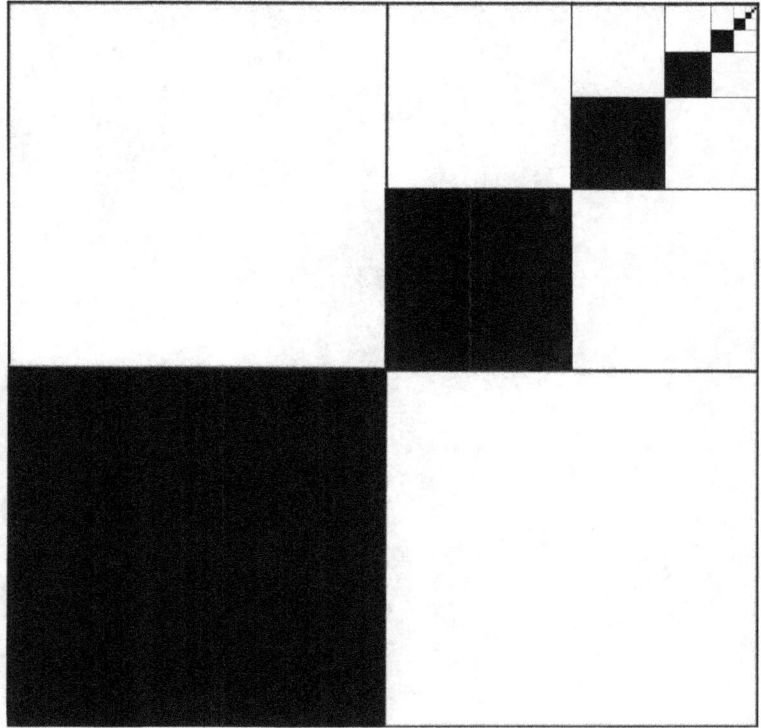

Figure 6.1 Box fractal.
Image courtesy of Annika Harney.

Mathematical fractal patterns are also discernible in nature (see Figures 6.2, 6.3, and 6.4).

Initiate a think-pair-share sequence, guiding students to reflect individually, share with a partner, and finally review as a whole class. Direct students to define fractals, describe representative examples, and explain the key properties of self-similarity, repetition, and scaling.

Introduce fractals in music. Just as mathematical fractals exhibit self-similarity, where portions of the fractal duplicate the whole at different scales, fractal structures in music are created when particular musical patterns or their symmetrical transformations recur at various time scales. In most compositions that exhibit fractal structures, those structures are present in fragmentary form, likely for aesthetic reasons. It is difficult to create a musical work that upholds the rules of fractal construction and is also aurally pleasing.

Common mathematical transformations of musical motives include augmentation (extending rhythmic durations), diminution (shortening rhythmic durations), transposition (shifting tonal centers), and employing inversion (a vertical mirror reflection of pitches) or retrograde (a horizontal mirror reflection of pitches). As seen in video example one, J. S. Bach's *14 Canons*, BWV 1087, demonstrates each of these techniques. Bach died in 1750, but this composition only came to light in 1974,

Figure 6.2 Magnified photo of snowflake.
© Chaoticmind/Dreamstime.com, ID 105689636.

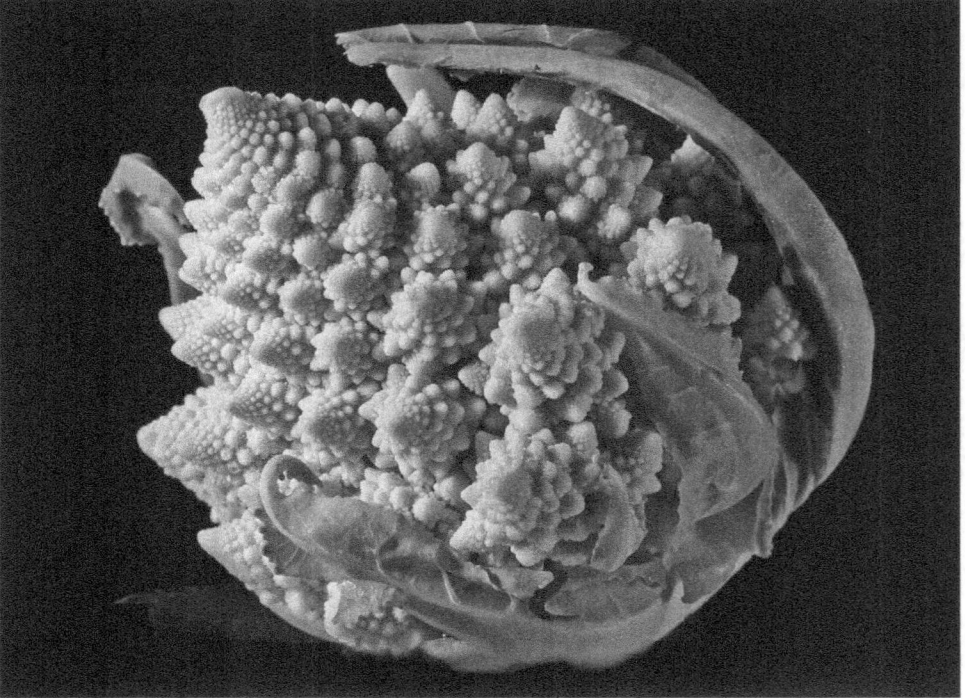

Figure 6.3 Romanesco broccoli.
Jon Sullivan/Wikimedia Commons, Creative Commons Attribution-ShareAlike License.

Figure 6.4 Fractal patterns in lightning.
Brezhnev30/Wikimedia Commons, Creative Commons Attribution-Share Alike 4.0 International.

when it was discovered in a private collection in France (Pearlman, 1990). On the back page of Bach's personal copy of the printed edition of his composition *Goldberg Variations*, he sketched another work he titled "Various Canons on the First Eight Bass Notes of the Preceding Aria" (see Figure 6.5). The pitches, rhythms, symbols, and notes that make up this composition outline the structure for fourteen unique canons based on the opening eight notes of the *Goldberg Variations*; however, the skeleton framework does not notate every part, specify the number of repetitions, designate specific instrumentation, or indicate where each canon should end, creating what Martin Pearlman labeled as "puzzles to be solved" (Pearlman, 1990). Inevitably, various recordings of the canons are similar, but not always identical. View video example six, *BWV 1087—14 Canons* (gerubach, 2013), which includes excerpts from Bach's manuscript and visually portrays their transformations. As the example is on the long side, feel free to watch the first few iterations, then skip to the last canon, which starts at 13:14.

As students become more familiar with the piece, listen to two short portions from video example seven, a recording of Bach's *14 Canons, J. S. Bach—14 Canons BWV 1087* (Montigiani, 2009). First play "Canon 1" and "Canon 2" (0:00–0:42), then "Canon 14" (5:49–6:21). Bach's written notation for the first canon presents the eight-note theme; however, the performance is not that straightforward, as Bach also included symbols that direct the performer to play the theme forward and backward simultaneously. Bach titled the second canon, "all' roverscio," meaning the performer must play the inverse of the theme backward and forward simultaneously.

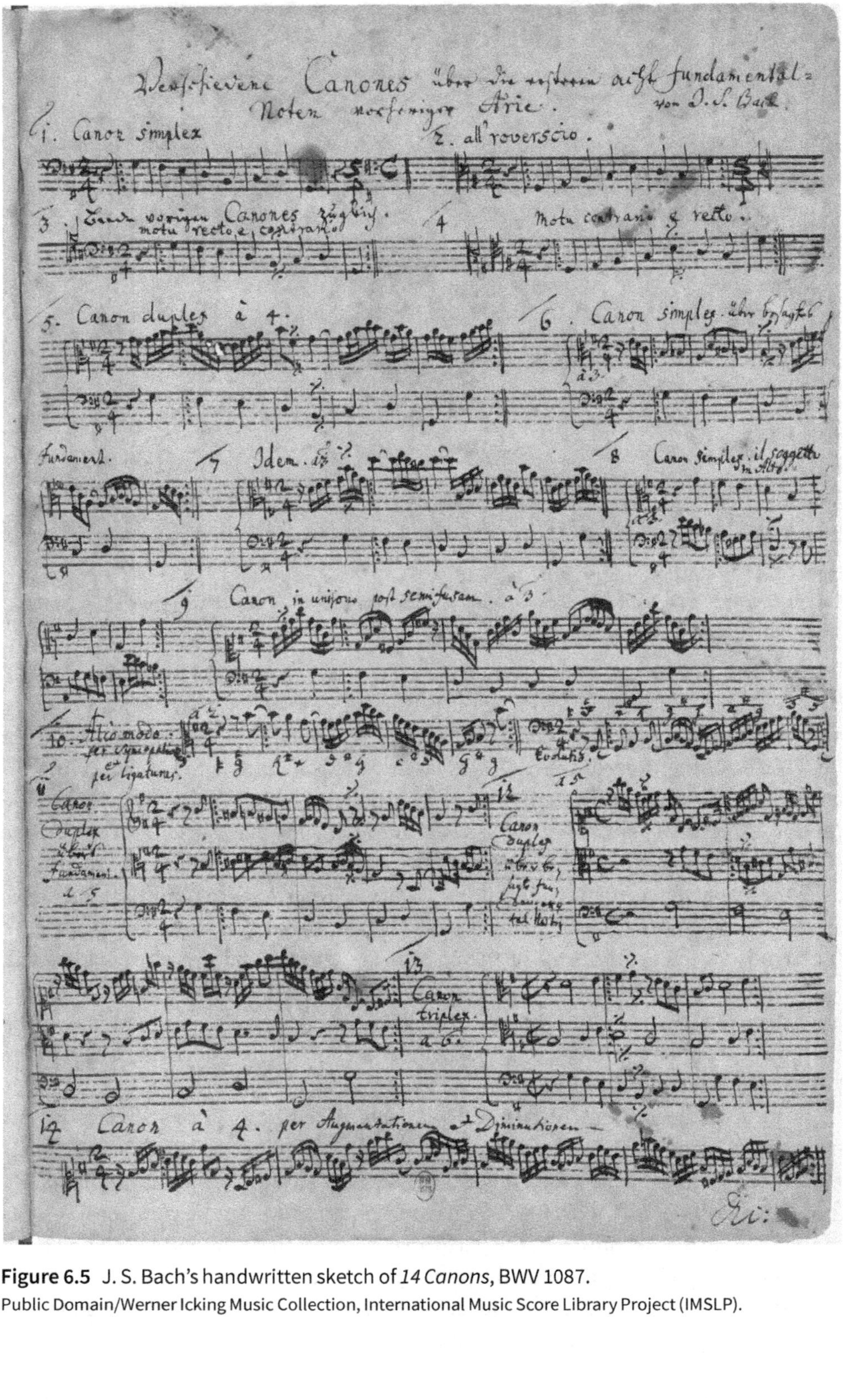

Figure 6.5 J. S. Bach's handwritten sketch of *14 Canons*, BWV 1087.

Public Domain/Werner Icking Music Collection, International Music Score Library Project (IMSLP).

Figure 6.6 Eight-note theme of Bach's *14 Canons*, BWV 1087.
Image courtesy of author.

Bach notated the last canon in the set, number fourteen, as a single melody line, but included instructions that the piece should be performed by four instruments, each playing at a different speed, and with two parts playing inversions. The ratio of tempos is 1:2:4:8, which aligns with fractal construction.

Replay the beginning of the example seven recording again, and direct students to sing along on the opening eight-note theme (see Figure 6.6). This will allow students to more easily discern the theme in its various iterations.

Next, watch video example eight, a short animation of just the last canon in the set, *Bach, Goldberg Canon à 4 per Augmentationem et Diminutionem (BWV 1087)* (smalin, 2024). The four parts are shown in different colors; the green ovals show the eight-note theme. During the last two repetitions of the theme, the other voices become gradually softer and softer, making it easier to hear and/or sing along with the theme.

Continuing with smalin's animation of "Canon No. 14" (video example eight), explore the fractal quality of the four rhythmic levels. Students might try performing each of these rhythmic levels in isolation, or for a challenge, try two, three, or four levels simultaneously.

- Level 1: The green shapes, representing the main theme, are the slowest. Tap one foot and count aloud, repeatedly saying "1, 2, 3, 4, 1, 2, 3, 4." Each tap and count should align with the moment an oval is illuminated.
- Level 2: The next level is twice as fast. It would be as if there were two equally spaced subdivisions for each of the green shapes. In the animation, this melody is shown by a light blue dot traveling through a portion of the red shapes; this melody does not appear until the third iteration. Tap the other foot and count aloud, repeatedly saying "1 and, 2 and, 3 and, 4 and." Again, the tempo of the tapping and counting should align with the animation. There are a few instances of embellishments in the melody but keep the tapping and counting steady for simplicity.
- Level 3: The next level is again twice as fast as the previous one. It would be as if there were four equally spaced subdivisions for each of the green shapes. In the animation, this melody is shown by a purple dot traveling through a portion of the green, red, and purple shapes; this melody does not appear until the second iteration. Pat one hand and repeatedly count "1 e and a, 2 e and a, 3 e and a, 4 e and a," with one pat and sound for each subdivision of the beat. Again, steadily pat and count.
- Level 4: The final level is once again, twice as fast as the previous one. It would be as if there were eight equally spaced subdivisions for each of the green shapes.

This melody begins the animation. Pat with the other hand and repeatedly speak "TI-ka ti-ka ti-ka ti-ka, TI-ka ti-ka ti-ka ti-ka," with one pat and sound for each subdivision of the beat, keeping patting and counting steady. The syllables "ti" (pronounced "tee") and "ka" (pronounced "kuh") will facilitate speaking at the quick tempo.

- Those familiar with standard notation might benefit from seeing an excerpt of the score of "Canon No. 14" showing the four concurrent rhythmic levels employing half notes, quarter notes, eighth notes, and sixteenth notes (see Figure 6.7).

Conclude the lesson by directing students to draw a fractal pattern, the Sierpiński Triangle, in two ways. Provide students with two different sets of directions to draw a Sierpiński Triangle (see Figure 6.8).

First, utilize the "removing triangles" method. Students first draw an equilateral triangle, then find the midpoint of each side. Connecting the midpoints will

Figure 6.7 Excerpt from J. S. Bach, "Canon No. 14," showing four rhythmic levels.
Image courtesy of author.

Figure 6.8 Method for constructing a Sierpiński Triangle.
Yoni Toker/Creative Commons, Attribution-Share Alike 3.0 Unported.

subdivide the shape into four equilateral triangles. Ignoring the center triangle, repeat the process on the remaining three remaining triangles, then on the nine remaining triangles, and so on, for as many iterations as are practically possible with fine-point pencil or pen. Students' drawings should display self-similarity: As they visually zoom in, each shape is an exact copy of the shape with which they started.

Next, try the "random dot" method. Again, students first draw an equilateral triangle. Next, they must choose a random point inside the triangle, then randomly select one of the vertices of the original triangle. Finally, they place a dot halfway between the randomly selected point and the randomly selected vertex. Direct students to continue to iteratively add points following this rule: add a point half the distance between the current dot and a randomly selected vertex. The image will emerge more quickly if students use a thicker-tipped marker to draw their dots, rather than the fine-point pencils or pens they used for the first drawing method. For teacher reference, see video example nine, *Man Demonstrates the Sierpinski Triangle in Mathematical Visual* (ViralHog, 2022).

If time allows, view two additional animations of Bach's *14 Canons* (video examples 10 and 11). Does either of the animations exemplify fractals? Which animations inform your understanding of the melody, the rhythm, or the structure of the music? For each video, feel free to watch the first couple canons, then skip to "Canon No. 14" at the end.

- *14 Canons/J. S. Bach* (onishikeita, 2021)
- *Bach: "14 Canons" Visualization* (Small Dots Ensemble, 2021)

Assessment

- Informally assess students' active participation in class discussion and activities, the accuracy of their responses related to self-similarity, repetition, and scaling in music and math, and the accuracy of their musical analysis and performance.
- Collect students' generated Sierpiński triangles and assess for accurate construction.
- Direct students to write brief responses to two reflection prompts: (1) Clearly explain the two processes you utilized to create fractal triangles; describe the fractal elements that you generated and (2) Does music with fractal patterns have value if those fractal patterns cannot be identified aurally? How might a mathematical analysis of music fractals enhance the listener's experience?

Extensions

- Explore Douglas Hofstader's *Gödel, Escher, Bach*, in which he tells the story of the fourteen canons.

- Examine and discuss the writings of John Cage related to indeterminacy in music and art.

Lesson 6.2: Applying Probability Distributions and Stochastic Processes to Musical Composition

Grade Level

Middle school, but may be adapted

Essential Question

How can non-deterministic mathematical models serve as creative tools in music and in what ways might that challenge ideas about creativity, control, and musical structure?

Objectives

- Students will explore the concept of chance procedures in music, identifying and describing how non-deterministic models can influence melody, rhythm, harmony, structure, and dynamics.
- Students will apply two non-deterministic models (a random walk and a stochastic process using dice) to create short musical compositions.
- Students will investigate chance processes by utilizing and evaluating a probability model to predict results.
- Students will present and share their created works with the class, accurately performing the products they generated and aurally demonstrating the use of chance procedures in the creative process.

Common Core State Standards for Mathematics Addressed

- CCSS.Math.Practice.1: Make sense of problems and persevere in solving them
- CCSS.Math.Practice.2: Reason abstractly and quantitatively
- CCSS.Math.Practice.4: Model with mathematics
- CCSS.Math.Practice.5: Use appropriate tools strategically
- CCSS.Math.Practice.8: Look for and express regularity in repeated reasoning
- CCSS.Math.Content.NS: The Number System
- CCSS.Math.Content.F: Functions
- CCSS.Math.Content.G: Geometry
- CCSS.Math.Content.SP: Statistics and Probability

National Core Arts Standards for Music Addressed

- MU:Cr2: Organize and develop artistic ideas and work
- MU:Cr3: Refine and complete artistic work
- MU:Pr5: Develop and refine artistic techniques and work for presentation
- MU:Pr6: Convey meaning through the presentation of artistic work
- MU:Re9: Apply criteria to evaluate artistic work

Materials

- Two-sided coin for each student
- Six-sided die for each student
- Optional: Table 6.1 or other template to record coin flip results
- Copy of Table 6.2 for reference
- Copy of Table 6.3 for reference
- Copies of Table 6.4, Figure 6.9, Table 6.5, Table 6.6, and Table 6.7
- Optional: Musical instruments or apps capable of playing melodies

Procedure

Background information: In mathematics, a deterministic model is one in which the output is always identical, given the same starting condition or initial state. In contrast, nondeterministic models depend on random chance. In this lesson, students will compose musical examples using two nondeterministic models, a random walk and a stochastic process using dice to randomly construct musical units based on systematized options. First, the random walk, is a model in which a point on the Euclidean plane moves a distance of one unit for each unit of time; however, the direction of each movement (+1 or −1) is random, meaning that the direction of future steps is independent of the direction of past steps and each step moves with equal probability. In probability theory, a stochastic process is one that involves the operation of chance, generating data that are indexed or organized against another variable or set of variables. Dice have been used to randomize musical output for centuries. One musical dice game is attributed to Wolfgang Amadeus Mozart. The game consisted of a given musical structure, a set of precomposed measures of music, and a procedure for selecting the specific sequence of measures based on the numerical outcomes from rolling dice. Although the authorship of the game is disputed, the name of the game attributed to Mozart reads (in English),

"Instructions for the composition of as many waltzes as one desires with two dice, without understanding anything about music or composition" (Hedges, 1978, p. 183).

1. Generate a melody with the random walk process.

First, establish parameters. Units for the walk are the pitches that make up the key of C major (CDEFGABC . . .). The starting point is the tonic (home tone) pitch C. Coin flips determine each step. A roll of heads dictates a move up the scale (C to D; D to E; E to F, etc.). A roll of tails dictates a move down the scale (C to B; B to A; A to G, etc.). Students will record eight total coin flips, then translate their results to the associated musical pitches.

Instruct students to commence their coin flips and record their results, perhaps using a template like Table 6.1. After students have translated the results of their coin flips to pitches in the key of C, depending on their musical background, they may wish to notate their melodies using traditional musical notation.

Table 6.1 Template for recording results of random walk melodies

Roll	0	1	2	3	4	5	6	7	8
Result		heads	tails	etc.					
Pitch	C	D	C	etc.					

Following the construction of random walk melodies, direct students to perform their examples for each other. Depending on classroom resources, students might play their melodies on keyboard apps for phones, tablets, or classroom computers; they might play on their band or orchestra instruments, you might obtain xylophones or keyboards for the class period, or students might simply sing their melodies. As students listen to each other's creations, guide them to aurally discern similarities and differences in the various melodies.

Finally, determine the probability distribution function that predicts the likelihood of the final note of an eight-note melody (starting C plus seven flipped opportunities) falling on a certain pitch. As a whole class, generate a version of Pascal's triangle to show the relationship between the pitches of the C scale and the number of flips of a coin (see Table 6.2). In the 0 column (zero turns), the only possible solution is the starting pitch C. In the 1 column (first coin flip), there is one chance of landing on the D above C and one chance of landing on the B below C. At two flips, a melody starting on D could move to E or move back to C. A melody on B could move to A or move back to C. Therefore, there is one chance of landing on E, two chances of landing on C, and one chance of landing on A. Continue in this fashion to construct probabilities through eight flips of the coin. As the number of flips increases, the probabilities approach a normal distribution.

2. Generate an eight-measure composition with stochastic processes.

Students will use six-sided dice to determine the musical elements of their compositions (rhythm, pitch, and dynamics). Help students visualize the stochastic process with a textual example (see Table 6.3). For this example, invite a student to

Table 6.2 Pascal's triangle showing relationship of melody to number of coin flips

	0	1	2	3	4	5	6	7	8
C								1	
B							1		8
A						1		7	
G					1		6		28
F				1		5		21	
E			1		4		15		56
D		1		3		10		35	
C	1		2		6		20		70
B		1		3		10		35	
A			1		4		15		56
G				1		5		21	
F					1		6		28
E						1		7	
D							1		8
C								1	

Table 6.3 Model for creating sentences using four dice rolls

	Roll 1	Roll 2	Roll 3	Roll 4
1	My	cat	loves	cheese
2	Our	dog	likes	crackers
3	The	baby	craves	noodles
4	A	kid	dislikes	cookies
5	Any	teen	avoids	apples
6	Every	adult	detests	salad

roll a die four times, noting the word from each column that aligns with the result of the roll for that turn. For example, if they roll 1, 2, 3, 4, the subsequent sentence is "My dog craves cookies." Each progression is essentially the same; the choices offered within each column are aligned, rather than being completely unrelated.

Follow the same process to create eight-measure musical compositions in 3/4 time (three quarter-note beats per measure). First, students roll eight times to determine rhythmic values, following the key provided in Table 6.4. Students will roll twice for column A (rolls one and five; measures one and five); twice for column B (rolls two and six; measures two and six); twice for column C (rolls three and seven; measures three and seven); and twice for column D (rolls four and eight; measures four and eight). They then must compare the results from Table 6.4 to find the associated rhythms in Figure 6.9. Students can record the results of their rolls (rhythms) on a template such as Table 6.5, or, again, depending on their musical background, they may wish to notate their work using traditional musical notation. Before moving on to the next step, allow students to rehearse their in-progress compositions, then spot-check to make sure students can accurately clap or tap their eight-measures of rhythms.

Next, students roll their dice eight more times to determine which pitch will be applied to each measure's rhythm (see Table 6.6). If, for example, the pitch C is designated for a given measure with three quarter notes, the pitch C would be repeated three times. If the pitch C is designated for a measure with a dotted half note, the pitch C would be played once and held for three beats. As in the random walk exercise, the pitches align with the key of C major.

Again, students can record the results of their rolls (pitches) on a template such as Table 6.5 or notate using traditional musical notation. Before going on to the next step, allow students to practice their melodies. Students might play on band instruments, orchestra instruments, keyboards, or xylophones; they could utilize keyboard apps on their phones, tablets, or classroom computers; or they could sing. Check to make sure students can accurately perform their creations.

Table 6.4 Key associated with Figure 6.9 rhythmic values for roll the dice composition

	A: Rolls 1 & 5	B: Rolls 2 & 6	C: Rolls 3 & 7	D: Rolls 4 & 8
1	a	a	a	d
2	b	b	b	d
3	c	c	c	d
4	d	d	d	f
5	e	e	e	f
6	f	f	f	f

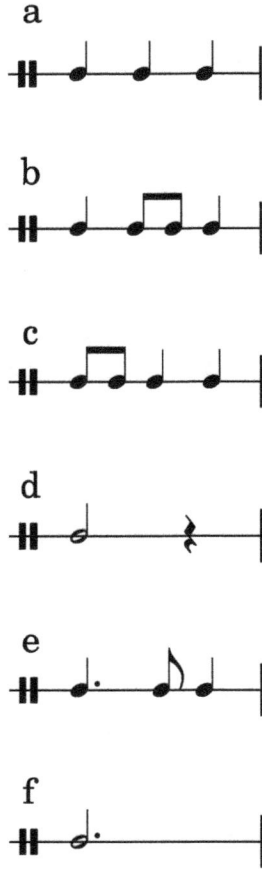

Figure 6.9 Rhythmic values for roll the dice composition.
Image courtesy of author.

Next, students will roll their dice twice to determine the dynamics that will be applied to each four-measure phrase of their composition (see Table 6.7). The choices include *p* (*piano*, or soft), *mp* (*mezzo piano*, or medium soft), *mf* (*mezzo forte*, or medium loud), *f* (*forte*, or loud), *p<mf* (a crescendo moving from soft to medium loud), and *mf>p* (a decrescendo moving from medium loud to soft). The results of the first roll will apply to the first phrase (measures 1–4) and the results of the second roll will apply to the second phrase (measures 5–8). As previously, students can record the results of their rolls (dynamics) on a template such as Table 6.5 or add to their notated musical scores.

At this point, allow a few minutes of individual practice time, then invite students to perform their entire eight-measure compositions for the class, demonstrating their selected rhythms, pitches, and dynamics. Because of the design, when multiple compositions are performed simultaneously, congruent harmonies will result. Invite pairs of students to perform together, then trios, quartets, and progressively larger groups. As a final performance, direct the entire class to play at once.

Table 6.5 Template to record dice roll results

	m. 1	m. 2	m. 3	m. 4
rhythm				
pitch				
dynamics				

	m. 5	m. 6	m. 7	m. 8
rhythm				
pitch				
dynamics				

Table 6.6 Pitches for roll the dice composition

	Rolls 1 & 5	Rolls 2 & 6	Rolls 3 & 7	Rolls 4 & 8
1	G	C	D	G
2	E	C	B	E
3	E	A	B	E
4	C	A	G	C
5	C	F	G	C
6	C	F	G	C

Table 6.7 Dynamics for roll the dice composition

	Rolls 1 & 2
1	*p*
2	*mp*
3	*mf*
4	*f*
5	*p<mf*
6	*mf>p*

In a follow-up class discussion, ask students to consider what aspects of the design of the roll-the-dice composition allowed for multiple iterations to sound compatible. Possible student answers include the overall similarity of the rhythmic values within each measure; consistent overall length; limited rhythmic options for the ends of each phrase contributing to a sense of finality; the options for pitches resulted in a harmonic structure I–IV–V–I (C chord, F chord, G chord, C chord); and more emphasis placed on the roots of chords (e.g., three chances for the pitch C in columns A and D).

Assessment

- Collect written evidence from students' random walk and stochastic dice trials, including musical notation, templates, or other records. Together with evidence from class discussions and activities, evaluate students' explanations and applications of non-deterministic models, checking for accurate, precise information; proper use of the given frameworks; and effective participation as presenters and listeners.
- Ask students to rate themselves with a thumbs up/thumbs down on a variety of items, including their precise application of chance procedures, transfer of numerical data to musical examples, and accurate musical performance. This activity allows the students to reflect about their learning and allows the teacher to informally assess student understanding.

Lesson 6.3: Developing, Conducting, and Analyzing Musical Surveys

Grade Level

Middle school, but may be adapted

Essential Question

How might the analysis of real-world musical data clarify statistical concepts such as mean, median, mode, standard deviation, and correlation? In what ways can statistics add to our understanding of musical data?

Objectives

- Students will collect and analyze real-world musical data, accurately calculating measures of central tendency (mean, median, mode).
- Students will visually represent statistical findings, identify trends and outliers, and share their interpretation of results.
- Students will apply their musical knowledge and skills to design survey questions that examine musical features, factors, or perceptions.

Common Core State Standards for Mathematics Addressed

- CCSS.Math.Practice.1: Make sense of problems and persevere in solving them
- CCSS.Math.Practice.3: Construct viable arguments and critique the reasoning of others
- CCSS.Math.Practice.5: Use appropriate tools strategically
- CCSS.Math.Practice.8: Look for and express regularity in repeated reasoning
- CCSS.Math.Content.RP: Ratios and Proportional Relationships
- CCSS.Math.Content.EE: Expressions and Equations
- CCSS.Math.Content.F: Functions
- CCSS.Math.Content.SP: Statistics and Probability

National Core Arts Standards for Music Addressed

- MU:Cr1: Generate and conceptualize artistic ideas and work
- MU:Pr4: Select, analyze, and interpret artistic work for presentation
- MU:Re7: Perceive and analyze artistic work
- MU:Re9: Apply criteria to evaluate artistic work
- MU:Cn10: Synthesize and relate knowledge and personal experiences to make art

Materials

Copies of Musical Preferences Survey (Table 6.8)

Table 6.8 Musical preferences survey

The following factors are important to me when I select music for listening (responses correspond to a scale of 1–5, where 1 = *strongly disagree*; 2 = *disagree*; 3 = *neutral*; 4 = *agree*; and 5 = *strongly agree*)					
1.	1	2	3	4	5	Artist/composer
2.	1	2	3	4	5	Popularity of the piece
3.	1	2	3	4	5	Genre
4.	1	2	3	4	5	Date created
5.	1	2	3	4	5	Length of piece
6.	1	2	3	4	5	Instrumentation
7.	1	2	3	4	5	Tempo
8.	1	2	3	4	5	Lyrics

Procedure

Part 1

Utilize musical content to promote real-world relevance and incorporate relatable content as students explore and study statistical analysis. A Likert scale is a rating system that allows survey respondents to express their level of agreement with specific statements. Responses typically correspond to a scale of 1–5, where 1 = *strongly disagree*, 2 = *disagree*, 3 = *neutral*, 4 = *agree*, and 5 = *strongly agree*. Pass out copies of the Musical Preferences Survey (see Table 6.8) and allow students time to complete the survey. Alternately, create an online version of the survey and provide students with a secure link.

Collaboratively analyze the survey responses as a whole class. First utilize the tally method to document responses. For question one, notate the number of "1" responses, "2" responses, "3" responses, "4" responses, and "5" responses. Record responses by hand on a whiteboard or project them electronically. Continue for all eight survey questions. A collection of tally marks is one way to present results, but to clearly display the distribution of responses (i.e., the number of responses at each level for each item), direct each student to create a bar chart or dot plot utilizing the collected data. As a follow-up, you might ask students to calculate and label each bar or line of dots with the associated percentage of total responses for each item.

In statistics, Likert scale data are sometimes analyzed as ordinal data and sometimes as interval data, with different preferred measures of central tendency for each classification. For the purposes of this exercise, direct individual students to solve for the mean, median, and mode associated with each item, then double-check solutions as a class. Reinforce students' understanding that the measures of central tendency they reported represent all the values associated with each survey item with a single number. In contrast, a measure of variation is a single number that describes how the values for a particular item diverge. Depending on the grade level or experience of your students, consider directing them to calculate and report values related to the variability of each item (interquartile range, mean absolute deviation, and/or standard deviation).

Next, divide students into groups of three and place one student in charge of median, one mean, and one mode. Direct students to create bar charts or dot plots to visually display the calculated values for their assigned measure of central tendency. Allow each group member to summarize and describe their visual display, then ask groups to compare and contrast their three displays, looking for overall patterns and deviations.

Conclude this portion of the lesson with a whole class discussion of the survey results. What do the results suggest about students' listening preferences? What results did they expect? What results surprised them? Which measure presents the most accurate picture of students' musical preferences? Why? What advantages and disadvantages of each type of measure can students identify? In what situations might one select each type of central tendency measure? What factors might influence the accuracy of Likert scale surveys? Depending on students' experience, you might discuss the distortion of results based on central tendency bias, acquiescence bias, or social desirability bias.

Part 2

Invite students to use their personal musical knowledge, skills, and interests to design a new survey, with each student responsible for creating one question. You might continue with Likert scale questions, or, depending on time and experience, you might decide to allow or require other types of questions such as dichotomous (e.g., yes/no), nominal (e.g., 1 = speakers; 2 = headphones, etc.), or ranking order of preference items.

Depending on students' musical background, they might design questions that examine pitch identification/discrimination; explore the aural identification of musical structures or styles; scrutinize student preferences for particular musical genres; explore listening habits; investigate playlist content; or quantify factors related to ensemble participation or private musical study. You might invite students to work together as they design their questions to allow for the eventual calculation of correlations. For example, one student might ask about length of time students typically spend on homework, and another might ask about students' music consumption during studying. Similarly, students might look for correlations between various musical features (tempo, instrumentation, etc.) and a song's streaming popularity.

Compile students' survey questions, then repeat the process from Part 1 of the lesson, collaboratively analyzing results, creating visual displays, and calculating means, medians, and modes. In addition, ask students to individually reflect about their particular results, sharing descriptions of the attribute under investigation and the specific results related to the question they designed.

Assessment

- At the end of the lesson, ask students to complete a table group exercise. At each table, place a set of index cards, each listing a topic from the lesson. Suggestions include: Likert scale, mean, median, mode, correlation, distribution, bar chart, and dot plot. Students draw cards and describe their selected topic using key details and terms.
- Additionally, collect students' calculations and visual representations of data. Evaluate students' accuracy in visually representing statistical findings, calculating central tendency (mean, median, and mode), and interpreting survey results.

Lesson 6.4: Exploring Ratios, Frequency, and Structure with Jack Johnson's "Better Together"

Grade Level

High school, but may be adapted

Essential Questions

How are mathematical ratios and frequencies related to the construction of a musical instrument? How might a composer incorporate the pitches of a descending major scale in a musical work?

Objectives

- Students will aurally analyze the structure, instrumentation, and scale-based ostinato pattern in Jack Johnson's "Better Together" and perform with in-tune singing and accurate rhythms.
- Students will construct, refine, and test water xylophones that produce an F major scale.
- Students will calculate the frequency in Hertz for each pitch of the F major scale, given the ratios between intervals.
- Students will improvise and perform melodies on water xylophones that align with given structural, rhythmic, and pitch guidelines.

Common Core State Standards for Mathematics Addressed

- CCSS.Math.Practice.2: Reason abstractly and quantitatively
- CCSS.Math.Practice.3: Construct viable arguments and critique the reasoning of others
- CCSS.Math.Practice.6: Attend to precision
- CCSS.Math.Practice.7: Look for and make use of structure
- CCSS.Math.Content.N: Number and Quantity
- CCSS.Math.Content.A: Algebra
- CCSS.Math.Content.M: Modeling

National Core Arts Standards for Music Addressed

- MU:Cr2: Organize and develop artistic ideas and work
- MU:Cr3: Refine and complete artistic work
- MU:Pr5: Develop and refine artistic techniques and work for presentation
- MU:Pr6: Convey meaning through the presentation of artistic work
- MU:Re8: Interpret intent and meaning in artistic work.

Materials

- For each group of students/station
  - Eight clear glass cups or jars (see procedure for suggestions)
  - Full water pitcher
  - Wooden stick, chopstick, or mallet
  - Ruler
  - Pipette (or dropper)
  - Markers and masking tape
  - Phone, tablet, or laptop app for measuring frequencies
  - Paper towels or rags
  - Clipboard with copy of Table 6.10 for recording observations
- Musical examples
  - "Better Together" by Jack Johnson
  - *105 BPM Drum Beat—Simple Straight* (youtube.com/watch?v=bGUcG0l4 q1M&t=0s)
- Content of Table 6.9 and notation in Figure 6.10 for reference
- Optional: keyboard, other instrument, or musical app to play melody

Background Information

Frequency is the property of a wave that determines the pitch of the sound. Higher frequencies produce higher sounds, and lower frequencies produce lower sounds. A wave that repeats itself 400 times per second (with each cycle of the wave taking 1/400th of a second) is labeled as having a rate of 400 Hertz (written as 400 Hz). For reference, the lowest note on a standard piano sounds at around 27.5 Hz and the highest note sounds at around 4,200 Hz.

The ancient Greeks discerned proportional mathematical relationships in the lengths of vibrating strings and the pitches they produced. In general, they noticed that shorter strings vibrated more quickly and produced higher pitches. More specifically, they noticed that a string that is half as long as another will vibrate twice as fast. The waves associated with these strings have frequencies with a 2:1 ratio, meaning that the shorter string is twice the Hz of the other and will sound one octave higher. For this lesson, students will explore pitch relationships with water glasses, rather than strings.

Procedure

First, play Jack Johnson's song "Better Together" and direct students to aurally analyze the style (students might classify it as folk, pop, or acoustic rock), tempo (relaxed, steady, slow), and instrumentation (guitar, bass, keyboard, percussion, voice). Lead a discussion to gather students' perceptions.

State that "Better Together" has an interesting feature regarding its construction: there is an ostinato accompaniment figure (a repeated pattern in the bass) that occurs twelve times over the course of the song. The pattern is based on a descending major scale and is repeated four times during each verse and twice during each interlude. The pitches of a descending F major scale are F-E-D-C-B♭-A-G-F. Since F is the tonic, or home tone of the key, the pitches of the descending one-octave scale start on high F and end on F (see Figure 6.10, segment A). In contrast, the pitches of the repeating pattern in "Better Together" are F-E-D-C-B♭-A-G-C. Note that the final pitch jumps back up to C (see Figure 6.10, segment B). The musical effect is a sense of forward motion, propelling the listener to the next repetition, rather than ending on the home tone of the key. Invite a student in the class to use a keyboard, other instrument, or app to play the descending pattern from the song, then direct everyone to sing along for a few repetitions.

Project Table 6.9 for students and direct them to follow along as they listen to "Better Together" again, ignoring the "Action" column for now. Guide them to discern the structure, noting the timing and/or lyrics that mark the start of each section, and ask them to quietly hum along on the ostinato pattern when it occurs.

Guide groups of students to construct an instrument that can play an F major scale, the same scale on which Jack Johnson's "Better Together" is based.

Figure 6.10 Descending F major scale (A) and ostinato accompaniment pattern (B).
Image courtesy of author.

Table 6.9 Musical features present in Jack Johnson's "Better Together" (Johnson, 2005, track 1)

Time	Structure	Instrumentation	Lyrics	Action
0:00	Introduction	guitar	N/A	rest
0:08	Verse 1 (A section)	voice + guitar	"There's no combination..."	play ostinato pattern 4×
0:43	Chorus (B section)	voice + guitar + percussion	"Mmm, it's always better..."	rest or tap the beat
1:00	Interlude	guitar + keyboard + percussion	N/A	play ostinato pattern 2×
1:17	Verse 2 (A section)	voice + guitar + percussion	"And all of these moments..."	play ostinato pattern 4×
1:52	Chorus (B section)	voice + guitar + percussion	"Yeah, it's always better..."	rest or tap the beat
2:10	Interlude	guitar + keyboard + percussion + hums	N/A	play ostinato pattern 2×
2:28	Bridge (C section)	voice + guitar + percussion	"I believe in memories..."	rest or tap the beat
3:03	Coda	guitar + percussion	N/A	rest or tap the beat

1. Demonstrate

- Fill two or three glasses with different levels of water.
- Tap one glass in a variety of places and with different levels of force; aurally evaluate the most suitable location for tapping and the ideal tapping force (the combination that produces the clearest sound).
- Tap each glass in succession to visually and aurally reinforce that glasses with more water produce lower pitches and glasses with less water produce higher pitches.

2. Divide students into groups and set up stations.

Each group needs a complete set of supplies as outlined in the materials section. Regarding the clear glass cups or jars that are the heart of the water xylophone construction, 64 oz growlers work well; a set of these jars can be tuned to all the pitches needed for the F major scale. Alternately, you might require two different sizes of glass containers for each station. For the lowest notes of the scale (F, G, A, and B♭), standard 16 oz glass tumblers, Tejava tea bottles, or Martinelli's sparkling cider bottles work well. For the highest notes of the scale (C, D, E, and F), consider using 5 oz Yoplait Oui yogurt jars or small 10 oz jelly jars.

3. Construct the water xylophone:

- Line up the glasses and/or jars in a row. If using two different sizes, place smaller containers on the right.
- Add a small amount of water to the glass on the far right. Add slightly more water to the next glass to the left, even more to the next, and so on. The glass on the far left should have the most water.
- Students may wish to use a ruler to double-check the water levels in their containers.

4. As a whole class, briefly review the mathematical relationships between the ratios, intervals, and frequencies of the pitches of the F major scale (see Table 6.10). Western music is rooted in the chromatic scale, successive sets of twelve notes. Notes of the major scale (Do, Re, Mi, Fa, Sol, La, Ti, Do) comprise a subset of the chromatic scale, and the interval relationships are constant. For example, the frequency ratio between Do and So, or F and C in this case, is always 3:2.

Ask students to calculate the frequency of each pitch in the F major scale, given the ratios between intervals and the internationally recognized standard tuning frequency of 440 Hz for the pitch A. Review answers as a class and note that there are some slight reductions (flattening) in the standardized frequencies of some pitches, resulting in frequencies that are lower than what students mathematically calculated based on their fundamental ratios. This is a result of equal tempering, a compromise that is necessary for instruments such as the piano to be played in any key. It would be impossible to tune all thirds, fifths, and so forth to their exact ratios and also have all octaves sound at perfect 2:1 ratios.

5. Tune the water xylophone:

- At this point, the water xylophones likely produce pitches that range from low to high, but do not align with the F major scale.
- To align the glasses with specific frequencies, students must adjust the water levels so that each glass sounds the correct pitch. Starting on the left, tune the lowest glass to play the pitch F by adding or removing water, remembering that adding water lowers the frequency and removing water produces a higher frequency. Direct students to use a tuner app or frequency analyzer to check the frequency of the sound. Use pipettes or droppers for fine tuning, then use masking tape to label the container as the pitch F.
- Continue in this fashion for the entire F major scale.

6. Measure and record the frequency associated with each note of the water xylophone in the final column of Table 6.10.

Allow for a few minutes of experimentation. Encourage each student to try playing the descending scale (see Figure 6.10, segment A), then the ostinato pattern (see

Table 6.10 Ratio, interval, and frequency data for each pitch of the F major scale

Pitch	Ratio	Interval	Calculated Frequency in Hz	Standardized Frequency in Hz	Measured Frequency in Hz
F′	2:1	octave		698.46	
E	15:8	major seventh		659.26	
D	5:3	major sixth		587.33	
C	3:2	perfect fifth		523.25	
B♭	4:3	perfect fourth		466.14	
A	5:4	major third	440.00	440.00	
G	9:8	major second		392.00	
F	1:1	unison		349.23	

Figure 6.10, segment B). Next, perform the ostinato pattern (Figure 6.10, segment B) along with recording of "Better Together." As the ostinato pattern repeats twelve times during the song, rotate through group members as needed to give everyone a turn playing their constructed water xylophone.

7. Direct students to improvise short four-measure melodies in F major. A common tendency is to rush the beat; a rhythmic backing track such as *105 BPM Drum Beat—Simple Straight* (LumBeat, 2024) can add appeal as well as maintain a steady beat in the environment.

- Before trying anything with the water xylophones, watch the beginning of the video and ask students to speak the rhythm, "ONE, two, three, four; TWO, two, three, four; THREE, two, three, four; FOUR, two, three, four," giving them a sense of the underlying pulse and how long their improvisation will last.
- Next, have students speak and clap that same sequence with the recording, then ask students to internalize the pulse, just thinking the count in their head while they clap.
- Once students can accurately clap along for four-measure segments, demonstrate how the rhythmic structure will transfer to the water xylophones. Each clap becomes a tap on whatever pitch they choose, equating to sixteen notes each student will play. Tell students that each individual will play their improvisation in succession, creating one long improvisatory piece.
- Allow for a few more minutes of practice time for students to experiment with the melodic sequences they will perform. Consider asking each student to incorporate a complete or partial descending scale within their improvisatory works. Also, recalling the ostinato accompaniment pattern from Jack Johnson's "Better Together," which ended on the pitch C and acted to drive the momentum forward, you might wish to direct students to end their segments on C, as well. To emphasize a sense of closure to the entire piece, the very last student to perform could end on the tonic of the key, F.
- Determine the order in which students will perform, start the rhythmic accompaniment backing track recording, and gesture to each student as their turn begins. Direct everyone to listen for the resulting melody segments as they strive to perform with rhythmic accuracy.

Following the final performance, enlist students' help cleaning up each water xylophone station.

Assessment

- Collect each group's recorded frequency measurements. Evaluate the accuracy of the frequencies, indicating the level of precision with which they were able to tune their water xylophones.

- Observe students' musical performances, listening for in-tune singing, accurate rhythms, and alignment with given structures.
- Informally assess students with a "roll the dice" activity. Project a set of six prompts. In their collaborative groups, each student takes turn rolling the dice and responding to the corresponding prompt:
  1. If I needed to explain today's lesson to a friend, I would say . . .
  2. I could apply what I learned today to other everyday objects by . . .
  3. The relationship between water levels in a container and the musical pitch produced is . . .
  4. The relationship between water levels in a container and the mathematical frequency is . . .
  5. I'm still confused about . . .
  6. The best thing about today's lesson was . . .

Inventory of Ideas

The following collection of ideas contains additional lesson topics, specific teaching strategies, and recommended activities.

1. Ask students to brainstorm different ways people use symbols to represent various phenomena. Guide the discussion by directing students to focus on mathematical and musical symbols; both systems utilize symbols to represent abstract concepts clearly and efficiently. Additionally, they both evolved from early, rudimentary systems (see Figure 6.11 and 6.12) to the sophisticated symbolic languages we use today.

Ask students to study each image and discuss their perceptions with a partner, using visual evidence to support their conclusions. What might the various shapes, images, and forms represent or suggest? What might the arrangement of symbols indicate? What might their functions be? Following student discussions, share the given descriptions of each image:

- Figure 6.11 shows a Sumerian clay cuneiform tablet, created around 3100–2900 BCE in Mesopotamia. The tablet was likely a mathematical record of grain distributed by a priest-king and includes impressions representing barley, a male figure, dogs, and boars.
- Figure 6.12 displays neume notation, inflective marks that indicate the general shape of a melody. The example was written by Cistercian monks living in the north of France during the twelfth century. The text translates as "Their sound has gone out into all lands, and their words to the ends of the world" and the symbols include a stylized letter F at the beginning of lines corresponding to that pitch.

Hand out, project, or direct students to locate charts cataloging basic musical symbols (e.g., symbols representing pitches, durations, dynamics, textures, articulations, key signatures, time signatures, or other aspects of staff notation) and mathematical symbols (e.g., symbols representing equivalence, similarity, comparisons, set theory, infinite numbers, brackets, or arithmetic operators). Pass out blank Venn diagrams and instruct pairs of students to organize the symbols, identifying overlaps in their functions and roles, as well as processes or characterizations unique to each discipline. Direct students to share their reasoning for the placement of each symbol, using musical and mathematical language to justify their decisions.

2. Explore negative numbers in math and music. First, have students create digital or physical number lines, moving counters or markers to signify positive and negative numbers. You might also have students explain negative numbers using examples such as hiking up and down in elevation or adding money to and withdrawing from a bank account to highlight the idea that positive and negative numbers describe quantities having opposite directions or values.

Next, direct students to transfer their understanding of positive and negative numbers to a real-world, musical context, explaining the structure of a retrograde

Figure 6.11 Proto-cuneiform tablet with cylinder seal impressions: Administrative account of barley distribution.

Image courtesy of The Metropolitan Museum of Art, Purchase, Raymond and Beverly Sackler Gift, 1988.

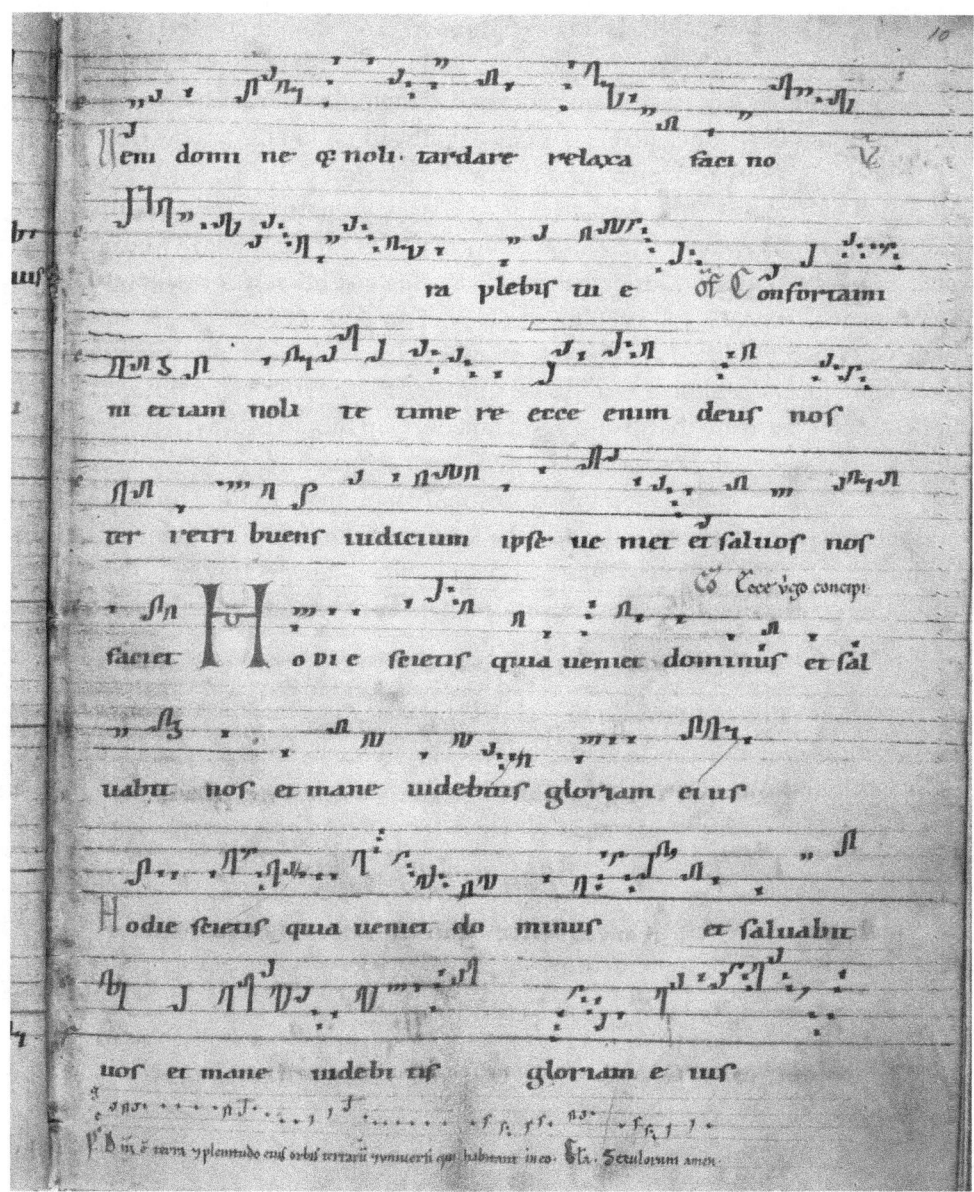

Figure 6.12 Twelfth-century Medieval Cistercian musical neumes, "Image 27 of Cistercian Gradual."
Public Domain/Image courtesy of the Library of Congress.

canon. First, invite students to sing a well-known simple canon (round) such as "Row, Row, Row Your Boat," or "Frère Jacques." Direct half the class to start singing the song, then cue the second half of the class to exactly imitate the melody, but to wait to start singing until the first group gets to the second phrase of the song. Next, describe a retrograde canon, where a tune is repeated backward, note for note, similar to the structure of the following phrases: "You should go" and "Go; should you?" The three words make sense forward and backward; each phrase is the exact reverse of the other. Ask students to connect this definition of retrograde canon with their understanding of negative numbers. Finally, listen to and watch two versions of J. S. Bach's "Canon a 2 Cancrizans" from *The Musical Offering*, BWV 1079, both performed by violinist Shunske Sato. The first is an animated graphical score, *Bach, Musical Offering, Canon 1 a 2 (cancrizans, BWV 1079)* by smalin (youtube.com/watch?v=b-0Tg8Y4VmQ), and the second is *Bach—Canon a 2 Cancrizans from The Musical Offering BWV 1079* by the Netherlands Bach Society (youtube.com/watch?v=29YwFjE2b1A&t=0s). Both examples clearly show the retrograde structure of the piece. If students would like a final challenge, the piece "Frère Jacques" can be sung forward and backward simultaneously in this same way; performing on a neutral vowel like "loo" or "la" will simplify the performance.

3. There are many songs and musical examples with math as their focus. Listen to these pieces and sing them with your students to encourage mathematical understanding and memorization of information, but also challenge students to examine conceptual connections between music and math such as pattern, repetition, shape, and structure. Some possible songs to explore:

- "Absolute Value and Linear Inequalities" by MathOdes
- "Algebra Song: Introduction to Variables" by Numberock
- "Algorhythm" by Emmy The Great
- "Asymptotic" by Louie Zong
- "Calculus" by The Depressants
- "Calculus Theme" by John Raskopf
- "Fibonacci Sequence" by the Beastie Boys
- "Infinity" by They Might Be Giants
- "Linear Algebra" by Ditch Effort
- "Linear Equations" by MathOdes
- "Mandelbrot Set" by Jonathan Coulton (download clean version)
- "Math Music" by kt3b, Aqua & Arctic
- "Multiplying Fractions" by Numberock
- "Order of Operations" by MathOdes
- "The Pi Song (100 Digits of Pi)" by AsapSCIENCE
- "Polynomials" by MathOdes
- "Polynomial-C" by Aphex Twin
- "Quadratic Inequalities" by MathOdes
- "Solving Equations Song: One-Step" by Numberock

4. The structure or form of a piece of music describes the way different sections of the composition are arranged. This organization can often be analyzed and depicted mathematically in terms of pattern, proportion, symmetry, or repetition. Lessons 3.1, 5.1, 5.3, and 6.4 demonstrated possible steps for analyzing the structure of

musical examples; utilize similar processes and apply a mathematical lens to analyze various pieces that align with numerical, algebraic, or geometric elements. For example, musical forms can be broken down into sequences of events, and these events can be analyzed in terms of their position within the overall structure of the piece. Often these events or sections are easy to identify aurally. In the solo piano work *Kinderszenen*, Op. 15, No. 11, "Furchtenmachen" by Robert Schumann, distinctions between the sections are straightforward to discern by their musical characteristics. You might relate this to the visual identification of congruent and incongruent geometric figures. You might also explore particular aspects of a song's construction such as the 5/8 meter in Taylor Swift's "Closure," the 7/8 meter of Peter Sandberg's "Lightdrops," the repeating ostinato pattern in "Come and Get Your Love" from *Guardians of the Galaxy* by Redbone, or the variations on a theme in G. F. Handel's Suite No. 5 in E major: "The Harmonious Blacksmith."

5. A Möbius strip is a one-sided, one-edged surface (see Figure 6.13). Their construction has connections with the geometry of musical chords, which can be described as unordered sets of pitch classes. In general, the configuration space of two unordered points on a circle is a Möbius strip. Therefore, by definition, the configuration of all two note chords is also a Möbius strip; musical notes act the same as points on a circle. Watch the short Simons Foundation video *Mathematical Impressions: Making Music with a Möbius Strip* (youtube.com/watch?app=desktop&v=8bgvRvh88-w), which illustrates these connections. Direct students to create Möbius strip songs. First, pass out a 12-by-3-inch strip of paper to each student. Tell them to hold the strip flat, then grasp one of the short ends and give it a half twist. Finally, bring both short ends

Figure 6.13 Photograph of Möbius strip.
David Benbennick/Wikimedia Commons, Attribution-Share Alike 3.0 Unported.

together and tape securely to make the Möbius strip. Prove that it is a one sided, one edged surface with two different colored markers. Use one color to draw a parallel line 1.5 inches from the side. The line will eventually return to its starting point. Next, use the other color, and holding the tip of the marker against any part of the edge of the Möbius strip, rotate the strip around while holding the marker still. Again, the coloring will eventually return to its starting point. To finish the lesson, ask students to write a set of lyrics along their Möbius strips, creating an endlessly repeating composition. Invite students to perform their lyrics as rhythmic chants.

6. Examine various philosophical debates about music and mathematics. Set up a Carousel of Consideration to encourage collaborative deliberation and reflection. Select several philosophical questions related to math and music. Write each question at the top of a large piece of paper, then tape the papers around the room. Divide your students into small groups, give each group a different colored marker, and direct them to different stations. At each station, allow students to reflect, discuss, and record their perceptions and viewpoints. After two to three minutes, groups rotate to the next station, read previous responses, discuss as a group, and add supporting or contrasting perspectives. Continue in this fashion until groups are back to their original papers. Conclude with a class discussion, summarizing responses and answering questions that arise. Suggested question prompts include:

- Is music a universal language?
- Is math a universal language?
- Is it possible to reduce all aspects of music to mathematical principles and formulas?
- Can math be considered an art form?
- Is music a product of the human mind or does it have an external reality?
- Is mathematics a product of the human mind or does it have an external reality?
- Can beauty be quantified?
- How do patterns in music and math help us understand the world around us?
- Is one system (music and math) more abstract or more complex than the other?

7. Lessons 6.1 and 6.4 examined connections between music and math with respect to ratios. Additional ways students might explore ratios in mathematics include scaling recipes up or down, creating scale models, or examining sports statistics. Connecting music to the study of ratios may also help students see how ratios apply in real-world situations and reinforce the idea that ratios are not just an abstract concept, but a fundamental part of music itself. At a basic level, for any song students perform, they could select ratios to guide their performances. They might choose 3:1 and perform three times louder, or 1:2 and perform half as loud. In addition to dynamics, ratios could also be applied to musical elements such as tempo or key. This challenge may focus students' attention and lead to more expressive, effective performances. Students could also create story problems related to ratios and music. For example: "Given a song of a specific number of measures, how fast would a musician have to play if they had a given amount of time to perform?" Finally, if

you have access to drums or other percussion instruments, invite students to experiment with various rhythms based on ratios. They might create a layered pattern with one drumbeat sounding twice as fast as another (2:1 ratio), or a polyrhythm in which one person plays paired eighth notes (two sounds) on one drum for every eighth-note triplet (three sounds) on another (2:3 ratio). For a challenge, ask students to try performing triplets with their right hand and eighth notes with their left at the same time.

8. Ask students to plot points on a Cartesian coordinate plane using the following ordered pairs: (1,0); (2,1); (3,2); (4,0); (5,0); (6,−1); (7,0). Figure 6.14 displays the result; for every ordered pair, the x-coordinate (abscissa) represents the horizontal distance of a point from the origin along the x-axis and the y-coordinate (ordinate) represents the vertical distance of a point along the y-axis.

Challenge students to transfer the previous mathematical example to music notation. First, assign each unit on the x-axis as a single beat in time. Note that each successive x-coordinate in the ordered pairs align with the musical beat (1, 2, 3, 4, 5, 6, 7). Next, label the units on the y-axis as the pitches of the major scale. If we define a major scale as ". . . Do Re Mi Fa Sol La Ti, Do . . ." and select the y-coordinate 0 as Do, it follows that a y-coordinate of 1 corresponds to the pitch Re, a y-coordinate of 5 corresponds to the pitch Sol, a y-coordinate of −1 corresponds to the pitch Ti below Do, and so forth. The pitches of the previous ordered pair sequence (0, 1, 2, 0, 0, −1, 0) correspond to the melody Do Re Mi Do Do Ti, Do. Invite students to sing

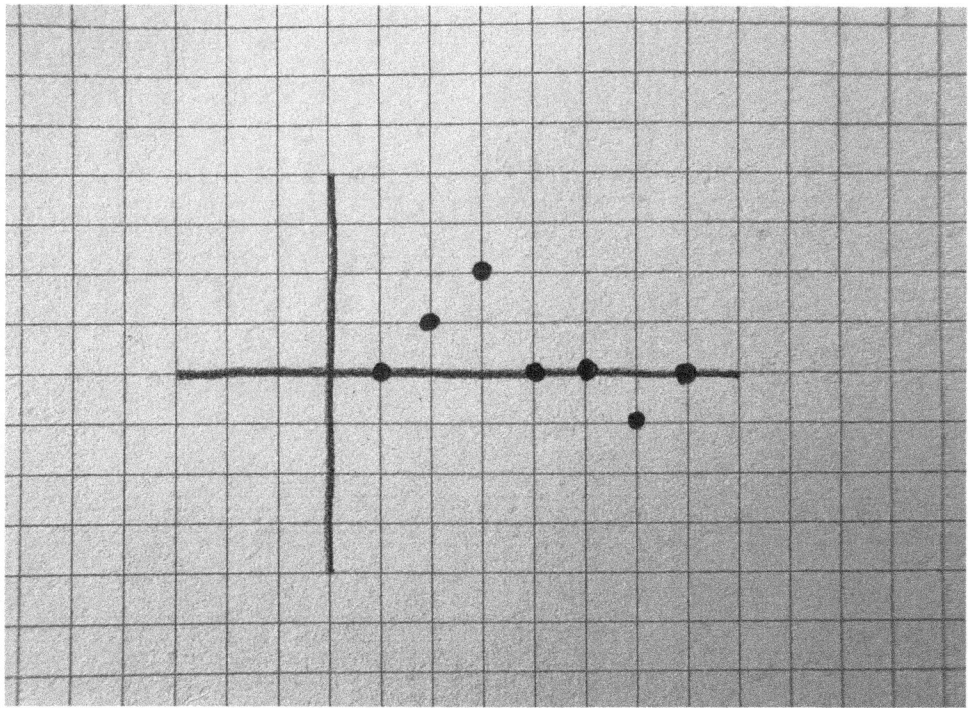

Figure 6.14 Hand-drawn realization of ordered pair set on a coordinate plane.
Image courtesy of author.

the short melodic phrase. As the data do not indicate a specific time signature or key, students will need to make some creative choices as they notate the melody on five-line staff paper using traditional musical notation. Figure 6.15 shows two possible solutions. The first answer uses the key of C major, a 4/4 time signature, and adds a rest at the end to fill out the second measure. The second solution uses the key of G major, a 3/4 time signature, and substitutes a dotted half note to complete the rhythm of the final measure. Both examples incorporate the given melody Do Re Mi Do Do Ti, Do. To extend this lesson, direct students to create simple melodies, notate them using graph paper or staff paper, then sing or play their compositions.

9. Analyze musical scores and recordings using mathematical techniques. Students can mathematically examine the structures, rhythms, melodies, and harmonies of various musical examples. For a given recorded example, such as the orchestral piece "Short Ride in a Fast Machine" by John Adams, students might connect the function rate × time = speed to calculate the tempo (beats per minute) of the performance. Direct students to locate additional recordings, solve for the tempo of each, and compare results. Given the tempo and total time of one recording, how accurately can they predict the tempo or total time of another recording, if one variable is known?

For a given musical score (see, e.g., Figure 6.16), direct students to solve various problems and calculate solutions. How many total beats are in the example?

Figure 6.15 Hand-drawn realizations of ordered pair set on musical staff paper. Image courtesy of author.

Figure 6.16 Two-measure musical example in the key of G major. Image courtesy of author.

(8). What are the three ways a four-beat measure is divided? (*four quarter notes; one dotted half with a quarter; one whole note*). Which rhythm occurs most frequently? (*quarter note*). Ignoring the fermatas (holds), tap the rhythm of the treble staff, then tap the rhythm of the bass staff. Sing or play the pitches of each part. Which pitch is most frequent? *(G)*. Still ignoring the fermatas, calculate how long in seconds the example would last given the tempo of 120 beats per minute. What is the impact of the fermatas on the rhythms, if they were added back in? Recalculate your solution and perform each line as written.

Students could also analyze songs of their choice, either aurally or from printed scores. Direct them to isolate various musical properties such as time signatures, tempos, note durations, pitches, phrases, and larger structures and to solve associated frequency, ratio, proportion, or rate problems. Check students' computations for accuracy and invite them to perform a portion of their selected examples.

References

ABBA. (2021). Bumblebee [Song]. On *Voyage*. Polar.

America's Independent Electric and Power Companies (AIELPC). (1959). More power to you [Advertisement]. *Time* (May 18).

Andreyev, S. (2022). *Livestream Q & A: 4 October 2022* [Video]. YouTube. youtube.com/watch?v=JohkrV2Jt1E

Angel, R. (1964). The chemical worker's song (process man) [Song]. Performed by Great Big Sea. On *Up*. Warner Music Canada.

aniMIDIfy. (2012). *Mozart—Fugue in G Minor KV 401/375e, Part 2* [Video]. YouTube. youtube.com/watch?v=gB5XqeEC1RU

AP Archive. (2018). *Barack Obama speaks at memorial service for John McCain* [Video]. YouTube. youtube.com/watch?v=7NxO_IyVabk

Arneauxtje. (2015). *Animated Julia set* [Video]. YouTube. youtube.com/watch?v=8O1y7FiNa6k

Avicii. (2013). Wake me up [Single]. PRMD, Columbia.

Barrett, J. R. (2001). Interdisciplinary work and musical integrity. *Music Educators Journal, 87*(5), 27–31.

Barrett, J. R. (2023). *Seeking connections: An interdisciplinary perspective on music teaching and learning*. Oxford University Press.

Barrett, J., McCoy, C., & Veblen, K. (1997). *Sound ways of knowing: Music in the interdisciplinary curriculum*. Schirmer.

Belshaw, S. (2017). *Music Machine 41* [Graphic musical score]. Simon Belshaw. https://simonbelshaw.co.uk/mm41/mm41Intro.html

BigBang. (2022). Still life [Song]. YG Entertainment.

Burnaford, G. (2007). *Arts integration frameworks, research & practice: A literature review*. Arts Education Partnership.

Carré, P. (2017). *Iannis Xenakis—Pithoprakta (w/ graphical score)* [Video]. YouTube. youtube.com/watch?v=nvH2KYYJg-o&t=14s

Childish Gambino. (2018). Feels like summer [Song]. On *FIFA 19 Soundtrack*. RCA.

Classic FM. (2024.) *Ludovico Einaudi: I Giorni* [Web page]. Classic FM. https://www.classicfm.com/composers/einaudi/music/i-giorni/

Clinton, G. (1982). Atomic dog [Song]. On *Computer Games*. Capitol.

Cooper, B. (1985). Newly identified sketches for Beethoven's tenth symphony. *Music & Letters, 66*(1), 9–18. http://www.jstor.com/stable/855432

Cooper, R. (Ed.). (1996). *The Hmong*. Bangkok: Artasia Press.

Corrigan, B. (2024). Elegy for one billion animals [Poem]. *Watershed Review (fall)*. https://watershedreview.com/poetry/brittney-corrigan-2/

Coulton, J. (2007). Still alive [Song]. On *The Orange Box Soundtrack*. Valve.

Crow Nation. (2024). Crow Apsaalooké [Language learning app]. Thornton Media.

Cslovjecsek, M., & Zulauf, M. (Eds.) (2018). *Integrated music education: Challenges of teaching and teacher training*. Peter Lang.

Cultural Property News. (2018). Mexico: Art in the time of restrictive export laws. [Web page]. Cultural Property News. https://culturalpropertynews.org/mexico-art-in-the-time-of-restrictive-export-laws/

Deutscher, A. (2021). *The mysterious barricades, arranged by Alma Deutscher* [Video]. YouTube. youtube.com/watch?v=Weauc3fVSFM

Dixon, V. (n.d.). Sir Peter Maxwell Davies: Sculpting sounds in Orkney. *Northlink Ferries*. https://www.northlinkferries.co.uk/orkney-blog/sir-peter-maxwell-davies-in-orkney/

Einaudi, L. (2016). *Ludovico Einaudi—"Elegy for the Arctic"—Official Live (Greenpeace)* [Video]. YouTube. youtube.com/watch?v=2DLnhdnSUVs

EncourageTV. (2021). *Alive inside: A story of music and memory [2014] documentary* [Video]. YouTube. youtube.com/watch?v=x9IHUPamCB4

Fautley, M., & Savage, J. (2011). *Cross-curricular teaching and learning in the secondary school—the arts: Drama, visual art, music and design.* Routledge.

Feinstein, S. (1996). From "Alabama" to a love supreme: The evolution of the John Coltrane poem. *The Southern Review, 32*(2), 315.

gerubach. (2013). *BWV 1087—14 Canons* [Video]. YouTube. youtu.be/6h6AabkLvEE?si=pquh6AFNWiihlReu

Gubicza, G. (2020). *Koch snow flake animation* [Video]. YouTube. youtube.com/watch?v=r6_dZHOHs4k

Harney, K. (2015a). A no-nonsense introduction to the new National Core Arts Standards. *Montana Music Educators Association Cadenza, 59*(3), 38–39.

Harpsichord Drawing. (2022). *J. S. Bach "14 Canons"—BWV 1087* [Video]. YouTube. youtube.com/watch?v=V4NFn4iGJIc

Hedges, S. A. (1978). Dice music in the eighteenth century. *Music & Letters, 59*(2), 180–187. https://www.jstor.org/stable/734136

Jacobs, H. H. (1989). The growing need for interdisciplinary curriculum content. In H. H. Jacobs (Ed.), *Interdisciplinary curriculum: Design and implementation* (pp. 1–11). Association for Supervision and Curriculum Development.

Johnson, J. (2005). Better together [Song]. On *In Between Dreams*. Brushfire Records.

Jurassic 5. (1998). Lesson 6: The Lecture [Song]. On *Jurassic 5*. Pan.

Kelly, P. (1991). From little things big things grow [Song]. On *Comedy*. Mushroom.

Kennedy Center. (2020). *Wu Man—"White Snow in Spring," Declassified: Ben Folds Presents, The Kennedy Center* [Video]. YouTube. youtube.com/watch?v=1Z-NLqbb8xA

Kennedy Center ArtsEdge. (n.d.). *What is arts integration?* John F. Kennedy Center for the Performing Arts. https://artsedge.kennedy-center.org

Library of Congress. (2017). Library of Congress medium of performance thesaurus for music [Online reference]. loc.gov.

LumBeat. (2024). *105 BPM Drum Beat—Simple Straight* [Video]. YouTube. youtube.com/watch?v=bGUcG0l4q1M

Ma, Y. (2016). *Silkroad Ensemble, Yo-Yo Ma—Heart and Soul ft. Lisa Fischer, Gregory Porter* [Video]. YouTube. youtube.com/watch?v=i3Z6LHtxN3U&t=10s

Ma, Y., & The Silk Road Ensemble. (2015). *The Music of Strangers* [documentary]. Silkroad. https://www.silkroad.org/tmos

MacFadden, L. [Cut Chemist]. (1997). Lesson 6: The lecture [Song]. On *Deep Concentration*. Distance; OM Records.

Margulis, E. H. (2018). *The psychology of music: A very short introduction.* Oxford University Press.

Martin, M. (2021). Team uses AI to complete Beethoven's unfinished masterpiece [Radio broadcast]. All Things Considered, National Public Radio (NPR). www.npr.org/2021/10/02/1042742330

Mathigon. (2020). *Mandelbrot Zoom Sequence* [Video]. YouTube. youtube.com/watch?v=b005iHf8Z3g

McCoy, C. W. (2000). The excitement of collaboration. *Music Educators Journal, 87*(1), 37–44.

Miller, B. (2022). *The rhythms of the river* [Documentary]. Manabu Inada, Director. benmillerartist.com.

Mitchell, J. (1970). Big yellow taxi [Song]. On *Ladies of the Canyon*. Reprise.

MoMA.org. (2024). Paul Klee *Twittering Machine (Die Zwitscher-Maschine)* 1922 [Artwork description]. The Museum of Modern Art.

Montgomery, J. (2008). Coldplay give track-by-track tour of Viva La Vida, explain handclaps, tack pianos, and the number 42 [Interview]. MTV.

Montigiani, J. (2009). *J. S. Bach—14 Canons BWV 1087* [Video]. YouTube. youtube.com/watch?v=8FEJHvq4-_g

Moore, J. K. (2003). The pipa [Artifact description]. Department of Musical Instruments, The Metropolitan Museum of Art. https://www.metmuseum.org/toah/hd/pipa/hd_pipa.htm

Mua, B. X. (1995). Tsaaj ntsaws/Tsi teb tsaws chaw (Song of the refugee) [Song]. On *The Music of the Hmong People of Laos*. Arhoolie Records; Smithsonian Folkways.

Myhre, S. (2023). Song of the week: Childish Gambino's feels like summer has a deeper message. Alliance for Sustainability. https://afors.org/2023/06/14/song-of-the-week-childish-gambinos-feels-like-summer/

National Coalition for Core Arts Standards. (2015). *National Core Arts Standards*. State Education Agency Directors of Arts Education.

National Council for the Social Studies (NCSS). (2010). *National Curriculum Standards for Social Studies: A framework for teaching, learning, and assessment*. Author.

National Council for the Social Studies (NCSS). (2013). *The College, Career, and Civic Life (C3) Framework for Social Studies State Standards: Guidance for enhancing the rigor of K-12 civics, economics, geography, and history*. Author.

National Governors Association Center for Best Practices, Council of Chief State School Officers. (2010a). *Common Core State Standards: English language arts*. Author.

National Governors Association Center for Best Practices, Council of Chief State School Officers. (2010b). *Common Core State Standards: Mathematics*. Author.

National Museum Australia. (2023) Wave Hill walk-off [Web page]. https://www.nma.gov.au/defining-moments/resources/wave-hill-walk-off

Nave for Eva. (2014). *John Cage "Water Walk"* [Video]. YouTube. youtube.com/watch?v=gXOIkT1-QWY

Next Generation Science Standards Lead States. (2013). *Next Generation Science Standards: For states, by states*. National Academies Press.

NOVA PBS Official. (2009). *Nova Short: Inside Oliver Sacks's brain* [Video]. YouTube. youtube.com/watch?v=wc6m0Uyis-8

onishikeita. (2021). *14 canons / J. S. Bach* [Video]. YouTube. youtube.com/watch?v=mdI7UM7Xubw

Oxford University Press. (n.d.). Art. In *Oxford English dictionary*. Retrieved June 18, 2024, from https://www.oed.com/search/dictionary/?scope=Entries&q=art

Pann. C. (2007). *Slalom* [Recording]. On *Redline Tango*. Performed by University of Kansas Wind Ensemble, John P. Lynch, conductor. Naxos Wind Band Classics.

Pann, C. (2008). *Slalom* [Score]. Mavlern; Theodore Presser Company.

Paramore. (2017). Fake Happy [Song]. On *After Laughter*. RCA.

PaulKlee.net (n.d.). Paul Klee and his paintings. [Web page]. https://www.paulklee.net/

Pearlman, M. (1990). *"Goldberg" Canons, BWV 1087*. Program Notes, Boston Baroque. https://baroque.boston/js-bach-goldberg-canons

Perspective Project. (2023). Marcia Angus [Web page]. Perspective Project. https://www.facebook.com/perspectiveproj/photos/pb.100063653762700.-2207520000/815212835769858/?type=

President's Committee on the Arts and the Humanities (PCAH). (2022). Executive Order on promoting the arts, the humanities, and museum and library services [Policy statement]. https://catalog.archives.gov/

Reimer, B. (2003). *A philosophy of music education: Advancing the vision*. Prentice Hall.

Relaxing White Noise. (2021). *Yellowstone National Park Water Sounds* [Video]. YouTube. (youtube.com/watch?v=1Jj22Tipe2Q)

Ritchie, H., & Roser, M. (2022). CO_2 and greenhouse gas emissions [Web page]. *Our World in Data*. https://ourworldindata.org/co2-and-greenhouse-gas-emissions#future-emissions

Robinson, S. (1970). The tears of a clown [Song]. On *Make It Happen*. Tamla.

Rolfe, G., Freshwater, D., & Jasper, M. (2001). Critical reflection for nursing and the helping professions: A user's guide. Palgrave Macmillan.

Scott, D. (2023). Xylophone Cat [Video]. YouTube. youtube.com/watch?v=-CUe8SUn3Wg

Seidl, J. (1983). Minnesota's newest immigrants. *Roots*, 20–26.

smalin. (2024). *Bach, Goldberg Canon à 4 per augmentationem et diminutionem (BWV 1087)* [Video]. YouTube. youtube.com/watch?v=3liLG2RpCSc

Small Dots Ensemble. (2021). *Bach: "14 Canons" visualization* [Video]. YouTube. youtube.com/watch?v=rqrZ9aeyQQc

Songfacts. (2024). Swimming pool, by Anna Calvi. [Web page]. https://www.songfacts.com/facts/anna-calvi/swimming-pool

SongsBackwards. (2014). *Sierpiński triangle zoom in* [Video]. YouTube. youtube.com/watch?v=wXBJfaZ2LvU

songsofmemory. (2016). *Hmong songs of memory by Victoria Vorreiter* [Video]. YouTube. youtube.com/watch?v=Dmhv6QyLJFg

SpadoCons. (2010). *Bobby McFerrin hacks your brain with music* [Video]. YouTube. youtube.com/watch?v=E2yAddhsLlg

SWNS. (2022). Relative of Ernest Shackleton composes on a violin made from the explorer's floorboards [Video]. South West News Service Media Group; YouTube. youtube.com/watch?v=R35f2epz5q0

tnsnamesoralong. (2013). *[Badura-Skoda-Demus] Mozart: Fuga for Piano Duet in g, K401(K375e)* [Video]. YouTube. youtube.com/watch?v=3sNE374O7ws

Torke, M. (n.d.). Michael Torke [Web page]. https://www.michaeltorke.com/

Toussaint, A. (1971). Workin' in a coal mine [Song]. On *Toussaint*. DJM.

Twin Cities PBS. (2021). *Hmong song poet of Kwv Txhiaj: Bee Yang* [Video]. YouTube. youtube.com/watch?v=K_acojZLSU8

ViralHog. (2022). *Man demonstrates the Sierpinski Triangle in mathematical visual* [Video]. YouTube. youtube.com/watch?v=Fgu5-3ihVVI

Watson, B. (2015). Made and played in Antarctica: People's music in a far-flung place. In B. Hince, R. Summerson, & A. Wiesle (Eds.), *Antarctica: Music, sounds and cultural connections*. Ed. ANU Press.

World Wildlife Federation (WWF). (2020). Three billion animals impacted by Australia's bushfire crisis [Report]. WWF. wwf.org.au

yourclassical.org. (2021). Team uses AI to complete Beethoven's unfinished masterpiece. [Radio broadcast]. Michel Martin, host. Minnesota Public Radio. https://www.yourclassical.org/

Index of Musical Examples

For the benefit of digital users, indexed terms that span two pages (e.g., 52–53) may, on occasion, appear on only one of those pages.

Subject Index

For the benefit of digital users, indexed terms that span two pages (e.g., 52–53) may, on occasion, appear on only one of those pages.

Tables, figures, and boxes are indicated by an italic *t*, *f*, and *b*